KING JOHN SEALING THE MAGNA CARTA

# DEDICATION

This book is dedicated to the memory of all the great American patriots who risked their freedom and fortune to preserve for every American citizen those "twin pillars of individual liberty" — representative democracy and trial by jury. Their names are written in letters of gold in the Honor Roll of Freedom: Richard Bland, Richard Henry Lee, Patrick Henry, Thomas Jefferson, James Madison and George Mason of Virginia; Andrew Hamilton, Thomas Paine, Thomas Hartley and James Wilson of Pennsylvania; Samuel Adams, John Adams and Elbridge Gerry of Massachusetts; John Jay and Alexander Hamilton of New York; Samuel Spencer and James Iredell of North Carolina; Charles Woodmason and Charles Pinckney of South Carolina; Alexander Hanson of Maryland; James Mitchell Varnum of Rhode Island; and John Dickinson of Delaware.

It is also dedicated to those Latter Day Patron Saints of the *Seventh Amendment* who have striven to preserve this "vital artery in the bloodstream of democracy" for the American citizen of today and for countless generations yet unborn: Justices Theodore Sedgwick and Joseph Story of Massachusetts; Chancellor James Kent, Justice Ward Hunt, Elihu Root and Joseph Choate of New York; Justices William Johnson and James Whitner of South Carolina; Chief Justice William Sharkey of Mississippi; Justice Levi Woodbury and Chief Justice Charles Doe of New Hampshire; Chief Justice Thomas Johnson of Arkansas; Justice Joseph Henry Lumpkin of Georgia; Justice John S. Teeney of Maine; Justice Asa O. Aldis of Vermont; Chief Justice Alexander W. Stowe of Wisconsin; Justices William Strong, Jeremiah S. Black and Robert Von Moschzisker of Pennsylvania; Justice David Davis and Dean John Henry Wigmore of Illinois; Justices Thomas M. Cooley and Frank Murphy of Michigan; Justices Stanley Matthews and Rufus P. Ranney of Ohio; Justices Elisha Carpenter and William O. Douglas of Connecticut; Justice Alphonso Avery of North Carolina; Judge Henry Clay Caldwell of Arkansas; Justice John S. Wilkes of Tennessee; Justices James Hazelrigg and John Marshall Harlan of Kentucky; Justice David J. Brewer of Kansas; Justice James A. McBride of Oregon; Justice Willis Van Devanter of Wyoming; Clarence C. Martin of West Virginia; Justices George Sutherland and J. Allen Crockett of Utah; Justices Hugo Black and James J. Mayfield of Alabama; Justice John H. Dimond of Alaska; Chief Justice Alfred Franklin of Arizona; Justice Harry E. Ackerson, Jr., of New Jersey; Chief Justice Wilfred C. Tsukiyama of Hawaii; Chief Justice Earl Warren of California; and Justice Tom C. Clark of Texas.

The American Jury Trial Foundation is a non-profit organization dedicated to the preservation of the right to trial by jury under the *Seventh Amendment*.

| | | |
|---|---|---|
| Richard A. Bieder | R. Ben Hogan, III | Barney O. Smith, Jr. |
| J. Kendall Few | Joe McLeod | Larry S. Stewart |
| O. Fayrell Furr, Jr. | Donald R. Moorhead | Daniel F. Sullivan |
| Bob Gibbins | Howard L. Nations | William L. Thorp |
| James R. Gilreath | Jerry R. Palmer | Ward Wagner, Jr. |
| | Peter Perlman | |

Trustees of The American Jury Trial Foundation

AMERICAN JURY TRIAL FOUNDATION

# TRIAL

*by*

# JURY

By J. Kendall Few

## THE REEDS OF RUNNYMEDE

At Runnymede, at Runnymede,
    What say the reeds at Runnymede?
The lissom reeds that give and take,
That bend so far, but never break,
They keep the sleepy Thames awake
    With tales of John at Runnymede.

At Runnymede, at Runnymede,
    Oh, hear the reeds at Runnymede:—
"You mustn't sell, delay, deny,
A freeman's right or liberty.
It wakes the stubborn Englishry,
    We saw 'em roused at Runnymede!

"When through our ranks the Barons came,
With little thought of praise or blame,
But resolute to play the game,
    They lumbered up to Runnymede;
And there they launched in solid line
The first attack on Right Divine—
The curt, uncompromising 'Sign!'
    That settled John at Runnymede.

"At Runnymede, at Runnymede,
Your rights were won at Runnymede!
No freeman shall be fined or bound,
    Or dispossessed of freehold ground,
Except by lawful judgment found
And passed upon him by his peers.
*Forget not, after all these years,*
    *The Charter signed at Runnymede.*"

And still when Mob or Monarch lays
Too rude a hand on English ways,
The whisper wakes, the shudder plays,
    Across the reeds at Runnymede.
And Thames, that knows the moods of kings,
And crowds and priests and suchlike things,
Rolls deep and dreadful as he brings
    Their warning down from Runnymede!

          —**Rudyard Kipling (1911)**

*Forget not, after all these years, the Charter signed at Runnymede.*

—**Rudyard Kipling (1911)**

## TABLE OF CONTENTS
## VOLUME I

- **A.** INTRODUCTION ............................................................................................. 1
- **B.** ORIGIN AND EVOLUTION OF TRIAL BY JURY ................................... 9
- **C.** WINSTON CHURCHILL ON THE *MAGNA CARTA* ........................... 37
- **D.** WILLIAM BLACKSTONE ON CONSTITUTIONAL LAW .................... 41
- **E.** THOMAS PAINE ON CIVIL RIGHTS ..................................................... 45
- **F.** PATRICK HENRY ON THE PRECIOUS JEWEL OF
  INDIVIDUAL LIBERTY ............................................................................. 49
- **G.** GEORGE SUTHERLAND ON THE LOSS OF
  FUNDAMENTAL FREEDOMS ................................................................. 52
- **H.** JOHN HENRY WIGMORE ON TRIAL BY JURY ................................. 57
- **I.** CHARLES S. MAY ON JUDICIAL REFORM .......................................... 61
- **J.** J. SYDNEY TAYLOR ON LEGISLATIVE UNDERMINING
  OF THE RIGHT OF TRIAL BY JURY ..................................................... 65
- **K.** A SUMMARY OF HISTORICAL REFERENCES ON
  TRIAL BY JURY ........................................................................................ 69
- **L.** A SUGGESTED METHOD FOR THE EVALUATION OF
  TRIAL BY JURY ........................................................................................ 81
- **M.** TRIAL BY JURY ON THE ROAD TO THE
  AMERICAN REVOLUTION ..................................................................... 89
- **N.** IMPACT OF THE CIVIL JURY ON RATIFICATION OF THE
  CONSTITUTION ...................................................................................... 177
- **O.** THE ADOPTION OF THE *SEVENTH AMENDMENT* ...................... 229
- **P.** A CHRONOLOGY OF QUOTATIONS ON TRIAL BY JURY ............ 237

## VOLUME II

- **Q.** TRIAL BY JURY AS A WEAPON IN THE
  ARSENAL OF DEMOCRACY .................................................................. 265
- **R.** TRIAL BY JURY VS. TRIAL BY JUDGE ............................................... 277
- **S.** THE JURY AS AN INSTRUMENT OF JUSTICE .................................. 289
- **T.** HOW HISTORY HAS VIEWED THE INSTITUTION OF
  TRIAL BY JURY ...................................................................................... 305
- **U.** A COMPARISON OF THE BRITISH AND
  AMERICAN CONSTITUTIONS .............................................................. 425
- **V.** THE RISE AND FALL OF THE JURY SYSTEM IN ENGLAND .......... 437
- **W.** THE RISE AND FALL OF THE JURY SYSTEM IN EUROPE ............ 441
- **X.** THE TYRANNY OF THE MAJORITY ................................................... 449
- **Y.** THE INSIDIOUS SCREW OF JUDICIAL ARISTOCRACY ................. 453
- **Z.** PRESERVATION OF THE CIVIL JURY ................................................ 457

### APPENDIX
- **A** Guarantees of Trial by Jury in State Constitutions .................................. 469
- **B** State Court Opinions on the Sanctity of Trial by Jury ............................ 477
- **C** U.S. Supreme Court Opinions on the Sanctity of
  Trial by Jury ............................................................................................... 497
- **D** Index of Quotations by State .................................................................... 505

**BIBLIOGRAPHY** ............................................................................................. 513
**TABLE OF ILLUSTRATIONS** ....................................................................... 533
**BIOGRAPHIES OF COMMISSIONED ARTISTS** ........................................ 536

## TABLE OF SUBHEADINGS
## VOLUME I

- A. INTRODUCTION .................................................................. 1
- B. ORIGIN AND EVOLUTION OF TRIAL BY JURY ...................... 9
- C. WINSTON CHURCHILL ON THE *MAGNA CARTA* ................ 37
- D. WILLIAM BLACKSTONE ON CONSTITUTIONAL LAW ........... 41
- E. THOMAS PAINE ON CIVIL RIGHTS ..................................... 45
- F. PATRICK HENRY ON THE PRECIOUS JEWEL OF INDIVIDUAL LIBERTY ....................................................... 49
- G. GEORGE SUTHERLAND ON THE LOSS OF FUNDAMENTAL FREEDOMS ................................................ 52
- H. JOHN HENRY WIGMORE ON TRIAL BY JURY ..................... 57
- I. CHARLES S. MAY ON JUDICIAL REFORM ............................ 61
- J. J. SYDNEY TAYLOR ON LEGISLATIVE UNDERMINING OF THE RIGHT OF TRIAL BY JURY ...................................... 65
- K. A SUMMARY OF HISTORICAL REFERENCES ON TRIAL BY JURY ................................................................. 69
- L. A SUGGESTED METHOD FOR THE EVALUATION OF TRIAL BY JURY ................................................................. 81
- M. TRIAL BY JURY ON THE ROAD TO THE AMERICAN REVOLUTION ........................................... 89
  1. The Tyranny of Divine Right ........................................ 90
  2. The Treason Trial of Nicholas Throckmorton (April 17, 1554) ... 100
  3. *The First Charter of Virginia* (April 10, 1606) ............... 101
  4. *The First Ordinance of Plymouth Bay* (1623) ................ 102
  5. *The Petition of Right* (June 7, 1628) ........................... 102
  6. *The Charter of Massachusetts Bay* (March 4, 1629) ........ 104
  7. *The Charter of Maryland* (June 20, 1632) ..................... 104
  8. The Abolition of the Star Chamber (July 5, 1641) ........... 105
  9. *The Massachusetts Body of Liberties* (December, 1641) ... 121
  10. *The Virginia Jury Act* (June, 1642) .............................. 122
  11. Rhode Island's Adoption of the *Magna Carta* (1647) ....... 122
  12. The Execution of Charles I (January 30, 1649) ............... 124
  13. The English Commonwealth and Protectorate (1649-1658) ... 125
  14. The Jury Trials of John Lilburne (1649, 1563) ............... 128
  15. Restoration of the Monarchy Under Charles II (1660) ..... 132
  16. *An Act Declaring the Rights and Privileges of Rhode Island* (March 1, 1662) ....................................... 133
  17. *The Charter of Connecticut* (May 3, 1662) .................... 133
  18. *The Charter of Rhode Island Plantations* (July 8, 1663) ... 133
  19. Resolutions of the House of Commons on the Punishment of Jurors (December 13, 1667) ................... 134
  20. *The Fundamental Constitutions of Carolina* (March 1, 1669) ... 134
  21. The Trial of William Penn (August 31, 1670) ................. 136
  22. *The General Laws and Liberties of Connecticut* (October, 1672) ... 140
  23. *The Charters of East and West New Jersey* (1677-1683) ... 140
  24. *The Laws and Liberties of New Hampshire* (March 16, 1680) ... 141
  25. *Certain Conditions or Concessions of the Province of Pennsylvania* (1681) ................................... 141

26. *The Frame of Government of Pennsylvania* (April 25, 1682) ............ 141
27. *The Charter of Liberties and Privileges of New York* (1683) ............... 142
28. The Trial of the Seven Bishops (June, 1688) ..................................... 144
29. The Abdication of James II (February 22, 1689) ............................... 148
30. The British *Bill of Rights* (December 16, 1689) ................................ 149
31. *The General Privileges of Massachusetts Bay* (October 13, 1692) ...... 152
32. Denial of Trial by Jury Redressed in Massachusetts
    (September 29, 1696) .................................................................. 153
33. *An Act for Establishing Courts of Massachusetts* (June 19, 1697) ...... 154
34. *An Act for Ascertaining Qualifications of
    Jurors of New Jersey* (November, 1703) ....................................... 154
35. South Carolina's Adoption of the *Magna Carta* and
    *Petition of Right* (December 12, 1712) ........................................ 154
36. *The Maryland Jury Act* (1715) ........................................................ 156
37. Delaware's Adoption of the *Magna Carta* (1727) ............................ 156
38. *The South Carolina Jury Act of 1731* ............................................. 156
39. *The Charter of Georgia* (1732) ...................................................... 157
40. The Trial of John Peter Zenger (August, 1735) ................................. 157
41. *An Act Establishing Courts of Justice of North Carolina* (1746) ......... 160
42. The South Carolina General Assembly's
    *Resolution of 1751* ................................................................... 160
43. *The Georgia Jury Act of 1760* ....................................................... 160
44. Resolution of the Town of Boston on
    Representation and Trial by Jury (1765) ....................................... 161
45. John Adams on the *Stamp Act* (October 14, 1765) .......................... 161
46. *A Declaration of Rights* by the Stamp Act Congress
    (October 19, 1765) ..................................................................... 162
47. The "Regulators": Charles Woodmason, Lawlessness
    on the South Carolina Frontier (1767) ........................................... 162
48. Resolutions of the Virginia House of Burgesses
    (May 16, 1769) ........................................................................... 164
49. The Regulators of Anson County, North Carolina
    (October 9, 1769) ....................................................................... 164
50. *Proceedings of the Town of Boston* (1772) ................................... 164
51. Samuel Adams With Sword in Hand (November 20, 1772) ............... 165
52. Thomas Jefferson, *A Summary View of the
    Rights of British America* (1774) ................................................. 165
53. The Provincial Congress of North Carolina
    (August 25, 1774) ....................................................................... 166
54. The Continental Congress' *Declaration of
    Colonial Rights* (October 14, 1774) ............................................. 166
55. John Jay, *An Address to the People of
    Great Britain* (October, 1774) ..................................................... 166
56. The Continental Congress on Representative
    Government and Trial by Jury (October, 1774) .............................. 169

**KING JOHN'S SEAL ON THE *MAGNA CARTA***

|   |   |   |
|---|---|---|
| | 57. | Patrick Henry Utters the Battle Cry of the American Revolution (March 23, 1775) .................. 169 |
| | 58. | *The Declaration of the Causes and Necessity of Taking Up Arms* (July 6, 1775) .................. 170 |
| | 59. | The Continental Congress Rejects Lord North's Offer of Reconciliation (July 31, 1775) .................. 170 |
| | 60. | *The Constitution of South Carolina* (March 26, 1776) .................. 172 |
| | 61. | *The Virginia Declaration of Rights* (June 12, 1776) .................. 173 |
| | 62. | *An Act to Abolish the Court of Appeals of New Hampshire* (June 28, 1776) .................. 173 |
| | 63. | *The First Virginia Constitution* (June 29, 1776) .................. 173 |
| | 64. | *The Declaration of Independence* (July 4, 1776) .................. 174 |
| | 65. | Arthur Schlesinger: "The Voice of the People" .................. 174 |
| **N.** | **IMPACT OF THE CIVIL JURY ON RATIFICATION OF THE CONSTITUTION** .................. **177** |
| | 1. | State Constitutions Adopted Between the *Declaration of Independence* and the Constitutional Convention of 1787 .................. 177 |
| | 2. | Life Under the *Articles of Confederation* (1781-1787) .................. 182 |
| | 3. | The Constitutional Convention (May-September, 1787) .................. 185 |
| | 4. | The Federalists (1782-1788) .................. 196 |
| | | (a) Alexander Hamilton .................. 196 |
| | | (b) James Madison .................. 198 |
| | | (c) John Jay .................. 200 |
| | | (d) John Dickinson .................. 201 |
| | 5. | The Anti-Federalists (1787-1788) .................. 204 |
| | | (a) Patrick Henry .................. 204 |
| | | (b) George Mason .................. 204 |
| | | (c) Richard Henry Lee .................. 205 |
| | | (d) Elbridge Gerry .................. 208 |
| | | (e) Melancton Smith .................. 208 |
| | | (f) Samuel Bryan .................. 209 |
| | | (g) Judge Alexander Hanson .................. 210 |
| | | (h) John DeWitt .................. 210 |
| | | (i) Impact of the Anti-Federalists .................. 210 |
| | 6. | The Views of Thomas Jefferson on Trial by Jury .................. 212 |
| | 7. | Ratification of the *Constitution* (1787-1788) .................. 216 |
| | | (a) The Pennsylvania Ratification Convention .................. 216 |
| | | (b) The Massachusetts Ratification Convention .................. 218 |
| | | (c) The Maryland Ratification Convention .................. 220 |
| | | (d) The Virginia Ratification Convention .................. 221 |
| | | (e) The North Carolina Ratification Convention .................. 224 |
| | | (f) The Margin of Victory .................. 225 |
| **O.** | **THE ADOPTION OF THE *SEVENTH AMENDMENT*** .................. **229** |
| **P.** | **A CHRONOLOGY OF QUOTATIONS ON TRIAL BY JURY** .................. **237** |
| | *Stand Up and Fight for Freedom Now* .................. 264 |

## VOLUME II

- Q. **TRIAL BY JURY AS A WEAPON IN THE ARSENAL OF DEMOCRACY** ......... 265
- R. **TRIAL BY JURY VS. TRIAL BY JUDGE** ......... 277
- S. **THE JURY AS AN INSTRUMENT OF JUSTICE** ......... 289
  1. The Trial of William Owen (1752) ......... 289
  2. The Trial of Gideon Henfield (1796) ......... 294
  3. The View from the Bar ......... 300
  4. The View from the Bench ......... 302
- T. **HOW HISTORY HAS VIEWED THE INSTITUTION OF TRIAL BY JURY** ......... 305
  1. Sir John Fortescue (1468) ......... 305
  2. Thomas Williams (1557) ......... 305
  3. Sir Edward Coke (1628) ......... 306
  4. William Walwin (1651) ......... 306
  5. Matthew Hale (1676) ......... 308
  6. Henry Care, *English Liberties* (1680) ......... 308
  7. Sir John Hawles (1680) ......... 309
  8. Sir John Maynard (1689) ......... 310
  9. Giles Duncombe (1725) ......... 310
  10. David Hume (1762) ......... 310
  11. Joseph Towers (1764) ......... 310
  12. *Blackstone's Commentaries* (1765-1769) ......... 312
  13. James Mitchell Varnum (1786) ......... 313
  14. Thomas Erskine (1788) ......... 316
  15. Charles Pratt (1792) ......... 316
  16. Thomas Jefferson (1801) ......... 317
  17. Theodore Sedgwick (1813) ......... 317
  18. Lord John Russell (1823) ......... 318
  19. Henry Hallam (1827) ......... 320
  20. Chancellor James Kent (1827) ......... 320
  21. Henry Peter Brougham (1828) ......... 321
  22. Sir Francis Palgrave (1832) ......... 322
  23. Jeremy Bentham (1832) ......... 322
  24. Justice Joseph Story (1833) ......... 324
  25. Justice William Johnson (1833) ......... 326
  26. Alexis de Tocqueville (1835) ......... 328
  27. John Quincy Adams (1839) ......... 332
  28. Henry John Stephen (1844) ......... 333
  29. Justice Levi Woodbury (1847) ......... 334
  30. William Forsythe (1852) ......... 336
  31. Lysander Spooner (1854) ......... 337
  32. Justice Joseph N. Whitner (1856) ......... 338
  33. John Norton Pomeroy (1863) ......... 338
  34. Eli K. Price (1863) ......... 340
  35. Jeremiah S. Black (1866) ......... 341

| | | |
|---|---|---|
| 36. | Justice David Davis (1866) | 342 |
| 37. | Emory Washburn (1871) | 344 |
| 38. | Justice Ward Hunt (1873) | 344 |
| 39. | John Proffatt (1877) | 345 |
| 40. | Edward P. Wilder (1879) | 346 |
| 41. | John Duke, Lord Coleridge (1879) | 346 |
| 42. | Sir James Fitzjames Stephen (1883) | 348 |
| 43. | Justice Stanley Matthews (1885) | 348 |
| 44. | D. H. Chamberlain (1887) | 349 |
| 45. | Elihu Root (1894) | 350 |
| 46. | Maximus A. Lesser (1894) | 352 |
| 47. | J.E.R. Stephens (1896) | 353 |
| 48. | James Bradley Thayer (1898) | 353 |
| 49. | Joseph Choate (1898) | 354 |
| 50. | Sir Frederick Pollock (1899) | 356 |
| 51. | Judge Henry Clay Caldwell (1899) | 357 |
| 52. | Justice John Marshall Harlan (1900) | 360 |
| 53. | Alfred C. Coxe (1901) | 361 |
| 54. | Justice David Josiah Brewer (1902) | 361 |
| 55. | William H. Holt (1905) | 362 |
| 56. | John F. Geeting (1907) | 362 |
| 57. | Justice E. C. O'Rear (1910) | 364 |
| 58. | Sam M. Wolfe (1911) | 364 |
| 59. | Justice James A. McBride (1912) | 365 |
| 60. | Frederic William Maitland (1912) | 366 |
| 61. | Delphin M. Delmas (1918) | 368 |
| 62. | Austin Wakeman Scott (1918) | 369 |
| 63. | Charles T. Coleman (1919) | 370 |
| 64. | James L. Coke (1922) | 372 |
| 65. | A. C. Umbreit (1924) | 373 |
| 66. | Francis L. Wellman (1924) | 374 |
| 67. | Lester P. Edge (1925) | 376 |
| 68. | John E. Wall (1926) | 376 |
| 69. | W. S. Holdsworth (1927) | 377 |
| 70. | Harold Corbin (1928) | 380 |
| 71. | Frederick Edwin Smith, Lord Birkenhead (1929) | 380 |
| 72. | Judge Frederick E. Crane (1929) | 381 |
| 73. | Justice Robert Von Moschzisker (1930) | 381 |
| 74. | Clarence E. Martin (1934) | 382 |
| 75. | Justice George Sutherland (1935) | 384 |
| 76. | Justice Hugo Black (1939) | 384 |
| 77. | Ashton File (1940) | 388 |
| 78. | Justice Frank Murphy (1942) | 388 |
| 79. | The Boston Bar Association (1943) | 389 |
| 80. | William Seagle (1946) | 389 |
| 81. | Justice Bernard Botein (1946) | 390 |

**The Magna Carta Memorial
Runnymede, England
Erected by the American Bar Association in 1957**
*To Commemorate Magna Carta — Symbol of Freedom Under Law*

|     |                                                   |     |
| --- | ------------------------------------------------- | --- |
| 82. | René Wormser (1949) | 390 |
| 83. | Clinton Rossiter (1953) | 392 |
| 84. | Justice William O. Douglas (1954) | 393 |
| 85. | Sir Winston Churchill (1956) | 394 |
| 86. | Theodore Plucknett (1956) | 396 |
| 87. | Albert Averbach (1956) | 396 |
| 88. | Judge David Edelstein (1956) | 397 |
| 89. | Clarence R. Runals (1956) | 398 |
| 90. | Sir Patrick Devlin (1956) | 398 |
| 91. | Judge William J. Palmer (1958) | 400 |
| 92. | W. S. Martin (1959) | 401 |
| 93. | Chief Justice Earl Warren (1962) | 402 |
| 94. | Charles W. Joiner (1962) | 404 |
| 95. | Harry Kalven, Jr. (1964) | 405 |
| 96. | Jefferson F. Meagher (1964) | 406 |
| 97. | Donald K. Ross (1965) | 408 |
| 98. | Stanley E. Sacks (1965) | 408 |
| 99. | Judge H. H. Grooms (1965) | 409 |
| 100. | Maurice Rosenberg (1966) | 409 |
| 101. | Justice Tom C. Clark (1966) | 410 |
| 102. | Morris J. Bloomstein (1968) | 412 |
| 103. | Joseph T. Karcher (1969) | 412 |
| 104. | Henry Marsh (1971) | 413 |
| 105. | Lloyd E. Moore (1973) | 414 |
| 106. | Justice E. L. Haines (1979) | 414 |
| 107. | Justice William H. Rehnquist (1979) | 416 |
| 108. | M.D.A. Freeman (1981) | 417 |
| 109. | Peter W. Culley (1983) | 418 |
| 110. | Judge Stephen Reinhardt (1986) | 418 |
| 111. | Judge John V. Singleton (1987) | 420 |
| 112. | Judge Morris S. Arnold (1987) | 420 |
| 113. | John Guinther (1988) | 421 |
| 114. | Paul B. Weiss (1989) | 421 |
| 115. | Alderman & Kennedy (1991) | 422 |
| 116. | Cynthia J. Cohen (1991) | 422 |
| SUMMARY | | 424 |

**U. A COMPARISON OF THE BRITISH AND AMERICAN CONSTITUTIONS** .................................................. **425**
**V. THE RISE AND FALL OF THE JURY SYSTEM IN ENGLAND** ............. **437**
**W. THE RISE AND FALL OF THE JURY SYSTEM IN EUROPE** ............... **441**
    1. The Jury System in France .................................................. 441
    2. The Jury System in Germany .............................................. 444
    3. The Jury System in Other Countries .................................. 448
**X. THE TYRANNY OF THE MAJORITY** .................................................. **449**
**Y. THE INSIDIOUS SCREW OF JUDICIAL ARISTOCRACY** ................... **453**
**Z. PRESERVATION OF THE CIVIL JURY** .............................................. **457**
    *The People's Prayer* .................................................................. 466
**BIBLIOGRAPHY** ................................................................................. **513**
**TABLE OF ILLUSTRATIONS** ............................................................... **533**
**BIOGRAPHIES OF COMMISSIONED ARTISTS** .................................. **536**

# INDEX OF QUOTATIONS*

Henry E. ACKERSON (1951) 488
John Dahlberg ACTON (1907) 449
John ADAMS (1765) 161, 239
John Q. ADAMS (1839) 180, 332
Samuel ADAMS (1772) 165, 363
Ellen ALDERMAN & Caroline KENNEDY (1991) 230, 422-23
Asa O. ALDIS (1860) 493
Roy C. ARCHER (1956) 493
ARISTOTLE (384-322 B.C.) 266-67, 539
Morris S. ARNOLD (1987) 420
Albert AVERBACH (1956) 396
Alphonso AVERY (1892) 72, 489
Bavarian Judge (1834) 445
Walter B. BEALS (1941) 494
Jeremy BENTHAM (1832) 278, 322-23
Andrew J. BETHEA (1937) 184
Vincent A. BIFFERATO (1981) 478
Lord BIRKENHEAD (1929) 168, 255, 282, 380
Hugo BLACK (1939-1963) 384-87, 425, 426, 428-29, 501, 502
J. S. BLACK (1866) 247, 341, 434
William BLACKSTONE (1765-1768) 9, 41-44, 48, 312, 437
Richard BLAND (1776) 74, 174, 392
James BLOODWORTH (1788) 224
Morris BLOOMSTEIN (1968) 4, 412, 415
Bernard BOTEIN (1946) 390-91
Henry de BRACTON (1268) 20
Louis D. BRANDEIS (1928) 120
William H. BRAWLEY (1897) 281
William J. BRENNEN (1958) 502
David J. BREWER (1881, 1902) 8, 251, 361, 482
Stanley F. BREWSTER (1934) 270
H. P. BROUGHAM (1828) 280, 287, 321
Samuel BRYAN (1788) 209
Henry C. BURMAN (1960) 481
George BUSH (1991) 2
Pierce BUTLER (1937) 500
Sigfredo A. CABRERA (1988) 285
Henry Clay CALDWELL (1899) 268, 281, 357-59
Harlan M. CALHOUN (1964) 494
Lord CAMDEN (1792) 187, 278, 280
Henry CARE (1680) 277-78, 308
Elisha CARPENTER (1878) 478-79
Edward F. CARTER (1959) 486
D. H. CHAMBERLAIN (1887) 274, 349
Salmon P. CHASE (1866) 342, 434-35
G. K. CHESTERTON (1909) 84, 278-79
Joseph CHOATE (1898) 77, 354-55, 515
Winston CHURCHILL (1956) 37-40, 97, 394-95, 453

CICERO (106-43 B.C.) 186
Tom C. CLARK (1966) 410-11
C. J. COHEN (1991) 263, 272, 422
Edward COKE (1628) 21, 306-07
James L. COKE (1922) 372
Charles T. COLEMAN (1919) 370-71
Lord COLERIDGE (1879) 346-47
Clinton COLLIER (1986) 189, 232
Francis B. CONDON (1964) 490
Henry G. CONNOR (1909) 166
J. J. COOK (1889) 444
Thomas M. COOLEY (1868) 302-03
James F. COOPER (1789-1851) 456
W. W. COPE (1861) 478
Harold CORBIN (1928) 380
Samuel T. CORN (1900) 494
Bill J. CORNELIUS (1975) 493
Corpus Juris 458
Monsieur M. COTTU (1822) 442
Grover L. COVINGTON (1977) 484
Noel COWARD (1938) 456
Alfred C. COXE (1901) 361
F. E. CRANE (1929) 282, 381
J. Allen CROCKETT (1957) 493
Peter W. CULLEY (1983) 285, 418
Louis W. CUNNINGHAM (1913) 478
Harry J. CURTIS (1940) 481
David DAVIS (1866) 342-43, 434, 498
Delphin M. DELMAS (1918) 8, 155, 284, 368
A. de TOCQUEVILLE (1835) 328-31
Patrick DEVLIN (1956) 398-99
John DeWITT (1788) 210
John H. DIMOND (1969) 468, 477
John DICKINSON (1788) 78$_n$, 170, 201-03
Paula Di PERNA (1984) 265
Charles DOE (1882) 163, 488
Wm. O. DOUGLAS (1954) 123, 393
Thomas H. DOYLE (1911) 490
Louis C. DRAPEAU (1954) 478
James DRISCOLL (1979) 438, 440
Giles DUNCOMBE (1725) 310
David EDELSTEIN (1956) 259, 397
Lester P. EDGE (1925) 300, 376
Thomas ERSKINE (1784) 77, 79, 316, 437
Stephen J. FIELD (1891) 498
Ashton FILE (1940) 388
Charles E. FLANDRAU (1860) 485
William FORSYTHE (1852) 10, 288, 336, 441, 444-46
John FORTESCUE (1468) 27, 305
Felix FRANKFURTER (1946) 501
Alfred FRANKLIN (1918) 477, 504
Benjamin FRANKLIN (1787) 171, 194
M.D.A. FREEMAN (1981) 270, 301, 417, 440

*Some quotations have been condensed due to space limitations.

xiii

**The Magna Carta**

**1215 A.D.**

William J. FULTON (1943) *481*
John F. GEETING (1907) *284, 362*
Elbridge GERRY (1787) *106-07, 193, 208*
Edward GIBBON (1776) *462*
GLANVILLE (1188) *10, 17, 48*
Lord GODDARD (1958) *282*
Ned GOOD (1981) *285-286*
Charles B. GRAVES (1910) *482*
Horace GRAY (1899) *498-99*
John C. GRAY (1899) *489*
H. H. GROOMS (1965) *409*
John GUINTHER (1988) *421*
E. L. HAINES (1979) *270, 414*
Matthew HALE (1676) *48, 308, 519*
Henry HALLAM (1827) *83, 320*
Alexander HAMILTON (1788) *74-75, 197-98, 429*
Dick HANEY (1896) *492*
Alexander HANSON (1788) *210-11*
John Marshall HARLAN (1882, 1900) *38, 360, 426-27, 436, 458-59, 498, 500*
Thomas HARTLEY (1787) *217*
John HAWLES (1680) *309*
James H. HAZELRIGG (1897, 1899) *281, 482, 483*
Patrick HENRY (1778) *49-51, 70, 71, 169, 204, 221, 243*
Howard T. HOGAN (1964) *282*
W. S. HOLDSWORTH (1927) *9, 24, 377-79, 535*
Oliver Wendell HOLMES, Jr. (1916, 1921) *6, 7, 82, 500*
William H. HOLT (1905) *281, 362*
David HOWELL (1786) *430, 490*
David HUME (1762) *310-11*
Ward HUNT (1873) *276, 344, 498*
James IREDELL (1787) *430-31*
Rudolph JANATA (1974) *285*
John JAY (1774) *166-67, 200, 543*
Thomas JEFFERSON (1788, 1801) *1, 86, 165, 212-15, 229, 230, 234-35, 317, 449, 457, 460*
Thomas JOHNSON (1848) *477*
William JOHNSON (1833) *326-27, 496*
Charles W. JOINER (1962) *404*
W. J. KALLBRIER (1916) *268*
Harry KALVEN, Jr. (1964) *405*
Joseph T. KARCHER (1969) *76, 285, 300, 412*
I. R. KAUFMAN (1967) *270-71, 302*
William E. KENNEDY (1831) *492*
James KENT (1827) *175, 320*
James W. KINDIG (1927) *482*
Richard S. KUHLMAN (1981) *273*
Rudyard KIPLING (1911) *iii*
Benjamin W. LACEY (1883) *494*

Arthur T. LaPRADE (1947) *477*
Thomas F. LAMBERT, Jr. (1963) *265, 453*
Emma LAZARUS (1883) *370*
Richard Henry LEE (1787, 1788) *205-07, 453*
Orville R. LEONARD (1877) *486*
Maximus A. LESSER (1894) *9, 352, 446*
James P. LEVINE (1992) *301*
John LILBURNE (1649-53) *128-131*
Abraham LINCOLN (1861-63) *450-51*
John LOCKE (1669) *134-35*
Charles D. LONG (1892) *485*
J. H. LUMPKIN (1849) *280, 480*
James MADISON (1787-89) *8, 74, 198-99, 229, 450*
F. W. MAITLAND (1912) *48, 366-67*
Henry MARSH (1971) *413*
John MARSHALL (1788) *222-23*
W. S. MARTIN (1959) *401*
Clarence E. MARTIN (1934) *382*
George MASON (1787) *204-05, 450, 454-55*
Stanley MATTHEWS (1885) *35, 348, 498*
Ralph L. MAXWELL (1954) *481*
Charles S. MAY (1875) *61-64, 106, 448, 462*
James J. MAYFIELD (1910) *477*
John MAYNARD (1689) *310, 523*
James A. McBRIDE (1912) *365, 490-91*
E. J. McCULLEN (1947) *486*
John C. McKENZIE (1985) *300*
Jefferson MEAGHER (1964) *272, 406-07*
Harold R. MEDINA (1954) *282-83*
John Stuart MILL (1859) *90-91, 452*
Irwin S. MOISE (1960) *488*
Chas. de MONTESQUIEU (1748) *511*
Lloyd E. MOORE (1973) *414*
Gouverneur MORRIS (1787) *70, 158-59, 450*
Frank MURPHY (1942, 1949) *xx, 388, 430, 501*
Ralph NADER (1966) *461*
Abraham NOTT (1822) *432*
E. C. O'REAR (1910) *364*
Henry PAGE (1899) *484*
Thomas PAINE (1777) *45-48*
Francis PALGRAVE (1832) *103, 322*
William J. PALMER (1958) *400*
William PENN (1644-1718) *449*
Ira PERLEY (1868) *488*
William C. PIERCE (1967) *480*
Charles PINCKNEY (1787) *194-95*
Wm. PITT, the Elder (1777) *86*
Wm. PITT, the Younger (1783) *80, 84*
Theodore PLUCKNETT (1956) *396*
Fred. POLLOCK (1899) *48, 356, 527*
John Norton POMEROY (1863) *8, 338-39*

xvi

W. H. POORMAN (1905) 486
Alexander PORTER (1825) 484
Roscoe POUND (1942) 14, 256
Chas. PRATT (1792) 278, 280, 316
Eli K. PRICE (1863) 278, 340
John PROFFATT (1877) 345
Alexander PULLING (1867) 438-39
Ralph Petty QUARLES (1915) 480
Edmund RANDOLPH (1787) 450
Rufus P. RANNEY (1853) 234, 489
Wm. H. REHNQUIST (1979) 194, 416, 465, 502
Stephen REINHARDT (1986) 418-19
Theodore ROOSEVELT (1890) 460
Elihu ROOT (1894) 350-51
Maurice ROSENBERG (1966) 409
Donald K. ROSS (1965) 408
Clinton ROSSITER (1953) 392
ROUSSEAU (1712-1788) 86
Truman B. RUCKER (1961) 272
Arthur P. RUGG (1929-35) 485, 507
Horace RUMPOLE (1990) 2-3
C. R. RUNALS (1956) 269, 398
John RUSSELL (1823) 318-19, 437
Stanley SACKS (1965) 269, 408
Carl SANDBURG (1878-1967) 456
Arthur SCHLESINGER (1968) 174
Bernard SCHWARTZ (1980) 220
Austin Wakeman SCOTT (1918) 369
William SEAGLE (1946) 389
Theo. SEDGWICK (1813) 8, 304, 317
Wm. L. SHARKEY (1834) 486-87
George SHARSWOOD (1870) 490
Roger SHERMAN (1787) 192-93, 450
Thomas A. SHRIVER (1960) 492
John SINGLETON (1987) 270, 420
John SMILIE (1787) 216
Adam SMITH (1776) 460
Melancton SMITH (1788) 208-09
Sydney SMITH (1824) 300
Harold F. SNEAD (1959) 494-95
Samuel SPENCER (1788) 224
Lysander SPOONER (1854) 337
Frank STENTON (1943) 10
Henry John STEPHEN (1844) 333
James F. STEPHEN (1883) 348
J.E.R. STEPHENS (1896) 353
George H. STEWART (1911) 481
Clyde E. STONE (1931) 481
Royal A. STONE (1923) 485
Joseph STORY (1830-1833) xix, 8, 227, 324, 497
Alex. W. STOWE (1850) 233, 494-95

Wm. STRONG (1862) 233, 475, 490
Alvin C. STRUTZ (1966) 489
William STUBBS (1880) 274
Supreme Judicial Court of New Hampshire (1860) 457
George SUTHERLAND (1930-37) 52-56, 384, 452, 462, 463, 500
Roger TANEY (1851) 88, 232, 497
J. Sydney TAYLOR (1839) 65-68, 438
John S. TEENEY (1853) 484
Glenn TERRELL (1937) 480
James THAYER (1898) 275, 353
E. P. THOMPSON (1980) 301
Joseph TOWERS (1764) 310
Harry S. TRUMAN (1955) 226
W. C. TSUKIYAMA (1960) 471, 480
A. C. UMBREIT (1924) 40, 270, 373
Willis VAN DEVANTER (1913) 188, 500
James M. VARNUM (1786) 313-15
Robert VOGEL (1978) 489
Robert VON MOSCHZISKER (1930) 254, 381-383
John E. WALL (1926) 376
Joseph T. WALSH (1975) 478
William WALWIN (1651) 306
Earl WARREN (1962) 402-03
George W. WARVELLE (1909) 269
Emory WASHBURN (1871) 344, 531
Geo. WASHINGTON (1789) 86, 218-19
S. M. WASSERSTROM (1974) 486
Daniel WEBSTER (1848) 456, 531
Paul B. WEISS (1989) 421
Francis L. WELLMAN (1924) 146-147, 374-75
William E. WERNER (1912) 489
William J. WERTZ (1965) 482
E. W. WHELPLEY (1860) 280, 488
Robert H. WHITE (1961) 300
Joseph N. WHITNER (1856) 179, 338, 492
John Henry WIGMORE (1924) 57-60
Edward P. WILDER (1879) 346
John S. WILKES (1899) 492
Thomas WILLIAMS (1557) 236, 305
Hugh WILLIAMSON (1787) 73, 192
James WILSON (1787) 217, 299
B. R. WISE (1948) 277
Sam M. WOLFE (1911) 364
Charles W. WOLFRAM (1973) 228
Levi WOODBURY (1847) 8, 280, 334-35, 497
Charles WOODMASON (1767) 162
René WORMSER (1949) 390

xvii

# THE *SEVENTH AMENDMENT* TO THE *CONSTITUTION OF THE UNITED STATES*

*In suits at common law, where the value in controversy shall exceed twenty dollars, the right of trial by jury shall be preserved; and no fact tried by a jury shall be otherwise re-examined in any court of the United States than according to the rules of the common law.*

**[Ratified December 15, 1791]**\*

\*The Constitutions of 49 states contain comparable provisions.

*The Seventh Amendment places upon the high ground of constitutional right the inestimable privilege of a trial by jury in civil cases, a privilege which is conceded by all to be essential to political and civil liberty.*
—U.S. Supreme Court Justice Joseph Story (1833)

*The right of jury trial in civil cases at common law is a basic and fundamental feature of our system of federal jurisprudence which is protected by the Seventh Amendment. A right so fundamental and sacred to the citizen should be jealously guarded by the courts.*
—U.S. Supreme Court Justice Frank Murphy (1942)

# A. INTRODUCTION

On the great plain at Runnymede, 777 years ago, a resolute band of rebel barons gathered on the banks of the Thames and extracted from King John his assent to the concept of constitutional government. In 1957, the American Bar Association erected a marble monument at the site commemorating this occasion as the greatest event in the history of human freedom. The base of the monument simply reads:

> To Commemorate Magna Carta — Symbol of
> Freedom Under Law

As the *"Symbol of Freedom Under Law,"* the *Magna Carta* is credited with the establishment of the "twin pillars of democracy," representative government and trial by jury. The centerpiece of the *Magna Carta* was the 39th clause which provided:

> *No freeman shall be seized, or imprisoned, or dispossessed, or outlawed, or in any way destroyed; nor will we condemn him, nor will we commit him to prison, excepting by the legal judgment of his peers, or by the laws of the land.*

This event became the rallying cry of individual liberty in England during the 17th century and so influenced the Founding Fathers of our country that the Seal of the *Magna Carta* was emblazoned on the cover of the *Journal of the Proceedings of the First Continental Congress*, held in Philadelphia on September 5, 1774, where our forefathers laid the foundation stone of individual liberty in the United States.

Individual liberty as we know it today means more than freedom from physical restraint. It consists of all rights necessary to ensure true human freedom. Under our *Constitution* and *Bill of Rights*, individual liberty encompasses such fundamental rights as representative democracy, the right of personal security, freedom of action, freedom of conscience, due process, equal protection and the impartial administration of civil justice.

Trial by jury is an essential ingredient of our fundamental right to the impartial administration of civil justice. Not only is it our constitutional right guaranteed by the *Seventh Amendment*, and by comparable provisions of our state constitutions, but it is the only way an individual citizen can ensure that his other fundamental rights are protected. As Thomas Jefferson said, trial by jury is "the only anchor ever yet imagined by man by which a government can be held to the principles of its *Constitution*."

Through seven centuries, trial by jury has been called "courthouse democracy," "the citadel of freedom," "the lamp of liberty," "the voice of the people," "the conscience of the community," "the cornerstone of our judicial process," "a vital artery in the bloodstream of democracy," and "the touchstone of contemporary common sense." In 1762, the English philosopher David Hume wrote that "trial by jury is the best institution calculated for the preservation of liberty and the administration of justice that was ever devised by the wit of man."

On December 15, 1991, in a speech commemorating the ratification of the *Bill of Rights*, President George Bush said:

> *Two hundred years after its ratification, this extraordinary document is recognized around the world as the great charter of American liberty and democracy. Indeed, as James Madison predicted, the principles enshrined in our Bill of Rights have become for all peoples "fundamental maxims of free government."*

Despite this lip service, our historic right to trial by jury is under attack today in Congress and in the legislatures of all 50 states. A "commercial coalition" of product manufacturers, professional groups and municipalities have joined forces with the liability insurance industry in the orchestration of a determined campaign to undermine our most fundamental constitutional right.

Today, a new wave of freedom sweeps across the face of eastern Europe. Millions yearn to throw off the yoke of oppression and to taste the forbidden fruits of individual liberty. But here at home, a different mood prevails. We have enjoyed them for so long that we take our fundamental rights for granted. Economic prosperity has become our primary goal. To many Americans, the *Bill of Rights* is but a semiconscious echo from our dim and distant past. The famous fictional barrister, Horace Rumpole, described us well when he recently lamented that "we seem prepared to chuck away those blessed freedoms we have fought for, bled for and got banged up in the chokey for down the centuries."

> *... We went to all that trouble with King John to get trial by our peers, and now a lot of lawyers with the minds of business consultants want to abolish juries. ... What must we do, I wonder. Go back to Runnymede every so often to get another Magna Carta and cut off King Charles' head at regular intervals to ensure our constitutional rights?...*[1]

---

[1]Mortimer, *Rumpole à la Carte*, p. 80 (1990).

*We went to all that trouble with King John to get trial by our peers, and now a lot of lawyers with the minds of business consultants want to abolish juries. What must we do, I wonder. Go back to Runnymede every so often to get another Magna Carta.*

—**Horace Rumpole (1990)**

Is "the cornerstone of our judicial process"[2] truly in jeopardy? Unfortunately, the answer is YES. In virtually every state of the union the so-called "tort reform" movement annually introduces a flood of legislation that is little more than a frontal attack on the *Seventh Amendment*. According to the Chicago *Tribune*, "in a campaign of increasingly enormous consequences," and "with increasing urgency, U.S. manufacturers, insurers, doctors and municipal officials" are "trying to overhaul the nation's tort system."[3]

Typical legislative proposals of this 'coalition of aspiring aristocrats[4] include arbitrary limitations on the amount of damages recoverable by victims of institutional negligence, irrespective of the extent of their injury or the gravity of the defendant's gross indifference to human safety. Other customary proposals include mandatory arbitration and penalties on the victims' exercise of their constitutional right to a civil jury trial.[5]

The claimed justification for these arbitrary infringements on individual liberty is that of economic necessity: our civil jury system is allegedly incompetent, irresponsible and out of control. Anecdotal illustrations of allegedly irresponsible jury verdicts bearing little relation to actual fact are broadcast to the world by the vast economic empire of the liability insurance industry. Insurance industry statisticians[6] generate mountains of *Alice in Wonderland* jury verdict statistics to convince the press and public of the validity of their grossly exaggerated claims.

---

[2]Bloomstein, *Verdict, The Jury System*, p. 29 (1968).

[3]*See* "Court of First Resort," a copyrighted article by the Chicago *Tribune*, August 4, 1991.

[4]Here, we adopt James Fenimore Cooper's definition of "aristocracy" as "a combination of many powerful men, for the purpose of maintaining and advancing their own particular interests." *Webster's New World Dictionary of Quotable Definitions*, p. 24 (Prentice-Hall Press 1988).

[5]*See, for example,* §202 of Senate Bill 640 in the 102d Congress, the so-called "Product Liability Fairness Act," which provides that "if a party refused unreasonably to participate in an [alternative dispute resolution] procedure, the refusing party shall be liable for the offering party's reasonable attorney's fees."

[6]A statistician has been defined as "a man who draws a mathematically precise line from an unwarranted assumption to a preconceived conclusion." *Webster's New World Dictionary of Quotable Definitions, supra n.4,* p. 544.

Without the protection of this so-called "tort reform," American industries, equipped with battalions of computer-assisted, M.I.T.-educated design engineers, are supposedly incapable of producing safe products, while medical doctors and other "sacred cow" segments of American society allegedly cannot perform their occupations in accordance with contemporary standards of professional care. These are the bizarre assumptions upon which current attacks on our civil jury system are based.

Rather than correcting these violations of the American citizen's right of personal security, this "commercial coalition" and the liability insurance empire are seeking immunity from civil responsibility, a privilege violative of the equal protection clause of the American *Constitution* and *Bill of Rights*.

In a day when the path to many politicians' ears is through their pocketbooks, industrial America is determined to reshape our *Constitution* in its own corporate image. This they cannot do without the effective elimination of our civil jury system. To accomplish this goal, a recent publication of the National Association of Manufacturers urges its membership to "turn up the heat."

> *If your representatives do not hear from you, we will never overcome our formidable opposition and general congressional lethargy. The late Senator Everett Dirksen said, "When I feel the heat, I see the light." It's time to turn up the heat and guarantee that Congress continues to hear our message for reform.*[7]

Through all of this, the American press, "the professional champions of the people," have slept. In his August, 1964, article entitled, "Trial by Jury Deserves a Fair Trial," Jefferson F. Meagher of Binghamton, New York, wrote:

> *In a day when greater professions of faith in pure democracy are abroad in the land than ever before, it seems odd that our one great democratic institution, apart from the free ballot, should not only be tampered with but even marked for destruction in the widest area of its operation without a whimper being heard from the professional champions of the people.*[8]

---

[7] *See* "The Campaign for Product Liability Reform," an "Issue Brief" of the National Association of Manufacturers (September, 1991).

[8] Meagher, "Trial by Jury Deserves a Fair Trial," 36 *N.Y.S.B.J.* 303, 308-309 (August, 1964).

The purpose of this book is to provide those who would defend our civil jury system with the historical background to do so. In the pages that follow we will trace the origin and development of trial by jury and explain its involvement in the long struggle for individual liberty in England and America. Also included are more than 250 quotations on trial by jury by distinguished English and American authors over more than 500 years of human history.

Among those quoted in honor and praise of the institution of trial by jury are five English Chief Justices, three Chancellors, two Prime Ministers, five American Presidents, and six Chief Justices and twenty-one Associate Justices of the United States Supreme Court. From across the Atlantic, they include Chief Justice John Fortescue (1468); Thomas Williams, Speaker of the House of Commons (1557); Chief Justice Edward Coke (1628); Chief Justice Matthew Hale (1676); Sir John Hawles, English Solicitor General (1680); David Hume, famous English philosopher (1762); Justice William Blackstone (1768); British barrister Thomas Erskine (1784); Chancellor Charles Pratt, Lord Camden (1792); Prime Minister John Russell (1823); Chancellor Henry Peter Brougham (1828); Chief Justice John Duke, Lord Coleridge (1879); Chancellor F. E. Smith, Lord Birkenhead (1929); and Sir Winston Churchill (1956).

Famous Americans who have praised the virtues of trial by jury include John and Samuel Adams (1772-1774), Thomas Paine (1777), Alexander Hamilton (1787), Richard Henry Lee (1787), Patrick Henry (1787-1788), James Wilson (1787), Elbridge Gerry (1788), John Dickinson (1788), Thomas Jefferson and James Madison (1788-1789), Justice Theodore Sedgwick (1813), Chancellor James Kent (1827), John Quincy Adams (1839), Jeremiah S. Black (1866), Elihu Root (1894), Joseph Choate (1899), and Dean John Henry Wigmore (1929).

Members of the United States Supreme Court who have defended the jury system include Justices James Iredell (1787), Joseph Story and William Johnson (1833), Levi Woodbury (1847), David Davis (1866), Ward Hunt (1873), Stanley Matthews (1885), John Marshall Harlan (1900), David J. Brewer (1902), Willis Van Devanter (1913), George Sutherland (1935), Hugo Black (1939), Frank Murphy (1942), William O. Douglas (1954), and Tom C. Clark (1966); and Chief Justices John Jay (1774), John Marshall (1788), Roger B. Taney (1851), Salmon P. Chase (1866), Earl Warren (1962) and William H. Rehnquist (1979).

In defending our civil jury system, we have relied in part upon the principle which Justice Oliver Wendell Holmes, Jr., recognized in *New York Trust Co. v. Eisner* (1921):

*Upon this point, a page of history is worth a volume of logic.*

*A page of history is worth a volume of logic.*
—Justice Oliver Wendell Holmes, Jr. (1921)

The enemies of individual liberty have placed the institution of trial by jury itself on trial. In its defense, we hope to show that trial by jury has served our country for more than 200 years as our primary protection against arbitrary injustice. In 1751, the South Carolina General Assembly declared "that any person who shall endeavor to deprive us of so glorious a privilege as trials by juries is an enemy to this province."

Fourteen years later, on the eve of the American Revolution, a Resolution of the Town of Boston proclaimed:

> *The most essential rights of the British subjects are representative government and trial by jury. These are the very pillars of the British constitution founded in the common rights of mankind.*

In 1789, James Madison said that trial by jury "is as essential to secure the liberty of the people as any one of the pre-existent rights of nature." In 1813, Justice Theodore Sedgwick of Massachusetts called trial by jury "the most cherished institution of free and intelligent government that the world has ever seen." In 1833, Justice Joseph Story wrote that trial by jury is "essential to political and civil liberty" and in 1847, Justice Levi Woodbury said that "our ancestors have resisted non-jury tribunals for reasons most vital to public liberty."

In 1864, Professor John Norton Pomeroy wrote:

> *We are bound to the jury trial by all the holiest traditions of our past history; we esteem it as the very bulwark of our liberties.*

In 1902, Justice David J. Brewer called the jury "one of the most valuable institutions in our history," and in 1918, Delphin M. Delmas, "the silver-tongued spell-binder of the Pacific Coast," declared:

> *Trial by jury is the most enduring of all political and judicial institutions which have flourished among English speaking peoples. No other institution ever struck its roots so deep in their hearts. Its decay would mark the decadence, and its overthrow would be the end of popular government.*

It is the solemn duty of every American citizen to preserve, protect and defend the *Seventh Amendment*. *The time has come. We must act now!*

# B. THE ORIGIN AND EVOLUTION OF TRIAL BY JURY

In his *History of Trial by Jury*, William Forsythe wrote that "few subjects have exercised the ingenuity and baffled the research of the historian more than the origin of the jury." Its origin, he says "is lost in the night of time."[9] René Wormser traced the jury to Solon, Athenian statesman of 638-558 B.C.[10] Maximus A. Lesser concluded that an institution resembling the modern jury originated among the Greeks at the earliest civilized period and was brought to England by the Romans.[11] Matthew Hale attributed the antiquity of trial by jury to the early Britons and later, to the Saxons long before the Norman Conquest.[12] William Blackstone noted that many are apt to impute its invention to "the superior genius of Alfred the Great" (871-899 A.D.), but concluded that trial by jury "hath been used time out of mind in this nation and seems to have been co-eval with the first civil government thereof."[13]

The more modern view is represented by Pollock and Maitland, who traced the history of the modern jury to the Frankish Inquest of the 9th century, later brought to England by William the Conqueror in 1066 A.D.[14] Likewise, William Holdsworth concluded that "though there may be more than one origin for the jury [and] though England may have been prepared for its introduction, it was definitely introduced by the Norman kings."[15]

---

[9] Forsythe, *History of Trial by Jury*, p. 2 (Lenox Hill Publishing Co. 2d ed. 1878) [New York Library Reprint 1971].

[10] Wormser, *The Law*, pp. 52-58 (Simon & Schuster 1949).

[11] Lesser, *The Historical Development of the Jury System*, p. 171 (Lawyers Cooperative Publishing Co. 1894).

[12] Hale, *The History and Analysis of the Common Law of England*, p. 264 (1713) [Legal Classics Library 1987].

[13] *Blackstone's Commentaries*, Vol. 3, pp. 349-350 (1768).

[14] Pollock & Maitland, *A History of English Law*, Vol. 1, pp. 141-142 (2d ed. 1899) [Legal Classics Library 1982]. *See also* Thayer, *A Preliminary Treatise on Evidence at the Common Law*, p. 48 (Little, Brown & Co. 1898); Roscoe Pound, "Jury: England and the United States," *Encyclopedia of Social Sciences*, Vol. 7, pp. 492-493 (Macmillan Co. 1942); Jenks, *A Short History of English Law*, pp. 47-48 (Methuen & Co. 1949); and Holdsworth, *A History of English Law*, Vol. 1, pp. 312-313 (Methuen & Co. 7th ed. 1956).

[15] Holdsworth, *supra* n.14, p. 313.

According to Forsythe's *History of Trial by Jury*, this ancient institution "does not owe its existence to any positive law," but arose "silently and gradually" out of the usages of society.[16] An institution similar in nature to the modern jury can be traced to the laws of King Ethelred around 997 A.D. A Saxon court was directed to be held in every local area in which 12 knights and a representative of the Crown swore upon a sacred object "that they will accuse no innocent man, nor conceal any guilty one." Although Stenton's *Anglo-Saxon England* acknowledges that "the sworn jury is unknown to pure old English law" and concludes that "the Norman kings established the jury as a regular part of the machinery of English government," he found sufficient evidence of the use of institutions resembling juries by the Saxons to believe that the ultimate establishment of the jury as a recognized institution resulted as much from old English practice as it did from the Norman Conquest.[17]

Regardless of its origin, the one point upon which all historians appear to agree is that our modern jury system owes much of its impetus to the laws of Henry II (1154-1189), great-grandson of William the Conqueror, and to the *Magna Carta* of King John in 1215 A.D. As Henry II's chief justiciar, Ranulf Glanville wrote in 1188, that trial by jury was "a royal benefit granted to the people by the goodness of the king."[18] For this "royal benefit," Henry II and his successors extracted a royal price until that practice was prohibited by the *Magna Carta*.[19]

---

[16] Forsythe, *supra* n.9, p. 1. For more on the early history of trial by jury, *see* Potter, *An Historical Introduction to English Law and its Institutions*, pp. 218-225 (Sweet & Maxwell, London 1932); "The Jury in Legal History," 180 *Law Times* 48-49 (July 20, 1935); Lawrence, "Development of Trial by Jury," 14 *Green Bag* 239-246 (1902); White, "Origin and Development of Trial by Jury," 29 *Tenn. L.R.* 8, 13 n.19 (1961) and Crabb, *A History of English Law*, Ch. 3, p. 22 *et seq.* (Baldwin & Craddock, London 1829).

[17] Stenton, *Anglo-Saxon England*, Vol. 2 in *The Oxford History of England*, pp. 510-511, 651-652 (Clarendon Press 3d ed. 1971).

[18] *See The Treatise on the Laws and Customs of the Realm of England Commonly Called Glanville*, p. 28 (Oxford University Press 1965) [Legal Classics Library 1990].

[19] *See* Thayer, *supra* n.14, p. 66. The 40th clause of the *Magna Carta* provides: *"To none will we sell,* to none will we deny, to none will we delay right or justice."

**Henry II, King of England (1154-1189)**
*Father of the Modern Jury System*

The five distinctive characteristics of the modern American jury system include: (1) the requirement of impartiality, (2) the administration of a judicial oath, (3) the application of established rules of evidence, (4) the sanctity of jury deliberations and (5) the separation of the duty of the judge to declare the law from the fact-finding function of the jury. As will be seen below, these five safeguards slowly evolved over several centuries.

According to one historian, "institutions ancestral to the jury are co-eval with history itself."[20] However, in the words of another authority, "of the origin and early history of juries but little is known with certainty, and much that has been said and written respecting them is pure conjecture."[21] With that word of caution, the chronology set forth below carries us from the *Kenbet* of ancient Egypt to the ratification of the *Seventh Amendment*. Over this period of almost 4,000 years, "our modern jury has been slowly evolved through the centuries of its 'great and strange career.'"[22]

**About 2000 B.C.** A form of jury called the *Kenbet* existed in ancient Egypt with eight jurors, four from each side of the Nile.[23] Also, according to Forsythe, in the Swedish *Nämbd*, which existed "from time immemorial," there are "many curious points of resemblance" to the English jury.[24] Similar institutions also existed in other Scandinavian countries.[25]

---

[20]Moore, *The Jury: Tool of Kings, Palladium of Liberty*, Preface, p. vii (W. H. Anderson Co. 1973).

[21]Warvelle, "The Jurors and the Judge," 23 *Harvard L.R.* 123, 124 (1909).

[22]Scott, "Trial by Jury and the Reform of Civil Procedure," 31 *Harvard L.R.* 69 (1918).

[23]Moore, *supra n.20*, p. 4.

[24]Forsythe, *supra n.9*, pp. 19-22. Forsythe notes that members of the Swedish *Nämbd* "were from time to time chosen from amongst the people, and their number was twelve; but still they were not 'jurymen' in the modern sense of the term." Forsythe, *supra*, p. 22.

[25]Forsythe, *supra n.9*, pp. 23-31. Forsythe discusses the *Tingmænd* and the *Nævinger* of Denmark, the *Sandemænd* of Jutland and the Icelandic *Tölftar-quidr*, but concludes that these "ancient courts of justice in Scandinavia" were "essentially different from our own jury."

**6th Century B.C.** Several scholars traced the concept of the modern jury to the Athenian statesman Solon (638-558 B.C.) and to the "*Dikasts*" of ancient Greece.[26]

**495-429 B.C.** Two treatises attributed advances in the jury system, including compensation for juries, to the Athenian statesman Pericles.[27]

**450 B.C.** A system called *Judices*, similar in some respects to the modern jury, existed under the *Twelve Tables of Rome*.[28]

**384-322 B.C.** One author found evidence of the continued existence of juries among the Greeks at the time of Demosthenes.[29]

**55 B.C.-395 A.D.** At least one scholar believed that the jury of the ancient Greeks was brought to England at the time of the Roman Conquest and occupation of Britain.[30]

---

[26]*See*, e.g. Bloomstein, *supra n.2*, pp. 2-3 and Wormser, *supra n.10*, pp. 52, 54, 56. *See also* Lesser, *supra n.11*, pp. 14-28, for a thorough discussion of this subject. Although Lesser states that the *Dikasts* of ancient Greece were "the first institution known to history which present characteristic features of jury trial" [pp. 26-27], he concludes that the direct influence of early Greek and Roman legal procedures on the formation of the British jury "could at best have been extremely slight." [pp. 17-18].

[27]Moore, *supra n.20*, p. 1; Lesser, *supra n.11*, pp. 14-28.

[28]Lesser, *supra n.11*, pp. 29-46. *See also* Moore, *supra n.20*, p. 3, citing John Pettingal, *An Inquiry Into the Use and Protection of Juries Among the Greeks and Romans* (London 1769). In accord, *see* Moore, *supra n.20*, p. 2, who wrote that a jury similar to that of the ancient Greeks was found in Rome around 450 B.C.

[29]Moore, *supra n.20*, p. 2.

[30]Lesser, *supra n.11*, p. 171. *See also* Moore, *supra n.20*, p. 1 et. seq.; Bloomstein, *supra n.2*, pp. 5-6; Wormser, *supra n.10*, p. 251 and Seagle, *The History of Law*, p. 75 (Tudor Publishing Co. New York 1946). Seagle believed that the *Frankish Inquest* "may have been derived from Roman sources"; but E. C. Lawrence, in his "Development of Trial by Jury," 14 *Green Bag* 239 (1902) writes that "this Roman jury, as well as the still earlier Greek jury, was in scarcely any respect, in form or duties, like the jury of our own time."

**400-550** History recorded little during these "Lost Centuries," but both Blackstone and Hale believed that some form of jury system existed in post-Roman Britain.[31]

**550-800** Blackstone wrote that trial by jury was "coeval" with the first civil government of England. Germanic tribes ruled large portions of England under a series of Saxon overlords for 2 centuries.[32] And there is authority for the fact that the "earliest constitution" of the English jury bears "some striking points of resemblance" to the old German courts of justice.[33]

**673-680** Alabama federal judge H. H. Grooms has written that "as far back as Hlothar and Eadrick, Kings of Kent (673-680 A.D.), there is evidence that something in the nature of trial by jury was employed" in England.[34]

**829** Emperor Louis the Pious, son of Charlemagne, established the *Frankish Inquest*, a "jury of administrative inquiry"[35] under which royal rights were to be determined by the sworn statement of twelve of the "best and most credible persons in the locality." According to the prevailing view, this is the seed from which our modern jury system has grown.[36]

---

[31] Lloyd E. Moore believed that the jury system in England survived from the days of the Roman occupation, or was brought over by the Angles and Saxons around 430 A.D. See Moore, *supra* n.20, p. 3.

[32] *Blackstone's Commentaries, supra* n.13, Vol. 3, p. 348.

[33] Forsythe, *supra* n.9, pp. 32-34. Still, Forsythe concludes that "it may be confidently asserted that trial by jury was unknown to our Anglo-Saxon ancestors" [Forsythe, p. 45]; and Stephens, "The Growth of Trial by Jury in England," 10 *Harv. L.R.* 150, 152 (1896) adds that "no trace of such an institution as the jury can be found in Anglo-Saxon times."

[34] Grooms, "The Origin and Development of Trial by Jury," 26 *Alabama Lawyer* 162, 163 (1965), stating, however, that "at most, it bore only a faint resemblance to trial by jury . . . as we know it today."

[35] Plucknett, *A Concise History of the Common Law*, p. 110 (Little, Brown & Co. 5th ed. 1956).

[36] Pound, *supra* n.14, p. 492-493. However, Plucknett writes that "more detailed study" of Anglo-Saxon writs indicates that the inquisition "certainly is to be found in England before the Conquest." Taswell-Langmead's *English Constitutional History*, pp. 102-103 (1960).

**Louis the Pious, Son of Charlemagne,** established the Frankish Inquest in 829 A.D.

**871-899** According to Blackstone, many attributed the invention of the jury to "the superior genius of Alfred the Great," King of Wessex.[37]

**911** Reeves, *History of English Law*, states that Rollo, the Norse chieftain, carried trial by jury with him when his troops occupied Normandy early in the 10th century.[38]

**997** The laws of King Ethelred the Unready provided that 12 knights shall swear upon a sacred object that "they will accuse no innocent man, nor conceal any guilty one."[39]

**1066** According to the prevailing view, William the Conqueror brought the *Frankish Inquest* across the Channel to England.

**1080** The first recorded use of the jury in a judicial trial in England took place in a civil action involving the disputed land title of the Abbot of Ely.[40]

**1085-1086** Juries were used to compile the *Domesday Book*, a survey of the value and ownership of English lands compiled by order of William the Conqueror.[41]

---

[37] *Blackstone's Commentaries, supra n.13*, Vol.3, p.350. *See also* Moore, *supra n.20*, pp. 27-28, citing the statutes of Ethelred I (866-871), Alfred the Great (871-879) and Ethelred the Unready (978-1016). Moore also cites the judgment of 12 witnesses during the reigns of King Edgar the Peaceful (959-975) and of Edward the Confessor (1042-1066). However, Busch, *Law and Tactics in Jury Trials*, p. 5 (Bobbs-Merrill 1950), says that statements attributing the origin of the jury to Alfred the Great "utterly lack historical support."

[38] *See* Stephens, *supra n. 33*, p. 150.

[39] Plucknett, *supra n. 35*, p. 108. *See also* Poole, *Domesday Book to Magna Carta*, pp. 397-398 (The Oxford History of England, Vol. 3, 2d ed. 1955).

[40] *See* Pollock & Maitland, *supra n. 14*, Vol. 1, pp. 143-144. However, according to Thompson, *A Historical Essay on the Magna Charta*, p. 228 (London 1829) [Legal Classics Library 1982], "the trial of equals is of great antiquity, and Sir Edward Coke cites an instance of its use in 1074."

[41] Thayer, "The Jury and its Development, Part I," 5 *Harv. L.R.* 249, 252 (1892). *See* Holt, ed., *Domesday Studies*, pp. 5, 26, 45 (Boydell Press 1987).

**1100-1135** Stephens cites an early instance of trial by jury in 1106 and states that the same expression found in the *Magna Carta* guaranteeing an Englishman's right to "the lawful judgment of his peers" can be found in a compilation of the laws of Henry I (1100-1135).[42]

**1101-1122** Jenks, *A Short History of English Law*, cites instances of civil jury trials in disputed land titles in 1101 and 1122.[43]

**1164** The *Constitutions of Clarendon* extended the use of the jury to private controversies in the 10th year of the reign of Henry II.[44]

**1166** The *Assize of Clarendon* in the 12th year of the reign of Henry II established the jury of presentment, forerunner to the modern grand jury.[45]

**1176** The province of the jury was extended under the *Assize of Northampton* by granting the heir of one dying in possession of land the right to "a verdict of his neighbors."[46]

**1177** The *Assize of Novel Disseisin* granted a recently dispossessed occupant of land the right to empanel a civil jury, "the first true step to jury trials."[47]

**1179** The Council at Windsor adopted the *Grand Assize* authorizing the use of civil juries to try title to land under a *Writ of Right*, one of Henry II's most significant contributions to the institution of trial by jury.[48]

**1188** Glanville's *Treatise On the Laws and Custom's of England* described trial by jury as "a royal benefit granted to the people by the goodness of the king."

---

[42]Stephens, *supra n.33*, pp. 153-155. *See also* Adams, Constitutional History of England, pp. 81-82 (1938).

[43]Jenks, *supra n.14*, pp. 48-49.

[44]Busch, *supra n.37*, p. 8. Forsythe writes that in the *Assize of Henry II;* "we first find the jury in its distinct form." Forsythe, *supra n.9*, p. 101.

[45]Holdsworth, *supra n.14*, Vol. 1, p. 321.

[46]Busch, *supra n.37*, p. 9.

[47]Warvelle, *supra n.21*, p. 124.

[48]Moore, *supra n.20*, p. 37.

**1202** The first documented use of the *Writ of Attaint* — both as a means of appeal from an adverse jury verdict and to punish jurors for unpopular verdicts in civil cases.[49]

**1215** Trial by Ordeal was condemned by Pope Innocent III.

**June 15, 1215** The *Magna Carta* established as a matter of constitutional right that no freeman shall be seized, imprisoned or dispossessed except by the legal judgment of his peers. The *Magna Carta* also provided "to none will we sell, to none will we deny, to none will we delay right or justice." According to Winston Churchill, the *Magna Carta* was confirmed on at least 38 separate occasions during the first 100 years of its existence.[50]

**November 12, 1216** The right of trial by jury as guaranteed by the *Magna Carta* was confirmed by the *First Great Charter* of King Henry III.[51]

**1217** The right of trial by jury was reconfirmed by the *Second Great Charter* of King Henry III.

**1219** Trial by Ordeal was prohibited by King Henry III.

**February 11, 1225** The right of trial by jury was again confirmed by the *Third Great Charter* of King Henry III.[52]

**January 28, 1237** The *Magna Carta* was reconfirmed for the fourth time by the *First Confirmation Charter* of Henry III.[53]

---

[49]Holdsworth, *supra n.14*, Vol. 1, p. 337.

[50]Churchill, *A History of the English Speaking Peoples*, Vol. 1, p. 254 (Dorset Press 1956). According to Churchill, throughout the *Magna Carta* "it is implied that here is a law which is above the king and which even he must not break." [p. 256]. In the 17th century, it became a "rallying cry against oppression" and "the Charter of an Englishman's liberties." [pp. 254-255].

[51]*See* Thompson, *supra n.40*, pp. 105-116. Henry III ascended to the throne at the age of nine and a series of barons ruled during his minority. *See* Cannon & Griffiths, *The Oxford Illustrated History of the British Monarchy*, p. 189 (Oxford University Press 1988).

[52]*See* Thompson, *supra n.40*, pp. 131-144.

[53]For notes on the *Confirmation Charters, see*, Thompson, *supra n.40*, pp. 376-393.

**KING HENRY THE III**rd

**Henry III, King of England (1216-1272),** *confirmed the Magna Carta on at least seven occasions.*

**1250** In his *Historical Development of the Jury System,* Maximus A. Lesser wrote that by the middle of the 13th century the jury had become "firmly established" and was regarded and used as an "important factor in the administration of justice."[54]

**May 13, 1253** In the *Second Confirmation Charter* of Henry III, a sentence of excommunication was threatened "against all who took even the humblest part in infringing" the *Magna Carta.*[55]

**March 14, 1265** The *Third Confirmation Charter* of Henry III reconfirming the *Magna Carta* was issued while the king was in the custody of Simon de Montfort.

**November 18, 1267** The *Statute of Marlborough* confirmed all rights granted under the *Magna Carta.*

**1268** Henry de Bracton was sometimes considered "the greatest medieval English jurist."[56] In 1268, he authored his famous treatise entitled, *On the Laws and Customs of England.* In it, he wrote that jurors could be disqualified for partiality, infamy or relation to the parties and that no judicial decree was valid if it was contrary to the *Magna Carta.*[57] He also recognized the distinction between the fact-finding function of the jury and that of the judge to expound upon the law, stating: "Truth is to be had from the jurors, justice and judgment from the judge."[58]

---

[54]Lesser, *supra n.11,* p. 112.

[55]Holdsworth, *supra n.14,* Vol. 2, p. 219.

[56]*Encyclopædia Britannica Micropædia,* Vol. II, p. 218 (15th ed. 1979). Holdsworth states that Bracton's works greatly influenced the later writings of Anthony Fitzhubert's *Grand Abridgment of the Laws of England* (1514), Edward Coke's *Institutes on the Laws of England* (1628), Matthew Hale's *History of the Common Law* (1676) and *Blackstone's Commentaries on the Laws of England* (1765-1768). As author of the doctrine that the king was subject to the sovereignty of the law, Bracton's works influenced "not only . . . the history of English law, but also . . . the general history of England." Holdsworth, *supra n.14,* Vol. 2, pp. 286-290.

[57]Holdsworth, *supra n.14,* Vol. 9, p. 186.

[58]*See* Plucknett, *supra n.35,* pp. 417-418, stating that the *Second Statute of Westminster* (1285) "was possibly the most potent single factor in forcing the distinction between law and fact."

**1272** According to Pollock & Maitland, when Henry III died in 1272, "the verdicts of jurors were rapidly expelling all the older [methods of] proof."[59]

**1275** The *First Statute of Westminster* made jury trials compulsory in criminal cases. The *Writ of Attaint* was extended to actions involving real property. Edward I found it "expedient to declare" that trial by jury was now "the common law of the land."[6]

**1284** The right of trial by jury was extended to actions for trespass by the *Statute of Wales*.[61]

**1285** The *Second Statute of Westminster* provided for civil jury trials to be held in the county in which they arose rather than at Westminster. It also empowered the clerks of the Court of Chancery to issue new writs authorizing "actions on the case" in which, "as well as all cases which were not covered by established rules, the jury was the mode of trial."[62] In the same year, King Edward I confirmed the *Magna Carta* by statute.

**1292** The first recorded instance of a trial judge's charge to the jury.[63]

**1294** Documents were introduced into evidence for consideration by the jury as early as 1294.[64]

**November 5, 1297** The *First Confirmation Charter* of Edward I provided that the *Magna Carta* as *The Great Charter of Liberties* "made by the common consent of all the kingdom" shall thereafter be considered "the law of the land," a clause which Sir Edward Coke said was "worthy to be written in letters of gold."[65]

---

[59]Pollock & Maitland, *supra n.14*, Vol. 2, p. 641.

[60]*See* Plucknett, *supra n.35*, p. 126.

[61]Thayer, *supra n.14*, p. 67. According to Plucknett, *supra n.35*, pp. 130-131, "all the civil trial juries now in use descend directly from the jury in trespass."

[62]Thayer, *supra n.14*, pp. 66-67.

[63]Thayer, *supra n.14*, p. 112.

[64]Thayer, "The Jury and its Development, Part II," 5 *Harv. L.R.* 296, 308 (1892).

[65]Thompson, *supra n.40*, pp. 369-373; 383-385.

**1299** Trial by battle was "practically obsolete by the end of the 13th century."[66]

**February 14, 1301** The *Second Confirmation Charter* of Edward I provided that all articles of the *Magna Carta* "shall be firmly held and observed" and "that if any statute shall be contrary to such charters," it shall be "annulled by the common council of our realm."[67]

**1306** Extension of the jury system occurred through development of newly-recognized "forms of action" in the common law courts.[68] In 1306, jury trials were extended to civil actions for false imprisonment.

**1327** The *Writ of Attaint* was extended to actions for trespass.

**1327-1377** During the 14th century, English juries were primarily composed of witnesses whose verdicts were based upon their own knowledge of the facts. The process by which the jury became impartial observers who based their decisions on sworn testimony presented in open court evolved over several centuries. The process of weeding-out witnesses and "leaving the decision in the hands of those having no prior knowledge of the facts" began during the reign of Edward III (1327-1377).[69]

**1349** Chief Justice William de Thorpe ruled that witnesses could testify to "nothing but what they knew as certain, *i.e.,* what they see and hear."[70]

**1350-1399** "By the middle of the 14th century, the ordinary civil action at common law was tried by a jury of 12 men."[71] During the second half of the 14th century, trial by jury assumed the "dominant position" in civil and criminal procedure.[72]

---

[66]Holdsworth, *supra n.14,* Vol. 1, p. 310.
[67]Thompson, *supra n.40,* pp. 374-375.
[68]Thayer, *supra n.14,* p. 60.
[69]Bloomstein, *supra n.2,* p. 17.
[70]Thayer, *"The Jury and its Development, Part II," supra n.41,* pp. 304-305.
[71]Jenks, *supra n.14,* p. 163.
[72]Gross, "Modes of Trial in the Medieval Boroughs of England," 15 *Harv. L.R.* 691, 705 (1902).

**Edward I's,** *Second Confirmation Charter provided that all articles of the Magna Carta "shall be firmly held and observed."*

23

**1351** The *Magna Carta* was reaffirmed by statute in the 25th year of the reign of Edward III.[73]

**1352** A statute prohibited concurrent service on grand jury and petit jury.

**1354** A statute required that all evidence be produced in open court and provided that after the jury had retired to deliberate "no person should be allowed to confer with them."[74]

**1360** The *Writ of Attaint* was extended to all civil actions.

**1361** Evidence of deeds and other documents were required to be produced in open court.

**1367** According to historian W. S. Holdsworth, it was "finally settled" in 1367 that the jury's verdict must be unanimous.[75]

**1369** The English Parliament enacted a statute voiding any act contrary to the *Magna Carta*.[76]

**1383, 1403** Statutes of 6 Richard II (1383) and 4 Henry IV (1403) required that all civil actions be brought either in the county of the defendant's residence or the county in which the action arose.[77]

---

[73]Kiralfy, *A Source Book of English Law*, p. 4 (Sweet & Maxwell, London 1957). "Whereas it is contained in the *Great Charter* that none shall be imprisoned or put out of his freehold, nor of his franchises nor free custom, unless it be by the law of the land; it is accorded, assented and established, that from henceforth none shall be taken by petition or suggestion made to our Lord the King, or his Counsel, unless it be by indictment or presentment of good and lawful people of the same neighborhood where such deeds be done. . . ."

[74]Holdsworth, *supra n.14*, Vol. 9, p. 182.

[75]Holdsworth, *supra n.14*, Vol. 1, p. 318. However, Stephens, *supra n.33*, pp. 150, 159, states that the difficulty of "procuring a verdict of 12 caused for a time the verdict of the majority to be received," but during the reign of Edward IV (1461-1483), "the necessity for a unanimous verdict of 12 was reestablished."

[76]Holdsworth, *supra n.14*, Vol. 2, p. 219 n.2.

[77]Holdsworth, *supra n.14*, Vol. 5, p. 118.

**1399-1413** "Early in the reign of Henry IV (1399-1413) . . . all evidence was required to be given in open court, so that the judges might be able to exclude improper testimony."[78] "From this period we may date the commencement of the modern law of evidence; the examination of witnesses, and the effective work of counsel in trial of causes."[79]

**1401-1599** Over a period of two centuries, English courts assumed the role of judicial review of jury verdicts either through a modification of verdicts or by the granting of a new trial on the issue of damages.[80]

**1410** By judicial decision, jurors were limited to consideration of evidence presented in open court.[81]

**1427** By statute in certain cases, sheriffs were required to furnish the parties with the names of jurors six days before each session of court.[82]

**1436** The preamble to a statute in the 15th year of the reign of Henry VI recites that "the trial of the life and death, lands and tenements, goods and chattels of every one of his subjects . . . touching matters of fact . . . is to be . . . made by the oaths . . . of 12 men duly summoned in his courts."[83]

**1450** According to Sir James Stephen, "trial by jury as we know it now was well established, at least so far as civil cases were concerned, in all essential features, in the middle of the 15th century."[84]

---

[78] Stephens, *supra n.33*, pp. 150, 159.

[79] Warvelle, *supra n.21*, p. 125.

[80] Plucknett, *supra n.35*, p. 135. *See also* reference to *Slade's Case* on p. 29 nn.99, 100 below.

[81] Forsythe, *supra n.9*, p. 131.

[82] Thayer, *supra n.14*, p. 97.

[83] Thayer, *supra n.14*, pp. 67-68.

[84] Stephen, *History of the Criminal Law*, Vol. 1, pp. 260, 263 (London 1883) quoted in Maximus A. Lesser, *supra n.11*, p. 124, n.54. To the same effect, *see* Warvelle, *supra n.21*, p. 125, stating that "about the middle of the 15th century the jury, much as we now know it, seems to have become an integral part of the king's courts."

**1465** Oaths administered to witnesses similar to our present practice were reported as early as 1465.[85]

**1468** Sir John Fortescue published *In Praise of the Laws of England* extolling the virtues of the English jury system. According to Plucknett's *Concise History of the Common Law*, "Fortescue gives us a picture of jury trial which is to all intents and purposes in modern form. By this date he is able to regard the jury as a body of impartial men who come into court with an open mind."[86]

**1483** An English statute required jurors to be freeholders of good repute.

**1500-1599** According to W. S. Holdsworth, "the practice of relying upon the sworn testimony of witnesses becomes general" during the 16th century.[87] Prospective jurors were selected from a panel by lot[88] and "in an age when political trials were becoming more frequent," royal prerogative courts such as the Star Chamber frequently undertook to punish independent juries who refused to convict enemies of the Crown.[89]

**1500-1699** Holdsworth also notes that "it was during the course of the 16th and 17th centuries that the jury definitely assumed its modern function as judge of the facts on the evidence presented in open court."[90]

**1509-1603** According to de Tocqueville's *Democracy in America*, during the reigns of Henry VIII (1509-1545) and Elizabeth I (1558-1603), "the civil jury did in reality, at that period, save the liberties" of England.[91]

---

[85]Thayer, "The Jury and its Development, Part III," 5 *Harv. L.R.* 357, 362 (1892).

[86]Plucknett, *supra n.35*, p. 129.

[87]Holdsworth, *supra n.14*, Vol. 1, p. 344. To the same effect, see Wigmore, *A Treatise on the System of Evidence in Trials at Common Law*, Vol. 1, p. 24 (Little, Brown & Co. 1904).

[88]Moore, *supra n.20*, p. 69.

[89]Plucknett, *supra n.35*, pp. 133-134.

[90]Holdsworth, *supra n.14*, Vol. 9, p. 127.

[91]de Tocqueville, *Democracy in America*, p. 265 (1838) [Legal Classics Library 1988].

*Trial by jury is the most rational and effective method for discovering the truth.*
   —**Sir John Fortescue, Chief Justice of the King's Bench (1468)**

**1512** Compulsory jury service was enforced in the city of London.

**1550-1699** As a result of a process of evolution during a large part of the 16th century and all of the 17th century, witnesses no longer sat upon English juries and "for practical purposes the jury depended very largely, if not entirely, upon evidence placed before it in court."[92]

**1554** Nicholas Throckmorton, charged with high treason in the Wyatt Rebellion, was acquitted by a London jury. The jurors were prosecuted for their verdict in the Star Chamber, severely fined and imprisoned for six months.[93]

**1562-1563** The right to subpoena witnesses was established by statute.

**1565** The *Writ of Attaint* was practically obsolete.[94]

**1580** Eleven jurors were fined in the Star Chamber for their verdict of acquittal in *Hodie's Case*.[95]

**1595** Certain actions of Sir Walter Raleigh as warden of Stannaries Prison were held contrary to the *Magna Carta* with the court holding that jury trials under the common law were "the surest and best inheritance that any subject hath."[96]

**1600-1699** Throughout the 17th century the observance of the *Magna Carta* "came to be regarded both by lawyers and politicians as a synonym for constitutional government."[97]

**April 4, 1606** The *First Charter of Virginia* guaranteed the protection of the *Magna Carta* to the inhabitants of that colony.

**June 7, 1628** The *Petition of Right* reaffirmed the right to trial by jury as a fundamental right of all English subjects.

---

[92]Plucknett, *supra n.35*, p. 136.
[93]*Besant's History of London*, pp. 61-62 (3d ed. 1989).
[94]Plucknett, *supra n.35*, p. 127.
[95]Plucknett, *supra n.35*, pp. 133-134.
[96]Holdsworth, *supra n.14*, Vol. 5, pp. 188-189 n.1.
[97]Holdsworth, *supra n.14*, Vol. 2, p. 216.

**March 4, 1629**  The *Charter of Massachusetts Bay* guaranteed the protection of the *Magna Carta* to the inhabitants of that colony.

**June 20, 1632**  The *Charter of Maryland* guaranteed the protection of the *Magna Carta* to the inhabitants of that colony.

**July 5, 1641**  The statute abolishing the Court of the Star Chamber "constituted an important reaffirmation of the concept of due process of law including the protection of trial by jury."[98]

**December, 1641**  The *Massachusetts Body of Liberties* provided for the right of trial by jury in civil and criminal actions.

**1648**  The record in *Slade's Case* "shows that the court regarded itself as possessing the right to grant a new trial as part of its usual powers."[99] In the early part of the 17th century, the practice of revising and setting aside the verdicts of juries as being contrary to the evidence was "clearly recognized and established," providing an additional judicial safeguard for the reliability of jury verdicts.[100]

**1655**  The Court of the King's Bench granted a new trial in *Wood v. Gunston* for excessive damages awarded in an action for slander.[101] According to Lloyd E. Moore, "it became common in the last of the 17th century to set aside the initial civil verdict and to call a new trial on various grounds [including] . . . excessive damages."[102]

**July 8, 1663**  The *Charter of Rhode Island and Providence Plantations* guaranteed the protection of the *Magna Carta* to the inhabitants of that colony.

**March 1, 1669**  John Locke authored the *Fundamental Constitutions of Carolina* which guaranteed the right of trial by jury to the inhabitants of that colony in all civil and criminal actions.

---

[98]Perry & Cooper, *Sources of Our Liberties*, p. 132 (American Bar Found. 1959) [Legal Classics Library 1991].

[99]Holdsworth, *supra n.14*, Vol. 1, p. 225.

[100]Thayer, *supra n.14*, p. 172.

[101]Plucknett, *supra n.35*, pp. 133-134.

[102]Moore, *supra n.20*, p. 77.

**1670-1688** Punishment of independent-minded juries continued throughout the 17th century until 1670[103] when, in *Bushel's Case*, Chief Justice John Vaughan held that the verdict of the jury was a judicial act for which they could not be punished.[104] Following *Bushel's Case*, manipulation of jury selection continued under Charles II and James II until it was curtailed by the adoption of the English *Bill of Rights*.

**March 13, 1677** The *Charter of Fundamental Laws of West New Jersey* guaranteed the right of trial by jury to the inhabitants of that colony.

**March 16, 1680** The *General Laws and Liberties* of New Hampshire guaranteed the right of trial by jury in civil and criminal cases.

**April 25, 1682** The *Frame of Government of Pennsylvania* guaranteed the right of trial by jury in all cases.

**1683** The *Fundamental Constitutions of East Jersey* guaranteed the right of trial by jury.

**June 30, 1688** In the *Seven Bishops' Case*, the defendants were charged with seditious libel for their "respectful petition" which questioned the legality of James II's royal prerogative to suspend the laws.[105] According to Winston Churchill, the jury's verdict of acquittal was "acclaimed with universal joy"[106] and played a substantial role in deposing "almost certainly the least popular of English monarchs"[107] and ensuring the "Glorious Revolution" and the adoption of the British *Bill of Rights*.

**December 16, 1689** The British *Bill of Rights* guaranteed the right of trial by an impartial jury to all English citizens.

**April, 1691** An act of the General Assembly of New York guaranteed the right of trial by jury to the inhabitants of that province.

---

[103] *See* Thayer, *supra n.14*, pp. 164-166.
[104] Holdsworth, *supra n.14*, Vol. 1, pp. 345-346.
[105] Holdsworth, *supra n.14*, Vol. 6, p. 193.
[106] Churchill, *supra n.50*, Vol. 2, p. 403.
[107] Cannon & Griffiths, *supra n.51*, p. 124.

**Charles II, King of England (1660-1685)**
*Manipulation of jury selection continued under Charles II and James II until it was curtailed by the adoption of the English Bill of Rights.*

**1692**  The right of trial by jury was reaffirmed in the *New Charter of Massachusetts*.[108]

**1700**  Hearsay rules date from about 1700.[109] Professor Wigmore wrote that "the final establishment of the right of cross examination by counsel, at the beginning of the 1700's, gave to our law of evidence the distinction of possessing the most efficacious expedient ever invented for extraction of truth."[110]

**1726**  The first treatise on the law of evidence was published by Chief Baron Gilbert.

**1727**  Delaware adopted the *Magna Carta*.

**1731**  The *South Carolina Jury Act of 1731* guaranteed the right of trial by jury.

**August, 1735**  An impartial American jury in the trial of John Peter Zenger established the right of freedom of the press in America.

**1751**  The South Carolina General Assembly declared that "any person who shall endeavor to deprive us of so glorious a privilege as trials by jury" was an enemy to the people of that province.

**1752**  Jury oaths similar to the present practice date from the mid-18th century.[111]

**1757**  English Chief Justice Lord Mansfield recognized that new trials in civil cases are "frequently granted,"[112] ensuring the continuation of the safeguard of judicial review of jury verdicts.

**October 19, 1765**  The Stamp Act Congress asserted the right of every American to trial by jury.

---

[108]Kent, *Commentaries on American Law,* Vol. 2, pp. 1-2 (1827) [Legal Classics Library 1986].

[109]*See* Moore, *supra n.20,* p. 73. To the same effect, *see* Holdsworth, *supra n.14,* Vol. 9, pp. 217, 229.

[110]Wigmore, *supra n.87,* Vol. 1, p. 25.

[111]Moore, *supra n.20,* pp. 77-78.

[112]Plucknett, *supra n.35,* pp. 133-134.

**1765** The Town of Boston called representative government and trial by jury "the most essential rights of British subjects."

**October 14, 1774** The First Continental Congress reasserted the right of every American citizen to trial by jury.

**March 26, 1776** The *Constitution of South Carolina* guaranteed the right of trial by jury in "all suits and processes pending in any court of law or equity."

**June 12, 1776** The *Virginia Declaration of Rights* guaranteed the right of trial by jury in civil and criminal cases.

**July 2, 1776** The *New Jersey Constitution* guaranteed the right of trial by jury.

**July 4, 1776** The *Declaration of Independence* reasserted the right of trial by jury for all American citizens.

**August 16, 1776** The *Pennsylvania Constitution* guaranteed the right of trial by jury in civil and criminal cases.

**September 11, 1776** The *Delaware Declaration of Rights* guaranteed the right of trial by jury.

**November 3, 1776** The *Constitution of Maryland* guaranteed the right of trial by jury.

**December 14, 1776** The *North Carolina Declaration of Rights* guaranteed the right of trial by jury in civil and criminal cases.

**April, 1777** The *New York Constitution* guaranteed the right of trial by jury.

**July 8, 1777** The *Vermont Constitution* guaranteed the right of trial by jury in civil and criminal cases.

**August 25, 1780** The *Constitution of Massachusetts* guaranteed the right of trial by jury in civil and criminal cases.

**June 4, 1784** The *Constitution of New Hampshire* guaranteed the right of trial by jury in civil and criminal cases.

**September, 1786** In *Trevett v. Weeden*, the Supreme Court of Rhode Island declared the *Rhode Island Bank Act* unconstitutional for depriving the defendant of his right to trial by jury.

**May, 1787** The Superior Court of North Carolina declared the North Carolina *Forfeited Land Act* unconstitutional because it deprived the defendant of his right to trial by jury.[113]

**July 13, 1787** The *Ordinance of the Northwest Territory* guaranteed the right of trial by jury.

**September 17, 1787** Three members of the federal Constitutional Convention refused to sign the Plan of the Convention because it failed to guarantee the right of trial by jury in civil cases.

**December 12, 1787** Twenty-one members of the Pennsylvania Ratification Convention published objections to the failure of the Plan of the Convention to guarantee civil jury trials.

**August 2, 1788** The North Carolina Ratification Convention refused to ratify the *Constitution* for lack of a *Bill of Rights* guaranteeing the right of trial by jury in civil cases.

**December 6, 1788** The Massachusetts Ratification Convention proposed an amendment to the *Constitution* guaranteeing the right of trial by jury in civil cases.

**June 8, 1789** James Madison presented a proposed *Bill of Rights* to the House of Representatives including the guarantee of civil jury trials, stating that trial by jury was "one of the best securities to the rights of the people."

**September 25, 1789** The *Bill of Rights* was adopted by Congress.

**December 15, 1791** The *Bill of Rights* was ratified by the states guaranteeing through the *Seventh Amendment* that "in suits at common law, where the value in controversy shall exceed twenty dollars, *the right of trial by jury shall be preserved.*"

---

[113]*Bayard v. Singleton,* 1 Martin (N.C.) 42-44 (1787). The court held "that by the *Constitution* every citizen had undoubtedly a right to . . . trial by jury. For . . . if the legislature could take away that right, and require him to stand condemned in his property . . . , it might with as much authority require his life to be taken without a trial by jury." See Schwartz, *The Roots of the Bill of Rights,* Vol. II, pp. 429-431 (Chelsea House Publishers 1980).

*The right of trial by jury is expressly secured by the Seventh Amendment. The U.S. Supreme Court has always guarded this constitutional right with jealousy.*
—U.S. Supreme Court Justice Stanley Matthews (1885)

**The Magna Carta Memorial
Runnymede, England
Erected by The American Bar Association in 1957**

*The substance of Article 39 of the Magna Carta was adopted by all 13 American colonies. The specific language of the Magna Carta's guarantee of the right of trial by jury was adopted by Massachusetts (1641), Rhode Island (1647), New Jersey (1683), South Carolina (1712) and Delaware (1727).*

## C. WINSTON CHURCHILL ON THE MAGNA CARTA

Winston Churchill was a man whose well-considered opinions were almost universally respected. No modern-day statesman can eclipse his acclaim in the hearts of the free world. After bringing Britain through its darkest hour as Prime Minister during World War II, he wrote a four-volume *History of the English-Speaking Peoples*.[114] In the first volume entitled, *The Birth of Britain*, he describes how, on June 15, 1215, "on the great meadow at Runnymede," a small group of renegade English barons forced King John to sign a "short document" that this "handful of resolute men had drawn up." This document, now known as the *Magna Carta*, was "sealed in a quiet, short scene, which has become one of the most famous in our history." According to Churchill, during the next 100 years, the *Magna Carta* was reaffirmed on 38 separate occasions.[115] It was regarded as a shield against encroachments by the king upon the liberties of the people and "a rallying cry against oppression."

> *Thus was created the glorious legend of the "Charter of an Englishman's Liberties."*[116]

On November 5, 1297, King Edward I executed the *Confirmation Charter*. In it, the *Magna Carta* was confirmed as the Great Charter of Liberties:

> *Know ye that We, . . . for the benefit of our whole kingdom, have granted for us and our heirs . . . [t]hat Great Charter of Liberties . . . which [was] made by the common consent of all the kingdom, . . . [and which] shall be held in all their parts, without any blemish. . . .*[117]

---

[114]Churchill, *A History of the English Speaking Peoples* (Dorset Press 4 Volumes 1956).

[115]*See also* Thompson, *A Historical Essay on the Magna Charta*, pp. 369-393 (1829) [Legal Classics Library 1982].

[116]Churchill, *supra* n.114, Vol. 1, pp. 254-255.

[117]Thompson, *supra* n.115, pp. 369-370. The second clause of the *Confirmation Charter* of Edward I provided "that if any judgment shall be given for the future against the ordinances of the aforesaid *Charter* by the justices, or by others of our officers, who, contrary to the particulars of the *Charters*, do hold pleas before them, it shall be done away with, and held as none."

Three years later, King Edward I executed his second *Confirmation of the Charter of Liberties* in which he commanded that all articles of the *Magna Carta* "shall be firmly held and observed" and, that if any statute should be contrary to any article contained in the *Magna Carta*, "the same shall be amended, or even annulled by the Common Council of our realm."

The most significant provision of the *Magna Carta* was Article 39 which provided that "no freeman shall be seized, or imprisoned, or dispossessed . . . excepting by the judgment of his peers."[118] For more than seven centuries, this article has been construed as a guarantee of the right of trial by jury both in civil and criminal cases. The words "freeman" and "peers" have been interpreted in the United States as a guarantee of every American's fundamental right to a trial by an impartial jury of his fellow citizens.

> . . . [I]n view of the Constitution, in the eye of the law, there is in this country no superior . . . class of citizens. . . . In respect of civil rights, all citizens are equal before the law. The humblest is peer of the most powerful.[119]

The second important area in which this great *Charter of Liberties* has evolved over the last seven centuries is the jury selection process. In describing "the origin of the jury and the part it played in the triumph of the Common Law," Winston Churchill describes how jurors were first selected from the neighborhood in which the controversy arose, as a result of which, many jurors were witnesses to the facts in dispute. Gradually, this practice gave way to a selection process in which every citizen selected for jury service was required to be an independent and objective juror with no prior knowledge of the facts. Therefore, according to Churchill, this system which provides for fair and impartial juries in all civil or criminal actions "endures to this day" and acts as a guarantee that "law flows from the people."

> The jury system has come to stand for all we mean by English justice, because so long as a case has to be scrutinized by twelve honest men [and women], defendant and plaintiff alike have a safeguard from arbitrary perversion of the law. . . .[120]

---

[118]Thompson, *supra.n.115*, pp. 374-375, 383.
[119]Justice John Marshall Harlan, *dissenting opinion* in *Plessy v. Ferguson*, 163 U.S. 537, 559 (1896).
[120]Churchill, *supra n.114*, Vol. 1, pp. 218-219.

*The jury system has come to stand for all we mean by English justice, because so long as a case has to be scrutinized by twelve honest men [and women], defendant and plaintiff alike have a safeguard from arbitrary perversion of the law.*
—**Sir Winston Churchill (1956)**

Other significant provisions of the *Magna Carta* include Articles 12 and 40. Article 12 provided that "no *scutage* or aid shall be imposed on the Kingdom, excepting by the common council of the Kingdom." "*Scutage*" being a form of feudal taxation, Article 12 has been construed as a guarantee of no taxation without representation, a basic principle of representative democracy. Article 40 provided that "to none will we sell, to none will we deny, to none will we delay right or justice": in effect, the free and unrestricted right to a redress of injuries in the established courts of civil and criminal justice. These three great rights combine to insure that the law does in fact "flow from the people."

But the only way that the judicial administration of American law can continue to "flow from the people" is through the preservation of our civil jury system. As will be shown below, the designation of judges or arbitration panels as finders of facts in civil controversies will deprive us of the neutral and uninfluenced integrity of our current system of civil justice. It is only through the jury that the blessings of true democracy may be preserved for generations of future Americans.

It is through the jury system, the only means by which the people have an active voice in the judicial branch of our government, that individual rights are protected. As the conscience of the community, American juries establish reasonable standards for acceptable conduct based upon evidence presented in open court where both sides are afforded an equal opportunity to advocate and defend their respective positions. Impartial jurors with no prior knowledge of the facts, with varying backgrounds and professions, bring a broad array of experience and understanding to the decision-making process. They hear only such evidence as the trial judge determines to be relevant. Each side is allowed to confront and cross-examine every witness. The jurors are instructed in the applicable law by the trial judge. Their verdicts are subject to review by the trial judge and, on appeal, by one or more appellate courts.

Occasionally, unjust verdicts may occur, but "the damage done to the administration of justice by such verdicts has been greatly minimized if not entirely neutralized, by the power of the court to set aside such verdicts and grant new trials."[121] This intricate system of checks and balances assures us all that, to the extent humanly possible, every citizen is guaranteed a fair and impartial trial.

---

[121]Umbreit, "Is Trial by Jury an Ineffective Survival?" 8 *Marquette L.R.* 132-133 (April, 1924).

## D. WILLIAM BLACKSTONE ON CONSTITUTIONAL LAW

William Blackstone was born in London on July 10, 1723. He was elected a member of All Souls College at Oxford in 1743 and became a barrister in 1746. He was appointed judge of the Chancellor's Court in 1761 and, ten years later, became a member of the House of Commons where he successfully advocated the repeal of the *Stamp Act* in 1766. In 1770, he declined nomination as Solicitor General and was appointed Justice of the Court of Common Pleas.

Blackstone authored a treatise on the *Magna Carta* in 1759 and, between 1765 and 1769, he published his four-volume *Commentaries on the Laws of England*.

> *... His Commentaries on the Laws of England, a literary masterpiece ..., was the first complete description of English law ever written. It achieved immediate renown, shaped the future of legal education both in England and America, and is today a legal classic.*[122]

In the first volume of his *Commentaries*, published in 1765, Blackstone wrote on "The Rights of Persons" and "The Absolute Rights of Individuals." He said that "the principal aim of society is to protect individuals in the enjoyment of those absolute rights, which are vested in them by the immutable laws of nature."

> *Hence it follows, that the spirit and primary end of human laws is to maintain and regulate these absolute rights of individuals. ... And therefore the principal view of human law is, or ought always to be, to explain, protect and enforce such rights as are absolute, which in themselves are few and simple; and then such rights as are relative, which arising from a variety of connections, will be far more numerous and more complicated.*[123]

---

[122] *Encyclopædia Britannica Macropædia*, Vol. 2, p. 1098 (15th ed. 1979). Edmund Burke said that "nearly as many copies" of *Blackstone's Commentaries* were sold in America as in England. Connor, "The Constitutional Right to Trial by a Jury," 48 *Univ. of Penn. L.R.* 197, 198 (1909).

[123] Blackstone, *Commentaries on the Laws of England*, Vol. 1, p. 120 (1765) [Legal Classics Library 1983].

On the *Magna Carta,* Blackstone wrote:

*First, . . . the Great Charter of Liberties, which was obtained, sword in hand, from King John . . . , was for the most part declaratory of the principal grounds of the fundamental laws of England. Afterwards by . . . statute . . . the Great Charter is directed to be allowed as the common law; all judgments contrary to it are declared void; copies of it are ordered to be sent to all cathedral churches, and read twice a year to the people; and sentence of excommunication is directed to be constantly denounced against all those that . . . in any degree infringe it. . . .*[124]

On "the absolute rights of every Englishman," Blackstone listed first "the right of personal security" which "consists in a person's legal and uninterrupted enjoyment of his life, his limbs, his body, his health, and his reputation." The declaration of these absolute rights would be "in vain," he wrote, "and protected by the dead letter of the laws, if the *Constitution* had provided no other method to secure their actual enjoyment."

*. . . It has therefore established certain other auxiliary subordinate rights of the subject, which serve principally as barriers to protect and maintain inviolate these three great and primary rights, of personal security, personal liberty, and personal property. . . .*[125]

After the powers of Parliament and limitations on the king's prerogative, Blackstone's third subordinate right was access "to the courts of justice for redress of injuries."

*A third subordinate right of every Englishman is that of applying to the courts of justice for redress of injuries. . . . The emphatical words of Magna Carta spoken in the person of the king, [are that] "for injury done to him by any other subject, . . . [the victim] may take his remedy by the course of the law, and have justice and right for the injury done him, freely without sale, fully without any denial, and speedily without delay."*[126]

---

[124]Blackstone, *supra n.123*, Vol. 1, pp. 122-124.
[125]Blackstone, *supra n.123*, Vol. 1, pp. 125, 136.
[126]Blackstone, *supra n.123*, Vol. 1, p. 137.

*Justice William Blackstone*

43

*Blackstone's Commentaries* was cited by Chief Justice John Marshall in *Marbury v. Madison* in 1803 when he wrote:

> *The very essence of civil liberties certainly consists in the right of every individual to claim the protection of the laws, whenever he receives an injury. One of the first duties of government is to afford that protection....*[127]

Blackstone was a confirmed believer in the sanctity of trial by jury. He called it "a privilege of the highest and most beneficial nature" and "our most important guardian both of public and private liberty." He said that its establishment in England "was always so highly valued and esteemed by the people, that no conquest, no change of government, could ever prevail to abolish" it. "The liberties of England," he said, "cannot but subsist so long as this *palladium* remains sacred and inviolate, not only from all open attacks, ... but also from all secret machinations, which may sap and undermine it." He warned against the introduction of "new and arbitrary methods of trial" by judges or commissioners which, "however convenient they may appear at first," pose an insidious threat to individual liberty and are "fundamentally opposite to the spirit of our *Constitution*." To those who will listen, then and now, William Blackstone tells us that the supposed inconveniences and imperfections of our time-tested "forms of justice, are the price that all free nations must pay for their liberty in more substantial matters."[128]

---

[127] *Marbury v. Madison,* 1 Cranch 137, 163 (1803). Provisions from *Blackstone's Commentaries* were adopted essentially verbatim in the North Carolina Ratification Convention's *Declaration of Rights* on August 1, 1788, *see* pp. 252-253 below.

[128] Blackstone, *supra n.123,* Vol. 3, pp. 349, 350; Vol. 4, pp. 342-344, 407.

# E. THOMAS PAINE ON CIVIL RIGHTS

Thomas Paine was born in Norfolk, England, on January 29, 1737. In 1772, he met Benjamin Franklin, who advised him to seek his fortune in America. He arrived in November of 1774, where his first employment was editing the *Pennsylvania Magazine*.

His 50-page pamphlet, *Common Sense*, was published in January, 1776. With more than half-a-million copies sold, "more than any other single publication, *Common Sense* paved the way for the *Declaration of Independence*, unanimously ratified July 4, 1776."

> *During the war that followed, Paine served as a volunteer aide-de-camp to General Nathanael Greene. His great contribution to the patriot cause was the 16 "Crisis" papers issued between 1776 and 1783, each one signed "Common Sense." "The American Crisis. No. I," published on December 19, 1776, when George Washington's army was on the verge of disintegration, opened with the flaming words: "These are the times that try men's souls." Washington ordered the pamphlet read to all the troops at Valley Forge.*[129]

Thomas Paine was a great American patriot. He believed in the principles of individual liberty. He believed, as we do, that it should be beyond the power of our legislature, state or federal, to permit *any infringement, however slight*, upon our fundamental freedoms as expressed in our *Constitution* and *Bill of Rights*. In *Common Sense*, Paine wrote:

> *But where, says some, is the king of America? I'll tell you. Friend, . . . let a crown be placed . . . , by which the world may know, . . . that in America* **the law is king**. *For in absolute governments the king is the law, so in free countries the law ought to be king; and there ought to be no other. . . .*[130]

---

[129] *Encyclopædia Britannica Macropædia*, Vol. 13, p. 868 (15th ed. 1979).

[130] Robbins, *Law: A Treasure of Art and Literature*, p. 174 (Macmillan Pub. Co. 1990). *See* Thomas Paine's *Common Sense* and *The Rights of Man* (Classics of Liberty Lib. 1992).

Andrew Jackson later said of him that "Thomas Paine needs no monument in the hearts of all lovers of liberty." He was a man who "had known firsthand the poverty and injustice suffered by England's lower classes,"[131] and he believed in the fundamental concept of a *Bill of Rights*. In answer to a letter criticizing the Pennsylvania Constitution of 1776, he wrote:

> *Every free government should consist of three parts: first a Bill of Rights; secondly a Constitution; and thirdly laws. . . .*
>
> *The Bill of Rights should contain the general principles of natural and civil liberty. It should be to a community what the eternal laws and obligations of morality are to the conscience. It should be unalterable by any human power. . . .*
>
> *. . . Civil rights are derived from the assistance or agency of other persons: they form a sort of common stock, which, by the consent of all, may be occasionally used for the benefit of any. They are substituted in room of some natural rights, either defective in power or dangerous in practice, and are contrived to fit the members of the community with greater ease to themselves and safety to others . . . : For instance, a man has a natural right to redress himself whenever he is injured, but the full exercise of this, as a natural right, would be dangerous to society, because it admits him a judge in his own cause. . . . Therefore, the civil right of redressing himself by an appeal to public justice, which is the substitute, makes him stronger than the natural one, and less dangerous. Either party likewise, has a natural right to plead his own cause; . . . but the parties may not be able, . . . therefore the civil right of pleading . . . by a counsel, is an appendage to the natural right and the trial by jury, is perfectly a civil right common to both parties.*[132]

---

[131] Quoted from a bookmark insert by the Classics of Liberty Library in their recent edition of Thomas Paine's *Common Sense* and *The Rights of Man* (1992).

[132] Schwartz, *The Roots of the Bill of Rights, supra n.113,* Vol. 2, pp. 315-316.

*The Bill of Rights should contain the general principles of natural and civil liberty. It should be to a community what the eternal laws and obligations of morality are to the conscience. It should be unalterable by any human power.*

—**Thomas Paine (1777)**

This civil right of redress by an appeal to public justice has been an essential ingredient of Anglo-American law for more than 800 years. In the 12th century, Glanville wrote that the courts of Henry II (1154-1189) were "so impartial" that "a poor man is not opposed by the power of his adversary, nor does favor or partiality drive any man away from the threshold of judgment."[133]

Blackstone tells us that by "the emphatical words of the *Magna Carta*," a victim shall "have justice and right" for his injuries "freely without sale, fully without denial, and speedily without delay."[134] Commenting on the law in England in the 13th century, Pollock & Maitland refer to the right of the injured to bring an action for damages as the "panacea" of the common law.[135]

In his *History and Analysis of the Common Law of England*, written in the latter part of the 17th century, Matthew Hale, Chief Justice of the King's Bench, wrote that every man has a right to the sanctity of his person for which the law provides "a double remedy," that is, both "preventional" and "remedial" in an action for damages.[136] The United States Supreme Court then recognized in *Marbury v. Madison* in 1803 that the right of every citizen "to claim protection of the laws, whenever he receives an injury" is "the very essence of civil liberties."[137]

For more than 800 years, this right of redress in the established courts of civil and criminal justice has been recognized as our fundamental constitutional right and, as Thomas Paine wrote in 1791:

> ...*A government is only the creature of a constitution. The constitution of a country is not an act of its government, but of the people constituting a government....A constitution, therefore, is to a government, what the laws made afterwards by the government are to a court....The court does not make the laws, neither can it alter them; it only acts in conformity to the laws made; and the government is in like manner governed by the constitution.*[138]

---

[133] Glanville, *Treatise on the Law and Customs of the Realm of England*, p. 2 [Legal Classics Library 1990].

[134] *See* p. 70 above.

[135] Pollock & Maitland, *The History of English Law*, Vol. 2, p. 523 (2d ed. 1899) [Legal Classics Library 1982].

[136] Hale, *History of the Common Law of England*, Part II, pp. 114-115 (1713) [Legal Classics Library 1987].

[137] *See* p. 72 n.126 above.

[138] Paine, *The Rights of Man*, supra n. 130, pp. 53-54.

# F. PATRICK HENRY ON THE PRECIOUS JEWEL OF INDIVIDUAL LIBERTY

Patrick Henry was born in Hanover County, Virginia, on May 29, 1736, and was admitted to the Bar of Colonial Virginia in 1760. In the *Parson's Cause* (1763), he "astonished the audience in the courtroom with his eloquence in invoking the doctrine of natural rights, the political theory that man is born with certain inalienable rights."[139] Elected to the Virginia House of Burgesses, he offered a series of resolutions opposing the British *Stamp Act* (1765), "asserting the right of the colonies to legislate independently of the English Parliament." He became "an influential leader in the radical opposition to the British government" and was designated a delegate to the Continental Congresses of 1774 and 1775. At the Second Virginia Convention on March 23, 1775, "he delivered the speech that assured his fame as one of the great advocates of liberty":

> ... Is life so dear, or peace so sweet, as to be purchased at the price of chains and slavery? Forbid it, Almighty God! I know not what course others may take, but as for me, give me liberty or give me death![140]

He served with Thomas Jefferson on the committee that drafted the *First Virginia Constitution* which provided that all civil cases "shall be tried by a jury upon evidence given . . . in open court."[141] He was elected governor of Virginia in 1777, 1778 and 1784. He opposed ratification of the U.S. *Constitution* because it failed to provide specific guarantees of individual liberty. However, following its adoption and ratification, "he was largely responsible for the passage of the *Bill of Rights*."[142]

At the Virginia Ratifying Convention in June of 1788, he opposed the failure of the *Constitution* to include a *Bill of Rights* guaranteeing freedom of the press and the right to a civil jury trial. Without a guarantee of those fundamental rights, he believed that liberty might be lost forever.

---

[139] *Encyclopædia Britannica Macropædia*, Vol. 8, p. 775 (15th ed. 1979).

[140] *Encyclopædia Britannica*, supra n.139, pp. 775-776.

[141] *See Thomas Jefferson, Public and Private Papers*, p.17 (Vintage Books/Library of America 1990).

[142] *Encyclopædia Britannica*, supra n.139, p. 775.

Warning his fellow Virginians that the Plan of the Constitutional Convention, without a *Bill of Rights*, was a proposal "of a most alarming nature," he said:

> *. . . [Y]ou ought to be extremely cautious, watchful, jealous of your liberty; for instead of securing your rights, you may lose them forever. . . .*[143]

When proponents of the *Constitution* answered with the argument that *economic necessity* required ratification, Patrick Henry responded:

> *. . . You are not to inquire how your trade may be increased, nor how you are to become a great and powerful people, but how your liberties can be secured; for liberty ought to be the direct end of your government. Is it necessary for your liberty, that you should abandon those great rights by the adoption of this system? Is the relinquishment of trial by jury, and the liberty of the press, necessary for your liberty? Will the abandonment of your most sacred rights attend to the security of your liberty? Liberty, the greatest of all earthly blessings — give us that precious jewel, and you may take everything else! . . . Guard with jealous attention the public liberty. Suspect everyone who approaches that jewel. . . .*[144]

The need to guard the public liberty "with jealous attention" is no less today than it was in 1788. Economic prosperity is much to be desired, but not at the expense of individual liberty. Representative democracy assures majority rule, but not individual liberty. Throughout history, overbearing majorities have persistently infringed the rights of minorities. It is the *Bill of Rights* and only the *Bill of Rights* that has preserved individual liberty. And it is the civil jury that ensures that the theoretical protection of the *Bill of Rights* becomes a reality for every American citizen.

---

[143]William Wirt, *The Life of Patrick Henry*, p. 283 (Revised ed., DeSilver, Thomas & Co. 1836).

[144]Wirt, *supra n.143*, pp. 289-290. For additional quotations by Patrick Henry, *see* pp. 70, 71, 204 and 221 below.

*Guard with jealous attention the public liberty. Suspect everyone who approaches that jewel.*

—**Patrick Henry (1788)**

# G. GEORGE SUTHERLAND ON THE *BILL OF RIGHTS*

George Sutherland, son of a Scottish farmer, was born in England on March 25, 1862. He immigrated to the Utah Territory in 1864. "In elementary school, Sutherland was exposed to the individualistic ideals of *McGuffey's Readers*, which inculcated diligence and promised material reward."[145] He attended Brigham Young Academy and enrolled in the University of Michigan's "young and distinguished law school." He returned to Utah, was admitted to the bar, and helped organize the Utah State Bar Association. When Utah was admitted to the Union in 1896, he was elected to the state legislature and, in 1900, was elected to the U.S. House of Representatives.

> ... After one term in Congress Sutherland returned to Utah to work for the state senate nomination to the United States Senate. Successful once again, in 1905 he returned to Washington where he proceeded to cast ballots for a large number of reform bills. ...[146]

After failing to win renomination to the Senate in 1916, he was elected president of the American Bar Association in 1917, authored a book entitled *Constitutional Power and World Affairs* and advocated American membership in the World Court. On September 25, 1922, President Warren G. Harding appointed him an Associate Justice of the United States Supreme Court.[147]

During 16 years on the Supreme Court, he authored 295 majority opinions and 24 dissents. "A number of Sutherland's decisions were particularly solicitous of the rights of the isolated individual." It was our solemn duty, he believed, to protect those fundamental freedoms guaranteed by our *Bill of Rights* from "*any infringement, however slight.*"[148]

---

[145] *See* David Burner, "Biography of George Sutherland," pp. 2133-2143 in Vol. 3, *The Justices of the United States Supreme Court 1789-1969: Their Lives and Major Opinions* (Chelsea House Publishers 1969).

[146] Burner, *supra* n.145, p. 2135.

[147] Burner, *supra* n.145, pp. 2136-2137.

[148] Burner, *supra* n.145, p. 2139. It was Justice Sutherland who said: "If the provisions of the *Constitution* be not upheld when they pinch as well as when they comfort, they may as well be abandoned." de Gregorio, *The Complete Book of U.S. Presidents*, pp. 441-442 (2d ed. 1984).

As author of the majority opinion in *Powell v. Alabama*, 287 U.S. 45 (1932) — "the first 'Scottsboro' case" — Sutherland was "widely applauded for this influential decision" in which he "sustained the right of an accused to counsel in a criminal proceeding in a state court."[149] Citing the *Magna Carta*, the British *Bill of Rights*, *Coke's Institutes on the Laws of England*, *Blackstone's Commentaries*, the *Penn Charter of 1701*, the *Declaration of Independence* and the original constitutions of twelve states, Sutherland spoke of those "fundamental principles of liberty and justice which lie at the base of all our civil and political institutions."[150] He said "that there are certain immutable principles of justice which inhere in the very idea of free government which no member of the Union may disregard."[151]

It was of those same "fundamental principles of liberty" and those identical "immutable principles of justice" that Justice Sutherland spoke in his dissenting opinion in *Associated Press v. National Labor Relations Board*, 301 U.S. 103, 133-137 (1937), where he "argued forcefully that presidential control of the employment and discharge of editorial writers interfered with freedom of the press":[152]

*The first ten amendments to the Constitution safeguard [those] fundamental rights . . . [that] the framers of the Bill of Rights regard[ed as] certain liberties . . . so vital that legislative denial of them should be specifically foreclosed. . . .*

\* \* \*

*No one can read the long history which records the stern and often bloody struggles by which these cardinal rights were secured, without realizing how necessary it is to preserve them against any infringement however slight. For . . . "illegitimate and unconstitutional practices get their footing . . . by silent approaches and slight deviations from legal modes of procedure. . . . It is [our] duty . . . to be watchful for the constitutional rights of the citizen, and against any stealthy encroachments thereon. . . .*

---

[149] Burner, *supra* n.145, p. 2140.

[150] *Powell v. Alabama*, 287 U.S. 45, 67 (1932), quoting from *Herbert v. State of Louisiana*, 272 U.S. 312, 316 (1926).

[151] *Powell v. State of Alabama*, supra n.150, 287 U.S. at 65, quoting from *Holden v. Hardy*, 169 U.S. 366 (1898).

[152] Burner, *supra* n.145, p. 2142.

*"Experience should teach us . . . to be most on our guard to protect a public liberty when the government's purposes are beneficent. . . . The greatest dangers to liberty lurk in insidious encroachment by men of zeal. . . ." A little water, trickling here and there through a dam, is a small matter in itself; but it may be a sinister menace to the security of the dam, which those living in the valley below will do well to heed.*

\* \* \*

*Do the people of this land — in the providence of God, favored, as they sometimes boast, among all others in the plentitude of their liberties — desire to preserve those [freedoms] so carefully protected by the [Bill of Rights]. . . ? If so, let them withstand all beginnings of encroachment. For the saddest epitaph which can be carved in memory of a vanished liberty is that it was lost because its possessors failed to stretch forth a saving hand while yet there was time.[153]*

The citizens of this country must be awakened to the realization that we all live in that endangered valley that lies below the sacred dam of the *Seventh Amendment.* The enemies of individual liberty are indeed "a sinister menace" to the security of that sacred dam. Do the people of this favored land desire to preserve those fundamental freedoms so carefully protected by the *Seventh Amendment?* Or shall we slumber as the "commercial coalition" mounts a frontal assault on the citadel of freedom? There is yet time today. Tomorrow, perhaps not. For as the Walrus said unto the Carpenter, "The time has come."

---

[153]*See* Justice Sutherland's dissenting opinion in *Associated Press v. NLRB*, 301 U.S. 103, 134-141 (1937).

*For the saddest epitaph which can be carved in memory of a vanished liberty is that it was lost because its possessors failed to stretch forth a saving hand while yet there was time.*

—**Justice George Sutherland (1937)**

***John Henry Wigmore***, *Dean Emeritus of Northwestern University Law School, shown receiving the American Bar Association's Medal in 1932 for The Most Outstanding Contribution to American Jurisprudence.*

## H. JOHN HENRY WIGMORE ON TRIAL BY JURY

John Henry Wigmore (1863-1943), Dean of the Northwestern University Law School from 1901 through 1929, is best known as the author of *Wigmore on Evidence* (1904-1905), "generally regarded as one of the world's great books on law."[154] He authored 46 original volumes of legal literature, served as Illinois Commissioner for Uniform State Laws and wrote numerous articles on trial by jury.

In 1924, he defended trial by jury against those who advocate substitution of trial by judge:

> We are good friends of jury trial. We believe in it as the best system of trial ever invented for a free people in the world's history. In spite of all suggestions to substitute the trained judge of fact, we believe that a system of trying facts by a regular judicial official, known beforehand and therefore accessible to the arts of corruption and chicanery, would be fatal to justice. The grand solid merit of jury trial is that the jurors of fact are selected at the last moment from the multitude of citizens. They cannot be known beforehand, and they melt back into the multitude after each trial.[155]

In 1925, he posed the question: What is the American Bar going to do about trial by jury? His answer:

> ... Trial by jury must and shall be preserved! Amidst the throng of crude sacrilegisms .... that assail us nowadays in the legal sanctuary, none is more shortsighted, none more dangerous, than the proposal to abolish trial by jury.[156]

---

[154] *Encyclopædia Britannica Micropædia,* Vol. X, p. 669 (15th ed. 1979). "There was nothing before 1900 to match the magnificent *Treatise on Evidence* (1904-05) by John H. Wigmore." Friedman, *A History of American Law,* p. 626 (Touchstone Books 1985).

[155] Wigmore, "To Ruin Jury Trial in the Federal Courts," 19 *Ill. L.R.* 97, 98 (June, 1924), reprinted in 9 *J. American Judicature Soc.* 61 (August, 1925).

[156] Wigmore, "First Aid for Trial by Jury," 20 *Ill. L.R.* 106 (May, 1925), reprinted in 9 *J. American Judicature Soc.* 121 (December, 1925).

In 1929, in an article in the *Journal of the American Judicature Society*, Dean Wigmore revisited the question of whether trial by jury is superior to trial by judge. His answer shows a depth of understanding of the inherent merits of trial by jury shared by few, if any, of its detractors:

> The writer believes that . . . [trial by jury] possesses four merits that can never be possessed by a judge trial. . . .
>
> **1. Prevention of Popular Distrust of Official Justice.** . . . Hence, the popular attitude toward the administration of justice should be one of respect and confidence. Bureaucratic, purely official justice, can never receive such confidence. The one way to secure it is to give the citizen-body itself a share in the administration of justice. And that is what jury-trial does. . . .
>
> **2. Provision for Necessary Flexibility in Legal Rules.** Law and justice are from time to time inevitably in conflict. That is because law is a general rule . . . ; while justice is the fairness of this precise case under all its circumstances. And as a rule of law only takes account of broadly typical conditions and is aimed on average results, law and justice every so often do not coincide.
>
> . . . Now this is where the jury comes in. The jury, in the privacy of its retirement, adjusts the general rule of law to the justice to the particular case. Thus the odium of inflexible rules of law is avoided, and popular satisfaction is preserved . . . That is what jury trial does. It supplies that flexibility of legal rules which is essential to justice and popular contentment. . . .
>
> **3. Education of the Citizenry in Administration of Law.** In a democracy, where the operation of the law frequently becomes a political issue, it is important that the body of citizens should have a general acquaintance with court method. . . . Jury-duty will bring all respectable citizens sooner or later to have acquaintance with court methods, and in such a way as to compel serious thought and give the needed scrap of judiciary education common to all. . . .

Trial by jury must be preserved. It is the best system ever-invented for a free people in the world's history.
—**Dean John Henry Wigmore (1929)**

***4. Improved Quality of a Verdict Based on Reconciliation of Varied Temperaments and Minds.*** *. . . Ask any twelve intelligent friends any question of opinion or fact, calling for serious thought. . . . Will it ever happen that you do not glean from at least two or three of the twelve some argument or detail or judgment that the others . . . had failed to mention?*

*. . . [T]he conduct of human life has to be based on elusive averages or generalities, whether in politics, law, medicine, engineering, commerce or ethics. And when it comes to applying these generalities to concrete cases, the only safe machinery, that is dependable in the long run, is a machinery that embodies an average judgment, i.e., the reconciliation of several judgments taken at random.*[157]

    These principles, preservation of public confidence in the administration of justice, provision for needed flexibility in legal rules, education of the citizenry in the administration of law and the improvement of the quality of verdicts based on varied temperaments and minds, all are important, both to our country and to the individual citizen whose future may hinge upon the verdict of a civil jury. Lack of public confidence in the administration of the legislative and executive branches of government already exists. Arbitrary and inflexible rules and regulations we have in sufficient quantity now. An uneducated citizenry is exactly what we do not need. And the reconciliation of various temperaments, preconceived notions and points-of-view is what democracy is all about.

    What Dean Wigmore said in the 1920's is equally true today. Trial by jury must be preserved: not as a mere formality, stripped of its discretion by arbitrary and inflexible rules dictated by the captains of commerce and industry for the furtherance of their own selfish interests, but free to search out and find the truly essential justice of each individual case. That is the spirit of *true democracy* and *true democracy is the spirit of America.*

---

[157]Wigmore, "A Program for the Trial of Jury Trial," 12 *J. Am. Jud. Soc.* 166, 169-171 (April, 1929). For similar views on the advantages of "aggregate wisdom" *see* quotes from Charles S. May (p. 64), Eli K. Price (p. 278), James H. Hazelrigg (p. 281), Howard T. Hogan (p. 282), Matthew Hale (p. 308), Henry Peter Brougham (p. 321), Ward Hunt (pp. 344-45), Harold Corbin (p. 380), Robert von Moschzisker (pp. 381-82), and David Edelstein (p. 391).

# I. CHARLES S. MAY ON JUDICIAL REFORM

Charles S. May, former Lieutenant-Governor of Michigan and an advocate of national repute, has been described as "one of the most brilliant lawyers and eloquent orators" and "one of the ablest independent thinkers" of his day.[158] He delivered an address to the law students at the University of Michigan in March of 1875 on "one of the great institutions of English justice," trial by jury. In response to "the frequent demands of the press for a change or abolition of the jury system, and the unfounded attacks on 'ignorant' juries," he said that the institution of trial by jury had been "highly prized and sacredly preserved" as "a glory and boon to England" and "a blessing and glory to us."

Noting that the purpose of "every form of trial known to the law" is "a struggle and endeavor after the truth and justice of the case," he warned that the true purpose of reform is improvement, not merely change or destruction:

> Does it need that I should defend at this late day, an institution thus venerable in years and hallowed by popular affection? . . . To some restless innovators the mere fact that it is old is an argument against it. But every considerate and thoughtful man will . . . hesitate before condemning an institution which has been in continued daily operation for more than twenty generations of men; which has become intertwined with the history and traditions of his country and race, and whose germs are found away back in the earliest civilizations. Progress, reform, judicial reform — these are good and admirable things, but we should take care to know what we do in their name. John Randolph once said, in Congress, that "change is not reform" and adding to his words, I may say, with still greater truth, that destruction is not reform. To abolish the trial by jury, to sweep out of use and out of existence with one blow the jury system, would be a terribly destructive and radical measure, a direct impeachment of the wisdom of the past and a bold and hazardous experiment upon the future.[159]

---

[158] See J. W. Donovan, *Skills in Trials*, p. 7 (Williamson Law Book Company 1891). *See also* Charles Sedgwick May, *Speeches of the Stump, the Bar and the Platform*, pp. 244-284 (Battle Creek, Michigan 1899).

[159] Donovan, *Modern Jury Trials and Advocates*, pp. 165-168 (Banks & Brothers, Law Book Publishers 1881).

Concerning the origin of trial by jury, Mr. May credited the initiation of this institution in its present form to the reign of Henry II, that "sagacious, far-seeing and intrepid monarch":

> *Since the Grand Assize of 1176, a period of almost 700 years, trial by jury has been one of the sacred muniments of English liberty. . . . And since Magna Carta, in every struggle of the British people against the encroachments of the Crown, in every popular upheaval or revolution — in every advance toward a larger and broader liberty, the recognition and maintenance of this institution has ever been stoutly insisted upon, so that today it would be easier to uproot the foundation of the British throne itself than to tear this venerated landmark from the British Constitution or the affections of the British people.*

As to the role of trial by jury as a shield against tyranny in America, Mr. May concluded:

> *. . . We may never have tyrants, we may never have caesars, but if we should have them, they will seek to accomplish the downfall of free government, not by directly overriding the Constitution, but by using the forms of law to strangle and subvert its spirit. No central despotism, no rule of monied or political monopolies can successfully control for tyrannical or sordid purposes an institution which derives its life and power from the great, honest masses of the people. And here will be our safety.*
>
> *For the jury system is the handmaid of freedom. It catches and takes on the spirit of liberty, and grows and expands with the progress of constitutional government. . . .*
>
> *No; civil liberty cannot dispense with any of her armaments. She needs them all to battle with tyranny and oppression. Trial by jury is one of the chiefest of these. . . . Rome, Sparta and Carthage fell because they did not know it, let not England and America fall because they threw it away.*[160]

---

[160]Donovan, *Modern Jury Trials, supra n.159*, pp. 165-166, 189-190.

*The jury system is the handmaid of freedom. It catches and takes on the spirit of liberty, and grows and expands with the progress of constitutional government. Rome, Sparta and Carthage fell because they did not know it, let not England and America fall because they threw it away.*
—**Charles S. May, Address to the Michigan Law School (1875)**

Defending the trial jury as "the best and fittest tribunal" to find the facts of a case, Charles S. May proclaimed that, as triers of facts, juries were superior judges in civil cases:

> ... I believe that a jury is always the best and fittest tribunal to find the facts of a case. ... The facts to be found in a trial in the courts are generally the facts of common life. The deductions and conclusions to be drawn from these facts, in nine cases out of ten, are the deductions and conclusions of ordinary human experience. These do not so much require learning and logic as practical common sense, knowledge of human nature as seen in men and not in books, and intuitive perception of right and wrong — qualities oftener found combined, I think, in the jury box than upon the bench.
>
> ... For facts cannot be dealt with like principles or arbitrary scientific rules, and right and justice are not always to be arrived at like mathematical results. Often the very learning and discipline of the judge may have unfitted him for this work by educating him away from the people. ... [U]sually the facts in a case are narrated by living witnesses in court, whose look and manner and the probability of whose story should be scanned and weighed by men practiced in the ways of human nature, and not easily to be imposed upon. ... [I]s there nothing still in the fact that the verdict of a jury is the aggregate wisdom of twelve men, while the finding of a judge is but the wisdom of one man? Do the scriptures say untruly, then, and is there no safety in a multitude of counsel?[161]

There is indeed safety in a multitude of counsel just as there is true wisdom in the accumulated common sense and good judgment of the common people of America. With the escalating costs of post-graduate education, more and more each year those who enter our law schools, graduate, practice law and ultimately become judges on our state and federal Bench are from that exclusive category of citizens which we like to call "the well-to-do." How many have milked a cow or plowed a mule? How many have worked in a cotton mill? How many have cut pulpwood, or sold newspapers, or shined shoes, or changed a spark plug?
*Precious few indeed!*

---

[161] Donovan, *Modern Jury Trials*, supra n.159, pp. 168-169.

# J. J. SYDNEY TAYLOR ON LEGISLATIVE UNDERMINING OF TRIAL BY JURY

J. Sydney Taylor (1795-1841) was born in Ireland and educated at Dublin University. As a student, he earned "a considerable university reputation," and became a respected member of the Irish Historical Society. But he yearned to study for the Bar, whose "sacred office" he believed, was "the guardian and vindicator of civil and religious liberty."

In 1816, he moved to London and was admitted to studies at the Middle Temple, at the same time contributing to the columns of the *Morning Chronicle* and the *Morning Herald.* He was called to the London Bar in 1822, but continued his contributions to the daily press, that "great engine of public opinion and improvement." He soon rose to prominence in the legal profession where, although he died at age 45, his many accomplishments included the successful defense of a deranged youth who attempted to assassinate Queen Victoria and "his successful exertions in advocating the abolition of the punishment of death."[162]

J. Sydney Taylor believed that the institution of trial by jury was "the best and noblest of our ancient institutions" and, "in the hands of the people — a great bulwark against tyranny, prejudice and oppression." He was outspoken in his opposition to the attempts of King Louis Philip of France to undermine the effectiveness of trial by jury in that country in furtherance of what he termed the king's "bitter and implacable" persecution of the press.

> *The persecution of the press, almost ever since Louis Philip became king of the French, has been bitter and implacable — as if he could never forgive it for being instrumental in raising him to the throne. The 500 or 600 prosecutions, which he has instituted against the great organ of public opinion, were all, of course, according to law; but juries did not always make their verdicts conform to the wishes of the sovereign and the demands of his minions. Too often have honesty and independence in the jury box stood between power and its victim — too often has the vindictive persecutor been disappointed of his prey....*[163]

---

[162] *See* Biographical Sketch of the Late J. Sydney Taylor, A.M. in *Selections from the Writings of the Late J. Sydney Taylor, A.M., Barrister at Law* (London 1843).

[163] Writings of J. Sydney Taylor, *supra*, p. 133.

But J. Sydney Taylor's greatest contribution to the defense of trial by jury was his attack upon the *Metropolitan Police Courts Bill*. On November 12, 1838, he wrote:

> *No single institution that the wisdom of man has ever devised is so well calculated to preserve a people free, or make them so, as trial by jury....*

He wrote that a Parliament could become obedient to "the mandates of a venal minister, or the unreasoning impulses of an excited mob."

> *But trial by jury cannot be corrupted unless the whole body of the people be corrupt.... Instances of perverse or dishonest verdicts there will be, because the attribute of perfection does not belong to any human institution....Trial by jury... must always partake of the imperfectability of human nature. The class of "minute philosophers" see only those blemishes which are the casual specks of a glorious institution. The magnificent source of material light is not without its blemishes; but what should we say of the astronomer who would wish to reform the solar system by extinguishing the sun, because the face of that luminary is not free from spots.*
>
> *Yet such is the sort of logical processes by which the deprecators of trial by jury arrive at the conclusion, that the administration of justice would be reformed, as they have gravely argued, by substituting for it the individual responsibility, or rather irresponsibility, of a judge. They select instances of verdicts of a perverse or absurd character, and present them to the public as specimens of the working of the jury system. They prove nothing so conclusively as their own incapacity to take a more comprehensive view of a great subject, than the fly upon the column, whose microscopic glance perceived with painful accuracy, the minute inequalities that came within the scope of its vision, but was blind to the beautiful symmetry of the whole design. Every column of the British Constitution has its philosophic fly, that solemnly pronounces the condemnation of the magnificent structure which its pygmy faculties cannot comprehend.*

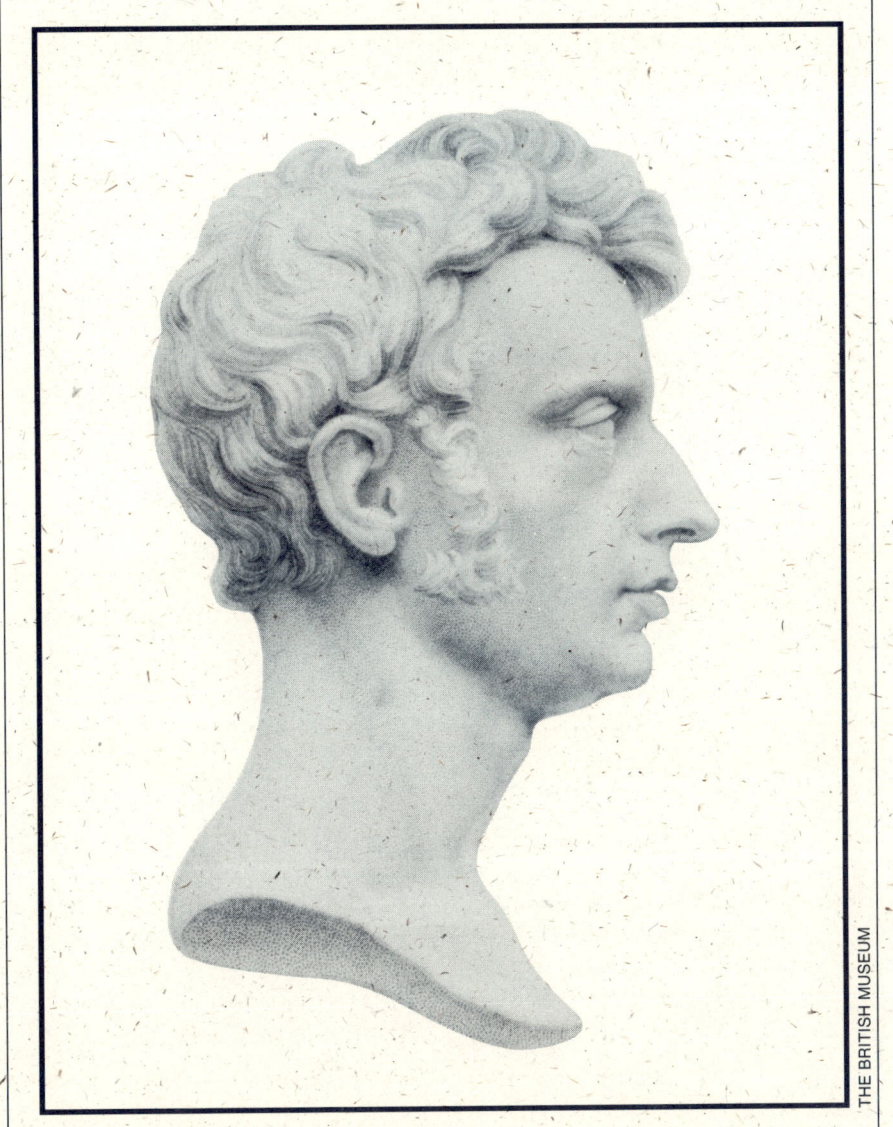

*No single institution that the wisdom of man has ever devised is so well calculated to preserve a people free, or make them so, as trial by jury.*

—J. Sydney Taylor (1838)

In a subsequent column entitled, "Dangerous Innovations Attempted on the Rights and Liberty of the Subject," appearing on March 9, 1839, he characterized the *Metropolitan Police Courts Bill* as "but the forerunner of a system of dangerous attacks upon the free institutions, and ancient rights of Englishmen" in order to "rob the people of the best and firmest securities for the due administration of justice." And on June 7, 1839, he called upon the spirits of Alfred the Great and Edward I, "the English Justinian," to save the institution of trial by jury from the misguided whims of a committee of Parliament:

> *Spirit of Alfred! August memory of that second Alfred — Edward I — the English Justinian! Mighty shades of Bacon and Burleigh — of Sydney and Hampden! if ye are allowed to look down upon the country which your magnificent wisdom and civil virtues adorned, enriched, and elevated, what must be your feelings on beholding the law, the justice, the freedom of Englishmen — all the venerable and sacred principles of her glorious Constitution threatened with extinction — not by the hands of a foreign conqueror — not by the splendid despotism of a Cromwell or a Napoleon, but by the laborious insignificance and presumptuous incapacity of . . . a committee of Parliament. . . .*[164]

In America today, that same question could be put to our own venerated ancestors. *Spirit of Samuel Adams! August memory of Patrick Henry! Mighty shades of Thomas Jefferson and James Madison!* If you could look down upon the country which your magnificent wisdom and civil virtues adorned, enriched and elevated, what would be your feelings upon viewing the great clamor to scuttle the *Seventh Amendment?*

> *Shock, disbelief, disappointment and despair — that it could all come to this in the short span of 200 years!*

Unfortunately, it has indeed come down to this in the short span of 200 years since the ratification of the *Seventh Amendment*. The mountain of so-called "tort reform" legislation sponsored each year by the captains of commerce and industry is "but the forerunner of a system of dangerous attacks upon the free institutions and ancient rights" of Americans in order to "rob the people of the best and firmest securities for the administration of justice."

---

[164]Taylor, *supra n.162*, pp. 392-393, 398-399, 401, 405.

# K. A SUMMARY OF HISTORICAL REFERENCES ON TRIAL BY JURY

The concept of constitutional rights began more than seven centuries ago with the adoption of the *Magna Carta*. Its most significant provisions include Article 12 which provided that no "scutage" [a feudal tax] should be imposed "unless by the common council of our kingdom" and Article 39 which guaranteed that no free man could be deprived of his life, liberty or property except by the judgment of his peers. As interpreted by ensuing generations, these two articles have provided a constitutional basis for "the twin pillars of liberty" — representative government and trial by jury.

During the first 100 years following its adoption in 1215 A.D., the *Magna Carta* was reaffirmed on 38 separate occasions. The people of England reasserted their historic right to trial by jury in the *Petition of Right* in 1628 and in the *Bill of Rights* in 1689. These ancient guarantees of the *Magna Carta* later became the basis for every American citizen's constitutional right to trial by jury both in civil and criminal cases when the right of trial by jury was reasserted in the *Declaration of Independence*, Article III, §2 of the *Constitution*, the *Sixth and Seventh Amendments* in the *Bill of Rights*, and comparable provisions of essentially all state constitutions.

In the 17th century, the British Crown believed in the *Divine Right of Kings*. They saw the right of trial by jury as an obstacle to the accomplishment of their arbitrary purposes. To undermine its effectiveness, they attempted to influence the administration of justice by packing English juries with subjects subservient to the king and by punishing jurors who did not submit to the Royal Will. Another of the favorite tools of tyranny was that infamous nonjury tribunal, the Court of Star Chamber.

These arbitrary acts contributed to the execution of Charles I in 1649 and the abdication of James II in 1689. To protect the people from further usurpations of power, Parliament required William and Mary's assent to the English *Bill of Rights* as a condition to their coronation.

Arbitrary rule in the 17th century contributed to English immigration to America. As the colonists crossed the Atlantic, royal abuse of the jury system was foremost in their minds. To protect themselves and their descendants, all colonial Charters guaranteed the right of trial by jury as the *palladium* of individual liberty.

In the 18th century, British tyranny turned its attention toward the American colonies primarily through attempted intimidation of the colonial press. Freedom of the press was a hollow right which only prevented prior restraints. The rule of law was: "Publish at your peril." Truth was no defense.

This abuse was confronted by a courageous American jury in the trial of John Peter Zenger in 1735. In its acquittal of Zenger of criminal libel, this jury lit the lamps of colonial liberty and fueled the fires of American freedom. In the words of Gouverneur Morris, a delegate from Pennsylvania to the Constitutional Convention of 1787, "the trial of Peter Zenger was the germ of American freedom, the morning star of liberty which revolutionized America." Trial by jury had established freedom of the press and a free press, in turn, brought about the birth of a new nation based upon principles of representative government and a guarantee of fundamental rights to every American citizen.

By the *Stamp Act* of 1765, the British Crown abridged the colonists' right to trial by jury by extending the jurisdiction of Admiralty Courts. The colonists considered this a violation of their historic rights under the *Magna Carta* as reconfirmed in their colonial charters. Their resistance led to the repeal of the *Stamp Act*, but the British Crown continued to undermine American juries.

In 1772, Samuel Adams declared that the *Magna Carta* had been "justly obtained of King John, sword in hand," and that "it must be one day, sword in hand, again rescued and preserved from total destruction." At his urging, British tea was dumped into the Boston Harbor. The British blockaded the Port of Boston and the die was cast.

In 1774, the Virginia House of Burgesses protested the British blockade. Thomas Jefferson authored *A Summary View of the Rights of British Americans*. In it, he faulted England for depriving the colonists of their right to trial by jury. The Continental Congress adopted a *Declaration of Colonial Rights* which complained of the same abuse. John Jay wrote *An Address to the People of Great Britain* stating that the colonists had "lost the advantage of being tried by an honest, uninfluenced jury." The Continental Congress declared that representative government and trial by jury were "the two most important principles on which to build a constitution of free people." Patrick Henry exclaimed:

> *Three millions of people armed in the holy cause of liberty . . . are invincible by any force which our enemy can send against us. . . . There is no retreat but in submission and slavery! Our chains are forged. The war is inevitable — and let it come!!*

*Three million people armed in the holy cause of liberty are invincible by any force which our enemy can send against us. There is no retreat but in submission and slavery! Our chains are forged. The war is inevitable — and let it come!!*

—**Patrick Henry (March 23, 1775)**

*In the Declaration of Independence, the King of Great Britain was arraigned before the world for depriving us of trial by jury. This language evinces the purpose of our representatives to risk their lives and their fortunes to secure the ancient right of trial by jury.*
—**Justice Alphonso C. Avery of North Carolina (1892)**

On July 4, 1776, the Second Continental Congress adopted the *Declaration of Independence*, indicting the English Crown "for depriving us, in many cases, of the benefit of trial by jury." The war was on. We won a glorious victory, but the price was dear. Many American lives were lost. We proved a historic truth. Fundamental freedom does not come cheap.

The constitutions of all American states guaranteed that the fundamental right of trial by jury would be held sacred. The *Articles of Confederation* soon proved unsatisfactory. A Constitutional Convention was convened at Independence Hall in Philadelphia in May of 1787. For four hot months, the Founding Fathers built the basic structure of our new government. It was only after the Committee of Style had hammered out the final draft that Hugh Williamson of North Carolina observed that "no provision was yet made for juries in civil cases and suggested the necessity of it." Then Elbridge Gerry of Massachusetts "urged the necessity of juries to guard against corrupt judges" and proposed a provision guaranteeing the right of civil juries. George Mason of Virginia joined in and suggested the *Constitution* be prefaced by a *Bill of Rights*.

Two days before the convention adjourned, Elbridge Gerry joined Charles Pinckney of South Carolina in a motion to amend Article III, §2, of the *Constitution* to add: "and a trial by jury shall be preserved as usual in civil cases." When their motion failed, Elbridge Gerry said that he would not sign the *Constitution* because nonjury trials would be a "Star Chamber" in civil cases.

However, on that hot day in September of 1787, the convention was unreceptive. They had haggled long and hard over the mechanics of government. The Continental Congress impatiently awaited the end result of their deliberations. The divisive battle over the perpetuation of slavery was fresh in their minds. They were tired and they wanted to go home.

Although this belated attempt to guarantee civil juries died in convention, it reappeared in the battle for ratification. For the anti-federalists, the failure to guarantee the right of trial by jury in civil cases was their primary rallying point. Patrick Henry, Richard Henry Lee and George Mason of Virginia, Elbridge Gerry of Massachusetts, Melancton Smith of New York, Samuel Bryan of Pennsylvania, Judge Alexander Hanson of Maryland, Justice Samuel Spencer of North Carolina and many others attacked the *Constitution* for its failure to guarantee civil juries. Following ratification by the Pennsylvania state convention, a 21-member minority published their objection to this omission in the *Pennsylvania Packet*.

Led by the initiative of Massachusetts, many state conventions proposed amendments guaranteeing the right of trial by jury in civil cases. It was only with assurance that a *Bill of Rights* would quickly follow that the required number of states ratified the *Constitution*. In *The Federalist* No. 83, Alexander Hamilton wrote:

> *The friends and adversaries of the plan of the convention, if they agree in nothing else, concur at least in the value they set upon the trial by jury; or if there is any difference between them it consists in this; that the former regard it as a valuable safeguard to liberty; the latter represent it as the very palladium of free government. . . .*

Following ratification of the *Constitution*, James Madison presented a proposed *Bill of Rights* to the House of Representatives on June 8, 1789. In his address to Congress, he characterized the civil jury as "one of the best securities of the rights of the people [which] ought to remain inviolate." He said that trial by jury was "as essential to secure the liberty of the people as any one of the preexistent rights of nature." The *Bill of Rights* was adopted by Congress on September 25, 1789, and ratified by the requisite number of states on December 15, 1791. The *Seventh Amendment* stipulates that "in suits at common law, where the amount in controversy shall exceed twenty dollars, the right of trial by jury shall be preserved." This is a sacred birthright of every American citizen.

For 500 years, trial by jury has been praised as the most cherished institution of free and intelligent government that the world has ever seen and as the best institution for the administration of justice ever devised by the mind of man. In the words of William Blackstone, trial by jury has been "the principal bulwark of English liberty" for so long that "the memory of man runneth not to the contrary." Winston Churchill wrote that "the jury system has come to stand for all we mean by English justice."

In 1776, Richard Bland of Virginia wrote that "trial by jury is hardly less important than representative government itself." The American Bar Foundation called it "a fundamental feature of the administration of American justice." In 1835, Alexis de Tocqueville said that "the practical intelligence and political good sense of the Americans are mainly attributable to the long use which they have made of the jury in civil causes." And in 1962, Chief Justice Earl Warren referred to the civil jury as one of "the keystones of America's strength" and "our main claim to moral leadership in the world community."

*The friends and adversaries of the plan of the convention, if they agree in nothing else, concur at least in the value they set upon the trial by jury; the former regard it as a valuable safeguard to liberty; the latter represent it as the very palladium of free government.*

—Alexander Hamilton (1788)

ILLUSTRATION BY DAVID JOHNSON

*For almost eight centuries trial by jury remains the best, safest, surest and perhaps the only bulwark to protect the basic rights of the average citizen. It is still the "Lamp of Liberty" and it must be preserved.*
—**Joseph T. Karcher,** *The Case for the Jury System* (1969)

Our jury system has been described as the sacred right of every American, a primary safeguard of individual liberty, a fundamental right of free and enlightened people, and the most rational and effective method for discovering the truth. According to Lysander Spooner, a jury ensures us of what no other court can: "that first and indispensable requisite of a judicial tribunal, integrity."

Tyranny implies the absence of civil responsibility for the actions of the tyrant. Therefore, whatever form tyranny may take, it cannot long coexist with the right of trial by jury. According to British Judge, Sir Patrick Devlin, it is a primary object of any tyrant "to overthrow or diminish trial by jury" because "no tyrant could afford to leave a subject's freedom in the hands of twelve of his countrymen."

> *... So that trial by jury is more than an instrument of justice and more than one wheel of the Constitution: It is the lamp that shows that freedom lives....*

But tyranny is not limited to individual dictatorship. The "tyranny of the majority" has long been recognized. It sets its course by the fickle winds of public opinion. Individual rights are its inevitable victim. It was primarily for this reason that Joseph Choate told the American Bar Association in 1898:

> *It is for the integrity, efficiency, and utility of trial by jury in civil causes that I am chiefly concerned. ... For I cherish as the result of a life's work ... that the old fashioned trial by jury of twelve honest and intelligent citizens remains today ... the best and safest practical method for the determination of facts ..., and that all attempts to tinker or tamper with it should be discouraged as disastrous to the public welfare.*

The civil jury brings to the bar of justice the collective wisdom of the community, integrity, impartiality, a broad body of human experience, and the common sense of the common people. It guards us against oppression, it protects us against those who threaten our safety and it sets standards for acceptable conduct.

Two hundred years ago, Thomas Erskine told England that its liberty would last only so long as trial by jury "remains sacred and inviolate not only from all open attacks, ... *but also from all secret machinations, which may sap and undermine it.*" The people of Great Britain failed to heed his warning and today the English civil jury is practically extinct.

For more than 100 years, our American civil jury system has been under attack and the danger is greater today than ever before. The benefits of "courthouse democracy" are poorly understood. To many Americans, the stirring defense of this *palladium* of individual liberty by the founding fathers of our country are a long-forgotten memory. The "citadel of freedom" has been stormed and the future of American democracy hangs in the balance.

In 1788, John Dickinson of Delaware demanded indignantly: "Who in opposition to the genius of united America shall dare to attempt [the] subversion" of trial by jury? The answer to that question today is all-too-painfully clear. A dedicated, determined and well financed coalition of commercial interests has united their efforts with those of the liability insurance industry in an attempt to undermine the effectiveness of the civil jury. They have many friends in Congress and in the legislatures of all 50 states. Anyone who would downplay the danger is courting impending disaster.

The question we must ask ourselves today is not who would attempt the subversion of the civil jury, but who will defend it? With every passing hour, the prognosis for individual liberty in America grows progressively dim. If our civil jury system is emasculated, what comes next? The grim reality of the experience in England since the curtailment of their civil jury in the 19th century should sober the most inveterate optimist.

In a world of constantly increasing centralization of power, we cannot afford to surrender our individual rights. Robbed of the protection of our civil jury system, the small businessman will be left at the mercy of the monopolists; the health and safety of the consumer will be placed in peril by the indifference of profit-oriented industrialists; the bewildered citizen will have no recourse from the injustice of a belligerent bureaucracy; and the disadvantaged, poor and helpless will be placed at risk by the insatiable appetite of the rich and powerful.

Unchecked by the right of effective civil recovery, the prevailing body of public opinion will stifle dissent and individuality will fall victim to the blind intolerance of enforced conformity. This is what we have to lose, along with our national pride and purpose as the guardians of individual liberty and the hope of all who aspire to achieve true freedom.

In the pages that follow, we will learn how England sacrificed its civil jury system. But we are not England. We have no king or queen. We harbor no House of Lords. We have no titled nobility. What we do have are those guarantees of individual liberty enshrined in the first ten amendments to our *Constitution*. In England, their motto is: "*God Save the Queen!*" In America, our motto must be: "*God Save the Bill of Rights!*"

*English liberty will subsist so long as trial by jury remains sacred and inviolate not only from all open attacks, but also from all secret machinations, which may sap and undermine it.*

**—Thomas Erskine, British Barrister (1784)**

*Necessity is the plea for every abridgment of human freedom. It is the argument of tyrants, the creed of slaves.*

—**William Pitt, Prime Minister of England (1783)**

# L. A SUGGESTED METHOD FOR THE EVALUATION OF TRIAL BY JURY

In their rush to judgment, the leaders of the "commercial coalition" have advanced arguments that challenge the underlying basis of democracy itself. For our civil juries are no more than a representative fraction of the public-at-large, chosen at random. If our civil jury system is irrational, then the entire American public must be irrational. If representatives of the American people, chosen at random, are not properly qualified to serve on American juries, then how can they be qualified to participate in the electoral process? If it makes good sense to substitute panels of "educated experts" for impartial American juries, then why does it not also make good sense to entrust the election of our representatives in our state and national legislatures to the same process?

Those who attack the civil jury are men of zeal, the leaders of great economic empires and members of our most respected professions. Their asserted justification for undermining our civil jury system is that of "economic necessity." But their rationalization is fatally flawed.

Physicians, whom the taxpayers provide with rent-free hospitals in which to practice their trade, and *exclusive* parking lots in which to park their foreign cars, supposedly cannot afford to pay their escalating liability insurance premiums. Therefore, rather than improving the quality of the professional care which they provide, they would have our lawmakers legislate away the constitutional rights of their patients.

American industrialists, by the same reasoning, can send a spaceship to the moon, penetrate the sanctuary of the atom, harness the energy of the sun and the wind, construct intricate electrical systems on a microchip, but cannot economically design and build a safe product. Consequently, they must have immunity from civil responsibility for their gory annual harvest of human hands, arms, legs and lives devoured by the hungry jaws of their unguarded industrial machines.

Does anyone really believe that a typical American jury equipped with that intuitive horse sense that comes from being born in the freest nation on the face of the earth would return a large verdict for an injured victim of an industrial machine unless it was truly defective and unreasonably dangerous? Does anyone believe that a typical American juror who literally worships the ground upon which the medical profession walks would render a verdict against a physician unless he had clearly departed from the accepted standard of medical care?

The propagandists of the commercial coalition would have us believe this, but anyone who does in fact swallow this line of preposterous propaganda is out of touch with the reality of everyday life. Jurors, as "the unadulterated voice of the people," are typical representatives of the American public and the American public is basically conservative and becoming more so with each passing day.

An American jury traditionally gives both sides of a civil dispute a fair and impartial hearing and renders a just and reasonable verdict. An indictment of our civil jury system is an indictment of America itself. Any attempt to limit the discretion of a fair and impartial jury, considering all of the relevant evidence, to reach the true justice of an individual case, flies in the face of reason and is faithless to the essential principles of democratic self-government.

But since the captains of commerce and industry have indicted our civil jury system in the Court of Public Opinion, those of us who would preserve the cornerstone of our judicial process can only hope that trial by jury itself will receive a fair trial. To ensure that it does, we would suggest the following for the consideration of those who may doubt the necessity of preserving the sanctity of our most fundamentally democratic institution.

**Consideration No. 1.** *The value of the civil jury can only be judged with a true understanding of its long and distinguished history.* If, as Oliver Wendell Holmes, Jr., has said, "a page of history is worth a volume of logic," then there is much indeed to learn from the history of trial by jury. Therefore, we have attempted here to tell that history, not only through the words of the greatest of English and American patriots and statesmen, but also by recounting the events of some of the most significant trials in England and America. These include the trial of Sir Nicholas Throckmorton in 1554,[165] the trials of Lt.Col. John Lilburne in 1649 and 1653,[166] the trial of William Penn and William Mead in 1670,[167] the trial of the Seven Bishops in 1688,[168] the trial of John Peter Zenger in 1735,[169] the trial of William Owen in 1752,[170] and the trial of Gideon Henfield in 1793.[171]

---

[165] *See* pp. 100-101 below.
[166] *See* pp. 128-131 below.
[167] *See* pp. 136-139 below.
[168] *See* pp. 144-147 below.
[169] *See* pp. 157-159 below.
[170] *See* pp. 289-293 below.
[171] *See* pp. 294-299 below.

*The sacred privilege of trial by jury is the unadulterated voice of the people which should be heard in the sanctuaries of justice as fountains springing fresh from the lap of earth.*
—Henry Hallam, **The Constitutional History of England** (1827)

In addition, we have documented the role of trial by jury in the long and rocky road to the American Revolution and the adoption and ratification of our *Constitution* and *Bill of Rights*. Following this are the testimonials of 116 English and American authors over a span of five-and-a-half centuries. What they have had to say on the subject is well worth the time and trouble that it takes to listen. G. K. Chesterton called this "tradition": the art of listening to the wisdom of our ancestors, or "*the Democracy of the Dead.*"

> *Tradition may be defined as an extension of the franchise. Tradition means giving votes to the most obscure of all classes, our ancestors. It is the Democracy of the Dead. Tradition refuses to submit to the small and arrogant oligarchy of those who merely happen to be walking about. All democrats object to men being disqualified by the accident of birth; tradition objects to their being disqualified by the accident of death. Democracy tells us not to neglect a good man's opinion, even if he is our groom; tradition asks us not to neglect a good man's opinion, even if he is our father.[172]*

**Consideration No. 2.** *Suspect anyone who attempts to deprive you of your fundamental rights.* Economic necessity was the alleged justification for the deprivation of individual rights in the fascist and communist regimes which dominated Europe in the early 20th century. The appeasement of those enemies of individual liberty led to one of the greatest holocausts in human history.

In the history of the human race, no nation has ever profited from the sacrifice of individual liberty. In 1783, Prime Minister William Pitt told the House of Commons that "necessity is the plea for every abridgment of human freedom." It was, he said, "the argument of tyrants" and "the creed of slaves."[173]

---

[172]*Oxford Dictionary of Modern Quotations*, p. 51 (Oxford University Press 1991).

[173]Speech before the House of Commons, November 18, 1783, *see* Bartlett's Familiar Quotations, p. 496a (14th ed. 1968). The *Encyclopædia Britannica* calls William Pitt "one of the most notable prime ministers in British history." He entered Parliament at age 21 and became prime minister at age 24 where his "outstanding gifts of oratory were . . . recognized by his colleagues." *Encyclopædia Britannica Macropædia*, Vol. 14, p. 477 (15th ed. 1979).

***Consideration No. 3.*** *Undermining an individual right may be the functional equivalent of its complete abolition.* This has been the experience of England. When the rising tide of commercial interests joined with the landed English aristocracy to clip the wings of the British civil jury in the middle of the 19th century, they essentially "did it in." The civil jury in England today is practically extinct and the English criminal jury system is not far behind.[174] The German jury system was dashed on the rocks of economic necessity in 1924,[175] and today, far in excess of 90% of all jury trials in the world are held in the United States.

There was, in theory at least, freedom of the press in England and America before the trial of John Peter Zenger in 1735.[176] But in actuality, the heavy hand of the British government dictated what could be written, just as our governmental bureaucracy would do today were it not for the *First Amendment.*

The true beauty of the American jury system lies in the degree of discretion allowed to those evenhanded "judges without robes" who are the ultimate finders of fact. An average American jury has an accumulated human experience of approximately 500 years and the combined I.Q. of eight Rhodes scholars. If the truth does not lie in the mouth of the witness, then they will ferret it out. No smooth-talking expert witness will ever convince an average American jury that water runs uphill.

But tie the jury's hands to some bureaucratic formula dictated by the liability insurance industry and justice is dead. And when justice dies, democracy dies. Unless the people are left in control of the administration of justice, then there will be no justice. Verdicts will be determined not by the unbiased minds of our objective and independent fellow citizens, but by partisanship, favoritism, animosity and influence.

The confidence of the American public in the administration of justice will be gone because what remains will be undeserving of confidence. The remaining rights of the people will be slowly swept away by the wealthy and powerful because there will be no civil jury system left to prevent it. What corporate America wants, corporate America will get and the land of the free and the home of the brave will be left completely at the mercy of the imminently corruptible power of government and industry. This is the clear and present danger which we must guard against at all costs.

---

[174]*See* pp. 437-440 below.
[175]*See* pp. 444-447 below.
[176]*See* pp. 157-159 below

***Consideration No. 4.*** *Individual rights are irretrievable.* This point was best made by the eminent French political philosopher Jean Jacques Rousseau (1712-1788).

> *Free people, remember this maxim: We may acquire liberty, but it is never recovered once it is lost.*

Although trial by jury once flourished on two continents, there is little left of it in Europe and our American jury system is under constant siege. It is only fitting that its final defense should be fought here, for as William Pitt the Elder said in 1777: "*You cannot conquer America.*" And it is also appropriate that the sacred fire of this ancient liberty be preserved and protected by the American people. In his first inaugural address, George Washington admonished Congress to "carefully avoid every alteration" of government inconsistent with "a reverence for the characteristic rights of freemen."

> *The preservation of the sacred fire of liberty . . . [is] justly . . . entrusted to the hands of the American people.*

In the history of Anglo-American law, those basic freedoms which we regard as fundamental rights have all been won through social, political or military revolutions, with the succeeding governments, once established in power, constantly seeking to abridge them. The right of representative democracy, trial by jury, and the uninhibited access to the established courts of justice have their constitutional basis in the revolution of the rebel barons against the tyranny of King John. Many of the fundamental rights of due process were won during the English revolutions and civil wars of the 17th century. Our American *Bill of Rights* resulted from the American Revolution and the *13th, 14th and 15th Amendments* were enacted in the aftermath of the American civil war.

Women's suffrage came at the conclusion of a century-long struggle ending with the adoption of the 19th amendment in 1920 and the poll tax was abolished as a result of the civil rights revolution of the 1960's. Based on this history, there is no reasonable basis to believe that a "victims' revolution" will resurrect the right of trial by jury once it has been lost. The principle that "eternal vigilance is the price of liberty" is attributed to Thomas Jefferson. Our only alternatives are to preserve the right of trial by jury *today*, or bid it farewell *forever*.

## HERE LIES THE CIVIL JURY

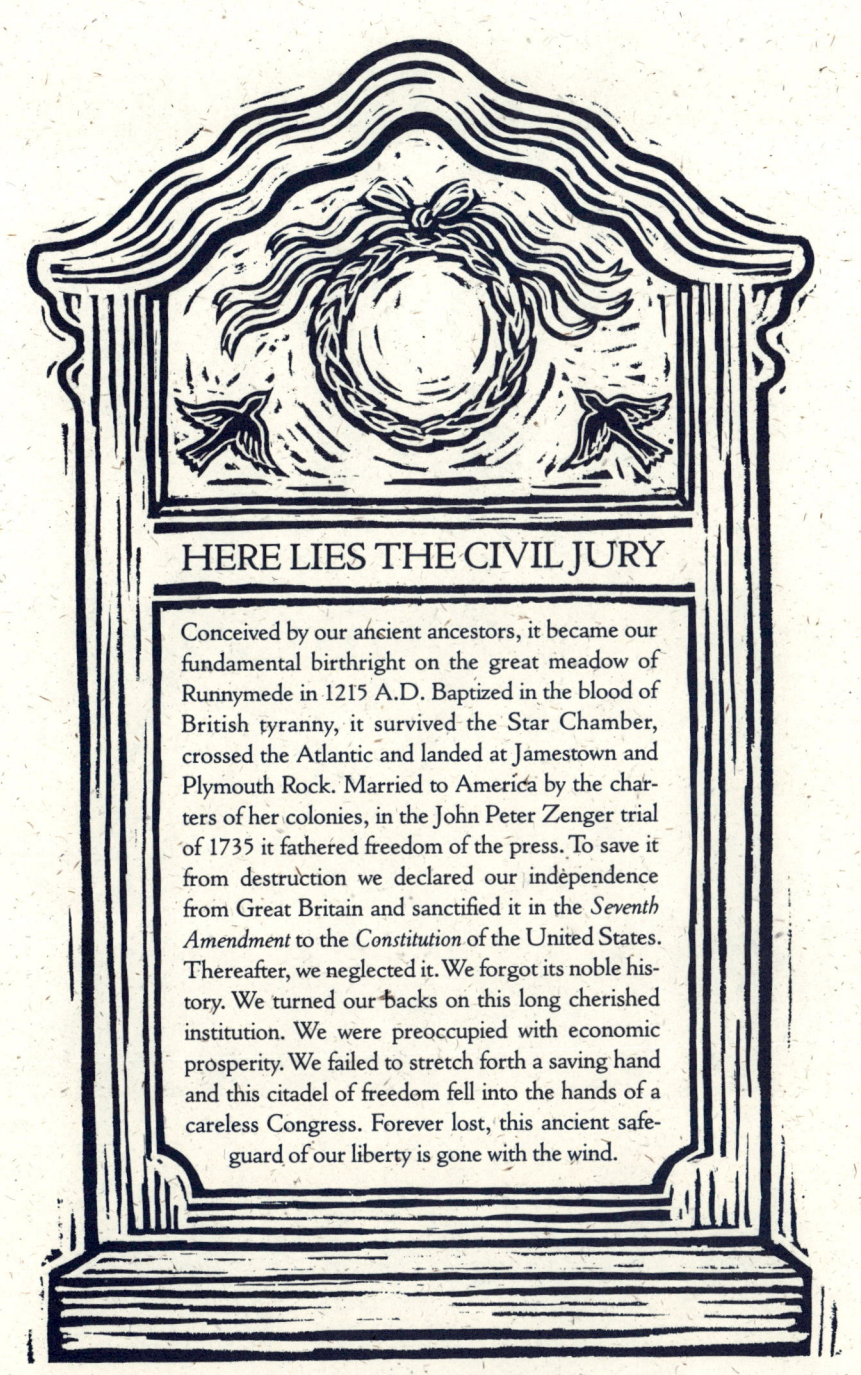

Conceived by our ancient ancestors, it became our fundamental birthright on the great meadow of Runnymede in 1215 A.D. Baptized in the blood of British tyranny, it survived the Star Chamber, crossed the Atlantic and landed at Jamestown and Plymouth Rock. Married to America by the charters of her colonies, in the John Peter Zenger trial of 1735 it fathered freedom of the press. To save it from destruction we declared our independence from Great Britain and sanctified it in the *Seventh Amendment* to the *Constitution* of the United States. Thereafter, we neglected it. We forgot its noble history. We turned our backs on this long cherished institution. We were preoccupied with economic prosperity. We failed to stretch forth a saving hand and this citadel of freedom fell into the hands of a careless Congress. Forever lost, this ancient safeguard of our liberty is gone with the wind.

*The saddest epitaph …*

*Among the most cherished principles of the common law was trial by jury in civil and criminal cases. It was regarded as a right of inestimable value, and the best and only security for life, liberty and property.*
　—U.S. Supreme Court Chief Justice Roger B. Taney (1851)

## M. TRIAL BY JURY ON THE ROAD TO THE AMERICAN REVOLUTION

The American Revolution was the culmination of the long struggle for individual liberty. But the road began much earlier in that ominous era of tumult and repression that hung like a dark cloud over Great Britain throughout the 15th and 16th centuries.

The Dark Ages were drawing to a close and a time of reformation and renaissance was about to awaken the western world to the realization that individual liberty was an attainable goal. Slowly, but surely, the minds of men turned toward the dawning of a new day of freedom. The end of an era was near.

There, among our English ancestors, were two institutions dating in a constitutional sense from the *Magna Carta*, which were the very essence of government by the people: trial by jury and representative government — "the twin pillars of liberty."

> *In the glow of inspiration which it provided during the later constitutional conflicts, Magna Carta came to be regarded as a deliberately designed declaration of political liberty.*[177]

With this inspiration as their guide, the great mass of the common people of England, from whom we have inherited many of our fundamental rights, began their long, slow, bitter, and agonizing journey. Beginning as little more than vassals of an English king, they gained encouragement and momentum with each small concession won. Their battles were our battles. Their defeats were our defeats and their victories were our victories.

With a grim determination that is peculiar to their race, they jealously guarded each new foothold, determined to pass it on to their descendants. They are the ones who shaped and molded these "twin pillars of liberty" and preserved them for us. From the *Magna Carta* to the *Petition of Right* to the *Declaration of Independence* and the *Bill of Rights*, the pathway of freedom was always onward and upward. Economies and kingdoms rose and fell, but liberty kept its steady course.

Today, we are free because that freedom was won for us. For every breath of liberty we take, someone paid a precious price. It is now our obligation to those who came before us to preserve those same freedoms for all who may follow after.

---

[177] Butt, *A History of Parliament: The Middle Ages*, p. 59 (Constable & Co. 1989).

**1.     The Tyranny of Divine Right.** Looking back on that long struggle, John Stuart Mill wrote in 1859:

> *The struggle between Liberty and Authority is the most conspicuous feature in the portions of history with which we are earliest familiar, particularly in that of Greece, Rome and England. . . . By liberty, was meant protection against the tyranny of the political rulers. The rulers were conceived . . . as in a necessarily antagonistic position to the people whom they ruled. They consisted of a governing One, or a governing tribe or caste, who derived their authority from inheritance or conquest, who, at all events, did not hold it at the pleasure of the governed and whose supremacy men did not venture . . . to contest, whatever precautions might be taken against its oppressive exercise. The aim, therefore, of patriots, was to set limits to the power which the ruler should be suffered to exercise over the community; and this limitation was what they meant by liberty. It was attempted in two ways. First, by obtaining a recognition of certain immunities, called political liberties or rights, which it was to be regarded as a breach of duty in the ruler to infringe, and which if he did infringe, specific resistance, or general rebellion, was held to be justifiable. A second . . . was the establishment of constitutional checks; by which the consent of the community . . . was made a necessary condition to some of the more important acts of the governing power. . . . To attain it more completely, became everywhere the principal object of the lovers of liberty. . . .*

To obtain these "constitutional checks," Great Britain had to overcome the tyranny of a long line of Divine Right Kings, and, having done so, the equally tyrannical governments of an omnipotent House of Commons. For as they soon learned, "the will of the people" was merely "the will of the most numerous or the most active *part* of the people; the majority, or those who succeeded in making themselves accepted as the majority."

> *. . . "The tyranny of the majority" is now generally included among the evils against which society requires to be on its guard.*[178]

---

[178]Mill, *On Liberty*, pp. 7-9, 13 (1859).

90

*The aim of patriots was to set limits to the power which the ruler should be suffered to exercise over the community. The establishment of constitutional checks by which the consent of the community was made a necessary condition to some of the more important acts of the governing power became everywhere the principal object of the lovers of liberty.*

—John Stuart Mill (1859)

The era of the "Divine Right of Kings" in England encompasses the reigns of the House of Tudor (1485-1603) and the House of Stuart (1603-1688). Henry VII, the first Tudor, came to power in 1485 when, according to popular legend, he snatched the fallen crown of Richard III from a bramble bush on Bosworth Field. "He took the throne of England by force of arms and held it by strength and skill."[179] But Henry VII was neither progressive nor popular.

> *... First, Henry VII (1485-1509) used penal bonds ... to enforce what he considered to be acceptable behavior of his subjects. These bonds had a dual purpose, namely to hold the political nation ... at the king's mercy, and to short-circuit due process of common law in case of offense by the victims. ...*[180]
>
> *Henry VII's death in 1509 was greeted with feasting, dancing, and universal rejoicing. ...*

Henry VIII followed in his father's footsteps. He had himself declared the *Supreme Head of the Church of England* and made it high treason to deny his royal supremacy.[181] According to Winston Churchill:

> *Early in his reign he declared, "I will not allow anyone to have it in his power to govern me." As time passed his willfulness hardened and his temper worsened. His rages were terrible to behold. There was no noble head in the country, he once said, "but he would make it fly," if his will were crossed. Many heads were indeed to fly in his 38 years on the throne.*[182]

Following the death of Henry VIII in 1547, those heads he had neglected to remove were governed for six years by his young son, Edward VI, who was "an intelligent, perhaps even promising child, but could be no more than a pawn in the hands of the Magnates."[183]

---

[179]Parker, *Britain's Kings and Queens*, p. 18 (Pitkin Pictorials 1990).
[180]Morgan, ed., *The Oxford Illustrated History of Britain*, p. 237 (Oxford University Press 1984).
[181]*Oxford Illustrated History*, supra n.180, p. 246.
[182]Churchill, "The New World", Vol. 2, p. 31 in *Churchill's History of the English Speaking Peoples* (Dorset Press 1956).
[183]Parker, *supra n.179*, p. 19.

When Edward VI died in 1553, "Bloody Mary" took his place and the persecution of English Protestants became the order of the day. Mary I "proclaimed herself queen" on July 10, 1553, after "a steady stream of defections from her rival Lady Jane Grey assured her accession."[184]

*Queen of England from 1553 to 1558, Mary I was the first woman to rule England in her own right, but she is chiefly remembered as "Bloody Mary," the instigator of a ruthless persecution of Protestants in a vain attempt to preserve Roman Catholicism in England.*[185]

Her marriage to Prince Philip of Spain led to an unsuccessful rebellion in 1554 in which 3,000 troops under Sir Thomas Wyatt marched on London. In the purge that followed, Lady Jane Grey was beheaded[186] and Sir Nicholas Throckmorton was tried for treason.[187] "After January, 1555, at least 280 persons (mainly commoners) were executed for heresy"[188] in her six-year "reign of terror."[189]

Next, came the "Virgin Queen," Elizabeth I (1558-1603). She executed Mary Queen of Scots, sank the Spanish Armada, and persecuted Puritans as "seditious revolutionaries."[190] Although Winston Churchill called her "Good Queen Bess,"[191] she was intolerant of Catholics,[192] repressed a popular Irish rebellion, arbitrarily exercised her royal prerogative, encouraged the censorship of the press, granted monopolies to her friends, and, in general, left a legacy of "endemic corruption."[193]

---

[184] *The Cambridge Historical Encyclopedia of Great Britain and Ireland*, p. 155 (Cambridge University Press 1985).

[185] *Encyclopædia Britannica Macropædia*, Vol. 11, p. 563 (15th ed. 1979).

[186] *Cambridge Historical Encyclopedia, supra.*

[187] *See* pp. 100-101 below.

[188] *Cambridge Historical Encyclopedia, supra.*

[189] *Encyclopædia Britannica, supra.*

[190] *See* Oxford Illustrated History of Britain, *supra* n.180, pp. 261, 266-269, 274-275.

[191] Churchill, *supra* n.182, Vol. 2, Ch. 7, pp. 102-120.

[192] Queen Elizabeth's Parliament "made it treason to bring into England or publish documents from Rome." *Oxford Illustrated History of Britain, supra* n.180, p. 275.

[193] *See* Oxford Illustrated History, *supra* n.180, p. 285; *see generally* Churchill, *supra* n.182, Ch. 7, pp. 102-120.

In many ways, Elizabeth I continued the autocratic rule of her father, Henry VIII. According to *Blackstone's Commentaries*:

> *The glorious Queen Elizabeth herself made no scruple to direct her Parliaments to abstain from discoursing of matters of state; and it was the constant language of this favorite princess and her ministers, that even that august assembly "ought not to deal, to judge, or to meddle, with Her Majesty's prerogative royal."*[194]

Yet through it all, the institution of trial by jury "defied the aggressions of time and man."

> *The institution of the jury, when once it is introduced into civil proceedings, . . . defies the aggressions of time and man. If it had been . . . easy to remove the jury . . . from the laws of England, it would have perished under Henry VIII and Elizabeth [I]; and the civil jury did in reality, at that period, save the liberties of the country. . . .*[195]

The only son of Mary Queen of Scots, James VI, King of Scotland, became James I of England on March 24, 1603, and ruled for 22 years. The first of the Stuart kings, "he believed that kings derived their authority directly from God and were answerable to Him alone for the discharge of that trust."[196] He put up with Parliament only because he could not abolish it and treated the common law judges as "lions under his throne."[197]

> *King James I, who had imbibed high notions of the divinity of regal sway, more than once laid it down in his speeches, that "as it is atheism and blasphemy in a creature to dispute what the deity may do, so it is presumption and sedition in a subject to dispute what a king may do in the height of his power: good Christians," he adds, "will be content with God's will, revealed in his word; and good subjects will rest in the king's will, revealed in his law."*[198]

---

[194] *Blackstone's Commentaries, supra n.123,* Vol. 1, p. 231.
[195] de Tocqueville, *Democracy in America,* p. 265 (1835) [Legal Classics Library 1988].
[196] *Oxford Illustrated History, supra n.180,* p. 304.
[197] Churchill, *supra n.182,* p. 156.
[198] *Blackstone's Commentaries, supra n.123,* Vol. 1, p. 231.

*James I (1603-1625)*

During the reign of James I, Jamestown was settled and the Puritans landed at Plymouth Rock. Driven from the Church of England by the Anglican bishops, they left Great Britain for Holland in 1607. Thirteen years later, they landed in the New World, bringing with them their unquenchable aspirations for individual liberty and their reverence for the institution of trial by jury.

Following the death of James I in 1625, there began one of the most eventful quarter centuries in England history. The reign of the "Martyr King," Charles I, witnessed the revolt of Parliament, the *Petition of Right* (1628), the abolition of the Star Chamber (1641), the English civil wars (1642-1648), the first execution of a reigning English king (January 30, 1649), and the creation of the English Commonwealth under Oliver Cromwell.

During his trial, Charles I was charged with "more transcendent treasons and enormous crimes than all the kings this part of the world has ever known." From the day of his coronation, King Charles had displayed "a design to alter and subvert the fundamental laws, and to introduce an arbitrary and tyrannical government." He was accused of packing the English courts with corrupt judges prone to inflict cruel and unusual punishments, including "such barbarous cruelties and unheard of punishments as brandings, slitting of noses, etc., among honorable men."

> *By his altering the patents and commissions to the judges, . . . he made them but during [his] pleasure, so that if the judges should not declare the law to be as he should have it, he might with a wet finger remove them, and put in such as should not only say but swear if need were that the law was as the king would have it. . . .*[199]

Following more than 150 years of repressive rule, led by an increasingly aggressive House of Commons, the common people of England finally revolted:

> *Charles I, king of Great Britain and Ireland from 1625 to 1649, by attempting to impose his authoritarian rule on a people with growing aspirations for political and religious liberty, brought about a civil war that ended with his execution by his subjects. . . .*[200]

---

[199] *Trial of King Charles the First*, pp. 235-238, 257 (William Hodge & Co. 1928) [Notable Trials Library 1990].
[200] *Encyclopædia Britannica Macropædia*, Vol. 4, p. 52.

But the execution of Charles I merely led to a transfer of the power of oppression from the Crown to the House of Commons. Oliver Cromwell's rule was an unmitigated disaster for individual rights. He had "a fatal disregard for civil and religious liberties,"[201] "trampled underfoot the *Constitution*,"[202] and left upon us all to this day "the Curse of Cromwell."[203]

After Oliver Cromwell's military dictatorship, the monarchy was restored under Stuart kings Charles II (1660-1685) and James II (1685-1689).

> *... Men forgot the despotism of the monarchy when the monarchy ... lay wrecked in common ruin. They forgot the tyranny of ... the Church [when it] was trampled underfoot by men who trampled underfoot the Constitution. By a strange turn of fate the restoration of ... the Crown became identified with the restoration of legal government and with the overthrow of a rule by brute force. And for such a restoration the vast majority of the nation were longing more and more. The old enmity of party and sect were forgotten in the common enmity of every party and every sect to the tyranny of the sword.*[204]

According to Winston Churchill, although "the doctrine of divine right was again proclaimed, that of absolute power had been abandoned" and "the victory of ... the common law was permanent":

> *A new conception of sovereignty had been born.... The common lawyers had borne the brunt of the struggle ... to ensure that the king should be under the law. This meant the law for which Magna Carta was felt to stand on ... traditional law, the kind of law which made Englishmen free from arbitrary arrest and arbitrary punishment.... [Chief Justice Edward Coke's] claim that the fundamental law of custom and tradition should not be overborne, even by Crown and Parliament together, ... survived in New England across the ocean, one day to emerge in an American revolution directed at both Parliament and Crown.*[205]

---

[201] *Oxford Illustrated History, supra* n.180, p. 328.
[202] Green, *History of the English People*, Vol. 3, p. 308 (1874).
[203] Churchill, *supra* n.182, Vol. 2, p. 292.
[204] Green, *supra* n.202, Vol. 3, p. 308.
[205] Churchill, *supra* n.182, Vol. 2, pp. 329-330.

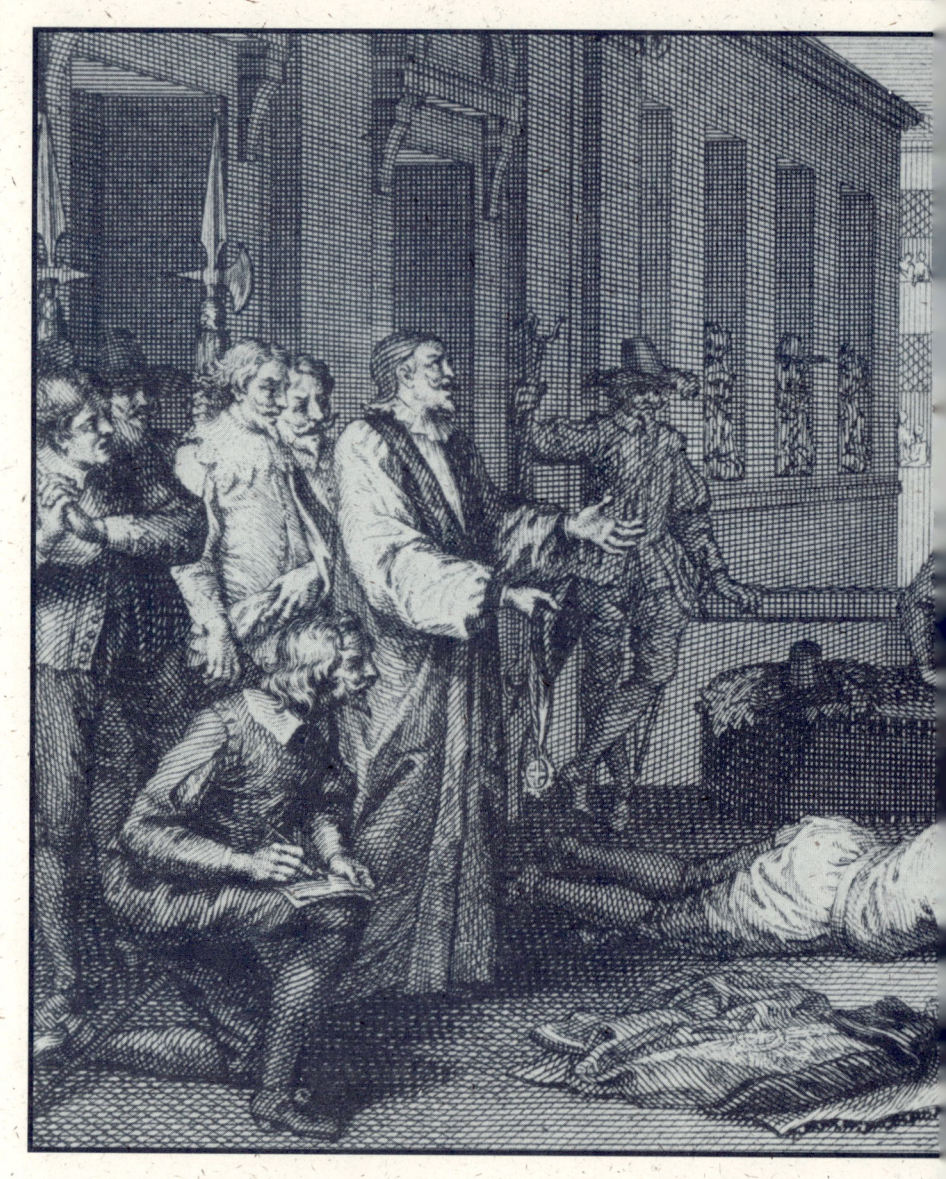

**EXECUTION OF CHARLES I, January 30, 1649**

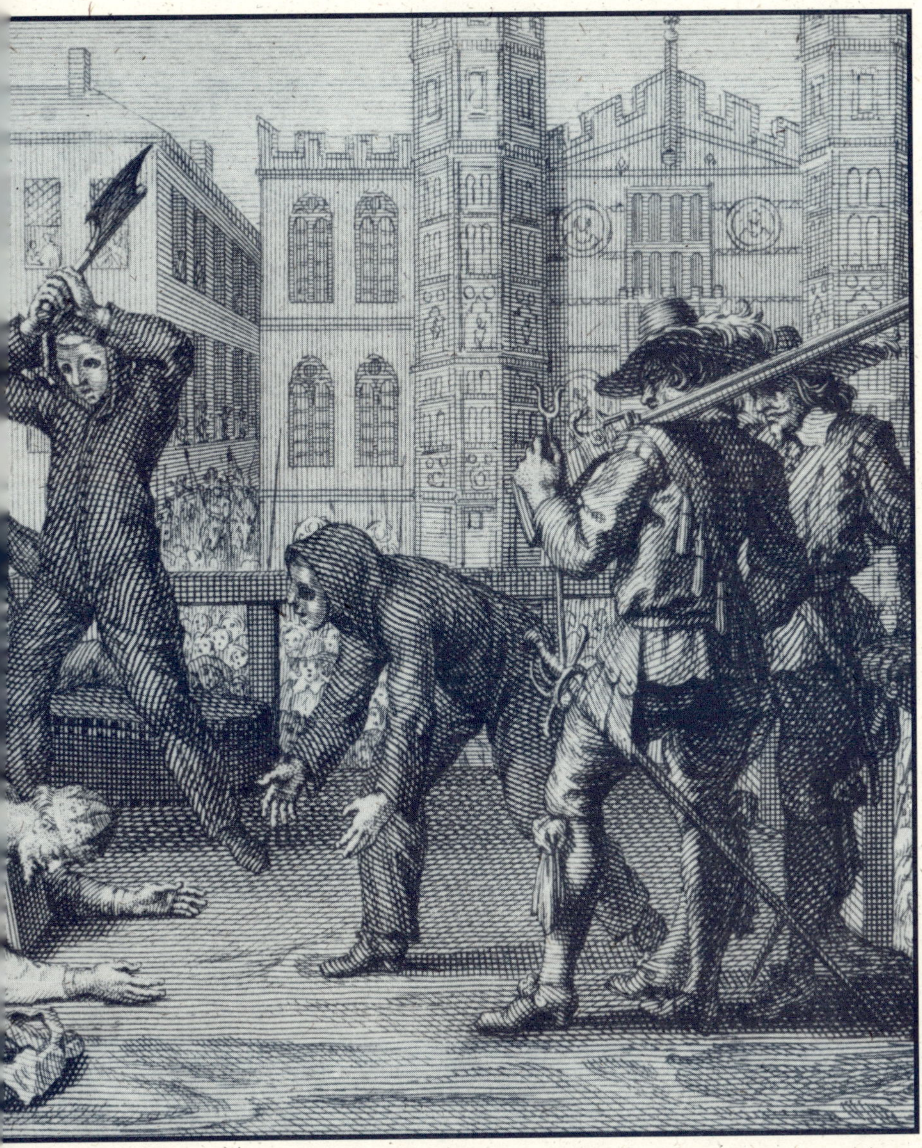

MARY EVANS PICTURE LIBRARY, LONDON

**2.  The Treason Trial of Nicholas Throckmorton (April 17, 1554).**  The great crime of Sir Nicholas Throckmorton appears to have been his opposition to Queen Mary's marriage to Prince Philip of Spain:

> *I confess I did mislike the Queen's marriage with Spain, and also the coming of the Spaniards into this Realm.*

Sir Thomas Wyatt took a more militant course. In January, 1554, he raised his standard in Kent and led an army of 3,000 to the gates of London.  When Wyatt's Rebellion was crushed, Throckmorton was charged with conspiracy to aid and comfort the enemies of the Queen and tried at the Guildhall of London before the Lord Chief Justice and 15 of his fellow benchmen.

From the outset, the panel of judges treated Throckmorton with great disrespect. Although they could prove no overt act on Throckmorton's part, the judges charged that Throckmorton was "a principal devisor, procurer and contriver of the late rebellion, and that Wyatt was but his minister."  The out-of-court statements of several witnesses were admitted as evidence despite Throckmorton's assertion of his right to cross-examine them:

> *Master Croftes is yet living, and is here this day; how happeneth it he is not brought face to face to justify this matter? Will you not know the truth?*

But the court was unmoved.  Moreover, when Throckmorton tried to call a witness in his behalf, the following occurred:

> **Attorney General:** *I pray you, my Lords, suffer him not to be sworn; we have nothing to do with him here.*
>
> **Throckmorton:** *Why should he not be suffered to tell the truth? Why not hear truth for me, as untruth against me?*
>
> **Court:** *Go your way, sir, the court hath nothing to do with you.*
>
> Then the witness departed the court and was not suffered to speak.[206]

---

[206] *Throckmorton's Case*, 1 How. St. Tr. 869, 885 (1554).

In his closing speech, Throckmorton entrusted his fate into the hands of the jury substantially as follows:

> *The gravity of my cause has occasioned me to trouble you here too long, and therefore I shall not detain you with a long oration. The trial of my innocence, my life, my property and my posterity, rests in your good judgments. Although many here today have inveighed against me, the determination of my fate now lies in your hands. The shedding of innocent blood is grievous in the sight of God. Therefore, do not defile your consciences with such a heinous crime. Lift up your minds. Believe that the queen and her magistrates are better served with impartial justice than with rash cruelty. As my fellow citizens I will leave you with Saint Paul's farewell to the Ephesians to whom he also professed his innocence. May it prove a lesson for your instruction, that every one of you may wash his hands of innocent bloodshed when you take your leave of this wretched world.*

To the great dismay of the judges, the jury found Throckmorton innocent. When the Lord Chief Justice threatened them, the foreman responded:

> *We have thoroughly considered the evidence against the prisoner, and his responses, and accordingly have found him not guilty, agreeable to all our consciences.*

According to the official report, "the court being dissatisfied with the verdict, committed the jury to prison."

**3.　The First Charter of Virginia (April 10, 1606).** Fifty-two years after the trial of Sir Nicholas Throckmorton, the protection of the *Magna Carta* began its great journey across the Atlantic when King James granted the *First Charter of Virginia*. In it, he decreed that any person who should inhabit that colony "shall have and enjoy all liberties" guaranteed to the inhabitants of England.[207] From that date, every colonist could legitimately claim the benefit of trial by jury as an individual right guaranteed by the English *Constitution*.

---

[207] *See* § 15 of the *First Charter of Virginia*, Harvard Classics, American Historical Documents, p. 56 (Grolier Enterprises 1910, 1938, 1980).

**4.    The First Ordinance of Plymouth Bay (1623).** At Cape Cod on November 11, 1620, the Pilgrims combined themselves together into "a civil body politic" under the *Mayflower Compact* to "enact, constitute and frame such just and equal laws" as "shall be thought mete and convenient for the general good of the colony."[208]

> *And it is an interesting fact that the first ordinance adopted by the Plymouth Colony in 1623 was one declaring, among other things, that "all criminal facts" should be tried "by the verdict of twelve honest men to be empaneled by authority, in the form of a jury upon their oaths."*[209]

**5.    The Petition of Right (June 7, 1628).** The same institution that saved Sir Nicholas Throckmorton's life and fortune in 1554 had crossed the ocean to Jamestown, Virginia, in 1607 and to Plymouth Rock, Massachusetts, in 1620. But back in England, trial by jury was under constant attack by the divine right Stuart kings. After James I died in 1625, Charles I ascended to the throne insisting, as his father had before him, on the exercise of his royal prerogative at the sacrifice of the individual rights of his subjects.

The will of the king was administered through such prerogative courts as the Star Chamber and the Court of High Commission where no juries sat. When heavy impositions were levied upon their subjects, their collection was enforced in the Star Chamber. But on June 7, 1628, the same independent spirit which had wrested the right of trial by jury, "sword in hand,"[210] from King John, forced Charles I's assent to the *Petition of Right.* The third clause of this *"Second Magna Carta"* provided:

> *And where also by the statute called the Great Charter of Liberties of England, it is declared and enacted, that no free man may be taken or imprisoned, or disseised of his freehold or liberties, or his free customs, or to be outlawed or exiled, or in any manner destroyed, but by the lawful judgment of his peers, or by the law of the land.*[211]

---

[208] *Harvard Classics, supra* n. 207, p. 59.
[209] *See* Dissenting Opinion of Justice John Marshall Harlan in *Maxwell v. Dow*, 176 U.S. 581, 605, 609 (1900).
[210] Samuel Adams, "The Rights of Colonists" (November 20, 1772) [*Annals of America*, Vol. 2, p. 219 (1976)].
[211] Perry & Cooper, *supra n.*98, p. 74.

ILLUSTRATION BY RAUL COLÓN

*As the great bulwark of English liberty, trial by jury is the best safeguard of a free Constitution. This mainspring in the machinery of remedial justice brings the law home to every man's door.*
—Sir Francis Palgrave, *On the English Commonwealth* (1832)

**6. The *Charter of Massachusetts Bay* (March 4, 1629).** As the *First Charter of Virginia* had done 23 years earlier, the *Charter of Massachusetts Bay* provided that all colonists should "have and enjoy all liberties and immunities of free and natural subjects . . . as if they . . . were born within the realm of England."[212]

**7. The *Charter of Maryland* (June 20, 1632).** The *Charter of Maryland*, similar in language to the *First Charter of Virginia* and the *Charter of Massachusetts Bay* had guaranteed to each citizen the right to exercise "all privileges, franchises, and liberties of this our kingdom of England, freely, quietly and peaceably . . . in the same manner as . . . [the subjects of the] kingdom of England." When referring to the "privileges, franchises and liberties" of the citizens of England, the *Charter of Maryland* had in mind those guaranteed by the *Magna Carta* and the *Petition of Right*.

> *Article X of the Charter of Maryland provided that the colonists should have the rights of Englishmen, and the efforts of the colonists to secure recognition of those rights constitutes one of the most important phases of the history of the colony. The struggle to secure those rights began at an early date, and the enactments of the early assemblies indicate that Magna Carta was considered to be their primary source. On March 6, 1639, the Act for the Liberties of the People was passed. It provided:*
>
> *"Be it enacted . . . that all the inhabitants of this province . . . shall have and enjoy all such rights, liberties, immunities, privileges and free customs within this province as any natural born subject of England. . . .*
>
> *"And shall not be imprisoned or disseised of their freehold goods or chattels or be outlawed, exiled or otherwise destroyed, forejudged or punished than according to the laws of this province. . . ."*
>
> *On March 19, 1639, it was provided . . . that "the inhabitants of this province shall have all their rights and liberties according to the Great Charter of England." . . .*[213]

---

[212]Perry & Cooper, *supra n.98*, pp. 82, 93.
[213]Perry & Cooper, *supra n.98*, pp. 101, 105, 109.

**8.     Abolition of the Star Chamber (July 5, 1641).** The existence and abolition of the Star Chamber and other prerogative courts of the English Crown in the 17th century was an important event in the constitutional history of England and a significant influence on the development of the *Constitution of the United States*. Just as the medieval *Inquisition* had been since Pope Innocent IV authorized the use of torture to extract confessions in 1252, the Star Chamber was synonymous with tyranny as evidenced by its current dictionary definition.

> ***Star Chamber, n. An early English court that illegally extended its jurisdiction and acted secretly, arbitrarily, and harshly. See court, tyranny.***[214]

Just as the creation of blue ribbon panels of expert arbitrators are advocated by the commercial coalition today, the need for more "learned" and efficient judicial panels like the Star Chamber were justified by their supporters in the middle ages. In 1899, U.S. Circuit Court Judge Henry Clay Caldwell called it a "curious and significant fact," that the reasons given then for denying the right of trial by jury "are precisely those given for the establishment of the Court of Star Chamber":

> *. . . History records the result. Its methods grew to be as cruel and pitiless as the Inquisition itself. It would have put an end to the liberties of the English people if it had not been abolished. . . .*[215]

For this reason, we have devoted significant space to the origin and history of the Court of the Star Chamber and the conditions from which it arose in medieval England during the lawlessness and political upheavals of the 14th and 15th centuries. The unmistakable conclusion from its one-and-a-half century career from its resurrection by Henry VII in 1487 until its abolition by Parliament in 1641 is that it was not initially intended to become the instrument of judicial savagery and oppression that it ultimately became. All of this only proves that *any court not controlled by the people themselves poses an inherent danger to individual rights.*

---

[214]Statsky, *West's Legal Thesaurus/Dictionary*, p. 713 (West Publishing Company 1986).

[215]Caldwell, "Trial by Judge and Jury," 33 *American L.R.* 321, 332 (1899).

The specter of the potential reoccurrence of the Court of the Star Chamber in the United States was raised in the closing days of the Constitutional Convention of 1787 by Elbridge Gerry of Massachusetts. Gerry listed the failure of the *Constitution* to guarantee trial by jury in civil cases as one of the three reasons "which determined him to withhold his name from the *Constitution*." He listed other objections, but concluded:

> *...He could, however, he said, get over all these, if the rights of the citizens were not rendered insecure, first by the general power of the legislature to make what laws they may please to call necessary and proper; secondly, to raise armies and money without limit; [and] thirdly, to establish a tribunal without juries... will be a Star Chamber as to civil cases.*[216]

While the Court of Common Pleas and the Court of the King's Bench developed as the ordinary and established courts of the common law,[217] the Court of the Star Chamber was an administrative tribunal which acted solely at the pleasure of the king and his council of close advisors. William Hudson, attorney, prosecutor and clerk of the Star Chamber from 1608 through 1625, published his *Treatise on the Star Chamber* in 1621. In it, he wrote that the court was established in the reign of Henry II (1154-1189) on the premise that a British monarch was "to be supreme judge of all... sitting in his throne of majesty with his wise men and sages, distributing justice in his royal person."[218] Named for the meeting room in Westminster Palace whose ceiling was ornamented with stars, it existed by that name at least as early as 1368.[219]

> *As early as the 14th century the name "Star Chamber" was used to designate the room in Westminster Palace where the council sat as a judicial body. The Star Chamber emerged as a separate court during the next century.*[220]

---

[216]Madison, *Records of the Debates in the Federal Convention of 1787*, p. 738 (Government Printing Office 1927).

[217]*See* Plucknett, *A Concise History of the Common Law*, pp. 147-151 (Little, Brown & Co. 1956).

[218]Hudson, *A Treatise of the Court of Star Chamber*, p. 10 [Legal Classics Library 1986].

[219]Holdsworth, *supra n.14*, p. 496.

[220]Perry & Cooper, *supra n.98*, p. 127.

*To establish a tribunal without juries will be a Star Chamber as to civil cases.*

—**Elbridge Gerry (1787)**

Fourteenth century England suffered through plague and revolt. In 1348, "the Black Death" reduced England's population by about a third.[221] This was followed by the Peasant's Revolt of 1381 in which the city of London was ransacked and the Archbishop was murdered.

The fourteenth century also witnessed an attempt by Parliament to curtail the power of the king and his council of advisors.[222] An ordinance in 1311 required Edward II to obtain Parliamentary consent to all appointments to the King's Council.[223] Edward III was forced to reaffirm the *Magna Carta* in 1352[224] and "Parliament attempted to render void any statute which infringed its provisions" in 1369.[225]

> *... The 14th century struggles against the Council helped to establish Magna Carta as the principal document of the English Constitution. Parliament passed a number of statutes which attempted to limit the Council's jurisdiction. These statutes were important ... because they developed the principle of due process of law building on Magna Carta ...*[226]

During the 15th century, England experienced an unparalleled period of civil strife. In 1399, Henry IV deposed Richard II, and his subsequent reign of 14 years was plagued by uprisings and beset by financial difficulties. Under Henry V, England's continental empire was briefly restored, but, upon his death in 1422, the remainder of the 15th century was an unmitigated disaster. Henry VI (1422-1461, 1470-71) was weak-willed and simple-minded and suffered from periodic bouts of nervous collapse.[227] The French rallied in 1429 under Joan of Arc, Normandy fell to the French in 1450 and Gascony in 1451. Four years later, Richard, Duke of York, rebelled and the War of Roses between the royal houses of York and Lancaster drug on for 30 years.

---

[221] *Oxford Illustrated History of Britain*, supra n.180, p. 186.

[222] *See generally* Butt, *supra* n.177, pp. 175-450.

[223] Butt, *supra*, p. 186.

[224] Plucknett, *supra* n.217, p. 32.

[225] Holdsworth, *supra* n.14, Vol. 2, p. 219.

[226] Perry & Cooper, *supra* n.98, p. 126. These statutes included 5 Edw. 3, c. 9 (1331): "That no man ... shall be attached by any accusation, ... nor his lands ... nor chattels seized into the king's hand, against the form of the *Great Charter*, and the law of the land."

[227] *See* Parker, *Britain's Rings and Queens*, pp. 16-17 (Pitkin Pictorials 2d. ed. 1990).

Henry VI was imprisoned and deposed in 1461, restored in 1470 and murdered in 1471. When Edward IV died suddenly in 1483, his 13-year-old son was murdered in the Tower of London by his uncle, Richard III. Two years later at Bosworth Field, Richard III died at the hands of Henry VII, who then proclaimed:

> *God and your arms be praised, victorious friends!*
> *The day is ours; the bloody dog is dead.*[228]

For the greater part of the 15th century, England had existed in a lawless state of society characterized by intrigue, insurrection and private wars in which "it was especially dangerous to be connected in any way, however humbly, with the administration of the law." The barrister who "chanced to be too successful in pleading the cause of his client against a powerful opponent" was threatened. The process server was "prevented from serving the writ entrusted to him by the king's court." Jurors were intimidated "to avoid the vengeance of powerful or passionate suitors." Powerful noblemen "wage[d] private war against each other." Prisoners frequently escaped and sheriffs were "unable to execute the directions or judgments of the court[s] of law."[229]

It was in this "barbarous state of society" that Henry VII ascended to the throne in 1485 and the Tudor dynasty began. His resurrection of the Court of Star Chamber soon followed:

> *. . . Henry [VII] had declared that private war and offenses against individuals were crimes against the state, and by the [re]institution of the Court of Star Chamber he had provided a machinery which should punish those who offended in this respect. . . .*[230]

The administration of the Star Chamber under Henry VII began innocently enough. C. G. Bayne described it "the mildest-mannered tribunal that ever sentenced a criminal, considerate in its procedure [and] gentle in its punishments."[231] However, under Henry VIII, the Court of Star Chamber was formally separated from the Council in 1526[232] and its jurisdiction was extended to impose "Henry's justice."[233]

---

[228] *Richard III*, Act V, Sc. 4-5.

[229] Denton, *England in the 15th Century*, pp. 306-08 (1888).

[230] Denton, *supra*, pp. 283-284.

[231] Plucknett, *supra n.217*, p. 182 n.3.

[232] *See* Perry & Cooper, *supra n.98*, p. 127 n.7.

[233] *Encyclopædia Britannica Micropædia*, Vol. X, p. 70 (1979).

*The Star Chamber, Westminster Palace*

*Destroyed by fire in 1834*

The repressive reign of the Tudors gave way to the Divine Right Stuart Dynasty in 1603.

> During the reign of James I (1603-1625), proclamations were issued more frequently than during the Tudor period. They were enforced by the Court of the Star Chamber.... Among the most important of these orders were those for the regulation of printing ... and the breakers and offenders of the same [were] severely and sharply punished and corrected.[234]

That the Star Chamber during the Stuart dynasty did in fact "severely and sharply punish" dissent is documented by the cases of John Lilburne, William Prynne and Dr. Alexander Leighton:

> Leighton, a Scots divine, published an angry libel against the church. He was sentenced to be publicly whipped at Westminster and set in the pillory, to have one side of his nose split, one ear cut off, and one side of his cheek branded with a hot iron.... Lilburne, who had issued pamphlets against the bishops, ... was set in the pillory and treated with great cruelty.... Prynne, already obnoxious to the Crown, was adjudged ... to be branded on the forehead, lose both his ears, ... and to suffer perpetual imprisonment. He later suffered further cruelties at the hands of the Star Chamber after he had used the leisure of jail to write fresh libels against the hierarchy.[235]

The most incriminating indictment of the Star Chamber comes from its most ardent defender. In his *Treatise on the Court of Star Chamber*, William Hudson documented "several contentions" that:

> ... this court is but an usurpation of monarchy upon the common law of England, and in prejudice of the liberties granted [by] the Great Charter, especially where persons are produced, without legal prosecution to punishment, ... without oath or testimony.[236]

---

[234] Perry & Cooper, *supra n.98*, p. 130.
[235] Perry & Cooper, *supra n.98*, p. 131 n.24.
[236] Hudson, *supra n.218*, p. 3.

Winston Churchill wrote that the Star Chamber "had in the lapse of time become oppressive to the people."[237] In its later years, according to W. S. Holdsworth, when the "occasion required, it habitually employed torture" and its punishments were often "excessive and brutal."[238] It "continually interfered in private disputes"[239] and, in the words of William Hudson, it constantly acted as "the curious eye of the state . . . prying into the inconveniences and mischiefs which abound in the commonwealth."[240]

Late in the reign of Elizabeth I (1558-1603), its summary punishments were attacked by the common law courts[241] and during the reigns of James I (1603-1625) and Charles I (1625-1649), it became "the most efficient means of prerogative government" as "the tyrannical proceedings of the Star Chamber aroused popular feelings against it."[242]

Even William Hudson himself admitted to close similarities between the Star Chamber and the *Spanish Inquisition*. In his 1621 *Treatise on the Court of the Star Chamber*, Hudson wrote:

> *An answer is not perfect without examination . . . ; for to any offense a man in a continued course may make a plausible answer; but where in his own excuses a short question is asked him to which he must answer, the nakedness of his excuse is discovered. . . . And of this kind of examination there are excellent precedents in the time of Henry VIII . . . but afterwards this advantage of examination was used like a Spanish Inquisition, to rack men's consciences. . . .*[243]

Charles I's use of the Star Chamber to stifle political dissent was a clear violation of the *Magna Carta* and the *Petition of Right*. His continued use of this court to inflict cruel and unusual punishments upon his enemies ultimately led to the abolition of the court and contributed to the English Civil Wars and Charles I's execution at the hands of his people.

---

[237] Churchill, *supra n.182*, Vol. 2, p. 222.
[238] Holdsworth, *supra n.14*, Vol. 1, p. 505.
[239] Holdsworth, *supra n.14*, Vol. 1, p. 506.
[240] *See* Hudson, *supra n.218*, p. 126.
[241] Holdsworth, *supra n.14*, Vol. 1, p. 509.
[242] Holdsworth, *supra n.14*, Vol. 1, p. 514.
[243] Hudson, *supra n.218*, pp. 168-169, emphasis added.

In March of 1629, Charles I dissolved Parliament and began the "Eleven Years' Tyranny" of "Personal Rule."[244] But financial demands resulting from the Scottish Rebellions (1638-40) forced him to call the "Short Parliament" of April, 1640, which "opened the world-famous struggle of Parliament against the king."[245] The "Short Parliament" was led by John Pym, a man of "political steel and administrative genius,"[246] and one of the "great champions of Parliament and liberty against the despotism of Charles I."[247]

Under the leadership of John Pym, Parliament refused to initiate appropriations until the Crown had redressed a long line of political grievances and within three weeks the "Short Parliament" was dissolved.[248] However, short of cash and facing upheaval at home and insurrection abroad, Charles I was forced to recall Parliament six months later. For him, this was a colossal mistake. In the words of Winston Churchill:

> *There is no surer way of rousing popular excitement than the holding of general elections in quick succession. Passions ran high; beer flowed. . . .*[249]

From the moment the "Long Parliament" first met in November of 1640, John Pym was the "central figure."[250] It was Pym who "forced Charles I to accept an act forbidding the dissolution of Parliament without its consent"[251] and it was under his leadership that Parliament abolished the Star Chamber in 1641.

> *By the abolition of the Court of Star Chamber the English Parliament, in dramatic fashion, reaffirmed the principle of due process of law as established by Magna Carta. Parliament did more than simply remove the principal instrumentality of oppression and persecution wielded by the Stuart kings; it established the ordinary courts of law as the rightful guardian of the liberties of the subject. . . .*[252]

---

[244] *The Cambridge Historical Encyclopedia, supra n.184,* p. 200.
[245] Churchill, *supra n.182,* Vol. 2, p. 208.
[246] *See Oxford Illustrated History, supra n.180,* p. 313.
[247] Halliday, *A Concise History of England,* p. 117 (1965).
[248] Cannon & Griffiths, *supra n.51,* p. 376.
[249] Churchill, *supra n.182,* Vol. 2, p. 212.
[250] Churchill, *supra n.182,* Vol. 2, pp. 208-209.
[251] *Encyclopædia Britannica Macropædia,* Vol. 15, p. 312.
[252] Perry & Cooper, *supra n.98,* p. 125.

**John Pym (1584-1643)**
*According to Halliday's Concise History of England, John Pym was one of the "great champions of Parliament and liberty against the despotism of Charles I."*

The abolition of the Star Chamber proved to be the greatest contribution to the cause of individual liberty in the 17th century. According to *The Oxford Illustrated History of Britain*, it "removed the teeth" of judicial tyranny from the Privy Council and was "the only really major weakening of royal power" in an age of constitutional crisis and civil war. With its abolition "almost all the methods by which Tudor and early Stuart kings could bring [their subjects] to heel had been taken away" and, thereafter, "government was more than ever by their active consent."[253]

> *The main effect of the abolition of the Star Chamber was to establish in England a system of justice administered by the courts instead of by the administrative agencies of the executive branch of government. The statute thus constituted an important reaffirmation of the concept of due process of law including the protection of trial by jury.*[254]

According to W. S. Holdsworth, the abolition of the Star Chamber also secured the supremacy of the common law and "afforded the best of all securities for the protection of the liberties of the subject."[255]

> *. . . As we have seen, it in effect deprived the Privy Council, and the various courts derived from the Privy Council, of all extraordinary jurisdiction in England. . . . Thus the most formidable rivals to the common law courts were removed, and the common law finally asserted its supremacy not only over the private, but over the public law of the state. . . .*[256]

Aside from the restoration of the right of due process and trial by jury, the abolition of the Star Chamber contributed to the doctrine of separation of powers in our own American *Constitution*,[257] and its death contributed to at least seven other sacred rights embodied in our *Constitution* and *Bill of Rights*.

---

[253]*Oxford Illustrated History, supra n.180*, pp. 341-342.

[254]Perry & Cooper, *supra n.98*, p. 132.

[255]Holdsworth, *supra n.14*, Vol. VI, pp. 262-263.

[256]Holdsworth, *supra n.14*, Vol. VI, p. 117.

[257]"The power of the [Star Chamber] to issue and enforce proclamations gave it important legislative and executive functions in addition to its judicial duties." Perry & Cooper, *supra n.98*, p. 239.

***a. Freedom of Speech.*** The Star Chamber had been the British Crown's main instrument of repression of political dissent and its abolition significantly contributed to the principles now embodied in our own *First Amendment*.

***b. Habeas Corpus.*** The eighth clause of the "*Act for Regulating of the Privy Council, and for Taking Away the Court Commonly Called the Star-Chamber*" adopted by Parliament on July 5, 1641, provided that the *Writ of Habeas Corpus* would be available to all persons restrained of their liberty.[258]

***c. The Right Against Self-Incrimination.*** According to the American Bar Foundation, "the abolition of the Court of the Star Chamber and the Court of High Commission also opened the way for the establishment of the privilege against self-incrimination."[259]

***d. The Right to Counsel.*** William Hudson wrote that in the Star Chamber, "to extenuate [an] offense, and mitigate [a] censure [the defendant] is and ought to be heard to speak for himself; but himself must only speak for himself, *his counsel may not.*"[260] The *Massachusetts Body of Liberties*, adopted five months after the Star Chamber was abolished, guaranteed the right of counsel.

***e. The Right of Confrontation.*** In his *Treatise on the Star Chamber*, William Hudson wrote:

> *But it is as much wondered, that this court suffereth not the parties to examine the credit of witnesses ... and the reason why it is not given way unto in this court is, for the causes of the king, if witnesses lives should be so ripped up, no man would willingly be produced to testify; and therefore many opinions ... are extant in this court, where it is adjudged that a witness deposing for the king upon an indictment shall not be questioned for perjury....*[261]

---

[258] *See* Perry & Cooper, *supra n.98*, pp. 141-142.
[259] Perry & Cooper, *supra n.98*, p. 132.
[260] Hudson, *supra n.218*, p. 128.
[261] Hudson, *supra n.218*, pp. 200-201.

***f. The Prohibition Against Cruel and Unusual Punishment.*** The specter of the Star Chamber's severed ears, split noses and branded cheeks was certainly on the minds of our founding fathers when they drafted the *Eighth Amendment*'s prohibition against "cruel and unusual punishments."

***g. Double Jeopardy.*** William Hudson notes with seeming pride the ability of the Star Chamber to retry and repunish criminal offenders already convicted and punished by the courts of the common law.[262]

In addition to its contribution to the establishment of these great rights, the statute abolishing the Star Chamber also charged that the court had "of late times assumed unto itself a power to intermeddle in civil causes and matters only of private interest between party and party . . . , contrary to the law of the land and the rights and privileges of the subject."[263]

The abolition of this court reestablished what William Blackstone called a "third subordinate right of every Englishman . . . that of applying to the courts of justice for redress of injuries." In *Blackstone's Commentaries* he wrote that "the emphatical words of *Magna Carta*" guarantee every citizen that "for injury done him . . . by any other subject, [he] . . . may take his remedy by the course of law, and have justice and right for the injury done to him, freely without sale, fully without any denial and speedily without delay."[264]

It is clear, however, that the primary purpose of the statute abolishing the Star Chamber was to preserve the right of trial by jury guaranteed by the *Magna Carta*. This is witnessed by the preamble to that statute which begins as follows:

*Whereas by the Great Charter many times confirmed in Parliament, it is enacted, that no free man shall be taken or imprisoned, or disseised of his freehold or liberties, or free customs, or be outlawed or exiled or otherwise destroyed, and that the king will not pass upon him, or condemn him; but by lawful judgment of his peers. . . .*[265]

---

[262]Hudson, *supra n.218.*

[263]Perry & Cooper, *supra n.98,* p. 139.

[264]Blackstone, *Commentaries on the Laws of England,* Vol. 1, p. 137 (1765) [Legal Classics Library 1983].

[265]Perry & Cooper, *supra n.98,* p. 138.

*English Puritan pamphleteer* **William Prynne** *was branded with the letters SL for "Seditious Libeler."*

We have written at length on the abolition of the Court of the Star Chamber for three reasons: first, because of its significant contribution to the individual liberties guaranteed under our *Constitution* and *Bill of Rights*; second, because of the important impact it had on the preservation of the historical right of trial by jury; and third, because of the close parallels that may be drawn between the Court of the Star Chamber of 1641 and the non-jury panels advocated by the commercial coalition today.

One lesson from the Star Chamber is the grim reality of what tribunals without direct citizen participation can easily become. A judge, commissioner, or arbitrator is a product of his own experience. He has prejudices, he believes his views are correct, and he rules accordingly. The jury, on the other hand, is a cross section of the community. Opposing views are discussed and reconciled and justice is administered by the people themselves.

The fundamental guarantees of our *Constitution* and *Bill of Rights* are America's greatest assets. The price for their attainment was extremely dear. The very thought that our representatives in Congress and the state legislatures would consider undermining these great rights should send shivers down the spine of every liberty-loving American.

In a speech before the United States Senate in January of 1848, John C. Calhoun warned that individual liberty is "harder to preserve than to obtain." Whatever the motives of those zealous men who would impair the administration of American justice by insidious encroachments on our constitutional right to trial by jury, they are equally as dangerous to the American ideal of popular justice today as Mrs. O'Leary's cow was to the city of Chicago in 1871 and as the San Andreas Fault was to the city of San Francisco in 1906.

> *The greatest dangers to liberty lurk in insidious encroachments by men of zeal. . . .*
> —**Justice Louis D. Brandeis (1928)**[266]

The early American colonists had learned this historic truth the hard way. That is why they displayed such an ardent attachment to the right of trial by jury, and that is why Elbridge Gerry of Massachusetts, when refusing to endorse the proposed *Constitution* in 1787 because of its failure to guarantee the right of trial by jury in civil cases, warned us against the inherent danger of creating little non-jury Star Chambers in the United States.

---

[266] *Holmstead v. United States*, 277 U.S. 438, 479 (1928).

**9. The *Massachusetts Body of Liberties* (December, 1641).** In May, 1635, a committee was appointed by the General Court of Massachusetts to draft legislation "for the well ordering of this plantation." The fruit of this committee's work was the *Massachusetts Body of Liberties* of 1641[267] which Justice William O. Douglas has called "a new *Magna Carta.*" Justice Douglas wrote that it "contained many of the seeds of the civil liberties which today distinguish us from the totalitarian systems" including the right to trial by jury.[268] As "the first code of laws established in New England," the *Massachusetts Body of Liberties* provided:

> *In all actions at law it shall be the liberty of the plaintiff and defendant by mutual consent to choose whether they will be tried by the bench or by a jury. . . . The like liberty shall be granted to all persons in criminal cases.*[269]

Of the *Massachusetts Body of Liberties*, the American Bar Foundation's 1959 publication *Sources of Our Liberties* states:

> *. . . We find in the Body of Liberties the idea that the fundamental law of the land should be embodied in a written instrument to which the people have assented; that this law should constitute a limitation upon the powers and discretion of administrators and judges; and that the liberties of the individual should be stated in the form of a Bill of Rights serving the same purpose as Magna Carta was thought to serve in England.*[270]

The *Body of Liberties* was followed by the *Book of General Laws and Liberties of Massachusetts*, commonly known as *The Code of 1648*. It provided that the constable of every town should "choose so many able and discreet men as the process shall direct" to be "empaneled and sworn truly to try betwixt party and party, who shall find the matter of fact with the damages and costs according to their evidence."[271]

---

[267] *See The Laws and Liberties of Massachusetts*, p. xi (1648) [Legal Classics Library 1982].
[268] Douglas, *An Almanac of Liberty*, p. 190 (Doubleday 1954).
[269] *See Harvard Classics*, supra n.207, pp. 66-70.
[270] *See* Perry & Cooper, *supra* n.98, p. 143.
[271] *Laws and Liberties of Massachusetts*, supra, pp. 31-32.

*The example set by Massachusetts was soon followed by other colonies. The Connecticut Code of 1650 and the New Haven Code of 1656, in particular, show the effects of the earlier Massachusetts codes. In both codes Chapter 39 of Magna Carta was given an important position as a protection of individual liberties. The codes of the later colonial periods such as the New York Charter of Liberties of 1683 and the Act of 1712 and the Act of 1715 in South and North Carolina included with Magna Carta such leading statutes as the Petition of Right and the Habeas Corpus Act, and thus enlarged the protection of individual liberties beyond the scope of the earlier colonial codes such as the Body of Liberties.*[272]

**10.    The *Virginia Jury Act* (June, 1642).** Six months after the adoption of the *Massachusetts Body of Liberties*, the General Assembly of Virginia adopted an Act providing for the right of trial by jury in civil cases "if either plaintiff or defendant desire the verdict of a jury for the determining of any suit pending within any of the courts of this colony." This Act was confirmed by the Virginia General Assembly in March of 1643 and subsequently reenacted in substantially the same language in March of 1658.[273]

**11.    Rhode Island's Adoption of the *Magna Carta* (1647).** Eleven years after the first settlers reached the colony of Rhode Island and Providence Plantations, the First General Assembly of that colony adopted the *Code of Laws of 1647* containing language identical in substance to the *Magna Carta* of 1215:

*That no person, in this colony, shall be taken or imprisoned, or disseized of his lands or liberties, or be exiled, or otherwise molested or destroyed, but by the lawful judgment of his peers. . . .*[274]

---

[272] Perry & Cooper, *supra n.98*, p. 147. In Thomas Cooper's edition of *The Statutes at Large of South Carolina*, Vol. 1, pp. 72-74 (1836), he lists nine confirmations of the *Magna Carta* and concludes that American *Constitutions* are "undoubtedly founded on this portion of the constitutional history of England."

[273] *The Statutes at Large of Virginia*, Vol. 1, pp. 273-274, 474 (1823).

[274] *The Earliest Acts and Laws of the Colony of Rhode Island*, p. 12 (Michael Glazier, Inc. 1977).

ILLUSTRATION BY AL PHILLIPS

*The Massachusetts Body of Liberties was a new Magna Carta. It contained many of the seeds of the civil liberties which today distinguish us from the totalitarian systems, including the right to trial by jury.*
—**Justice William O. Douglas (1954)**

**12.    The Execution of Charles I (January 30, 1649).**
Following the abolition of the Star Chamber, the classic struggle between Parliament and Crown continued. The *Petition of Right* of 1628 was a reaffirmation of the *Magna Carta*. "Its object was to curtail the king's prerogative." According to Winston Churchill, it embodied "the main foundation of English freedom." It prohibited executive imprisonment and reasserted the right to trial by jury. Churchill has said that "trial by [a] jury of equals, only for offenses known to the law, *if maintained*, makes the difference between bond and free."[275]

But Charles I would not maintain that right, and many atrocities were committed in his name. The ears of political dissidents were cropped, the noses of non-conformists were split, the cheeks of so-called "seditious libelers" were branded, many languished in London jails,[276] and popular uprisings were brutally suppressed. When "the hungry, downtrodden masses" rebelled in Ireland in 1641, the government of Charles I "struck back without mercy" and "a general slaughter of males and a policy of devastation was proclaimed throughout large parts of the countryside."[277]

Through all this, two institutions sustained the growing hunger for individual liberty: representative government and trial by jury. Frustrated by an independent Parliament, Charles I, accompanied by 300 or 400 swordsmen, invaded the House of Commons on January 4, 1642. He had come to arrest John Pym and four of his followers, but by the time the king arrived, "the birds had flown." Charles I had made a monumental mistake. "Upon this episode the wrath of London became uncontrollable."[278] Six years of civil war followed, closing with Charles I's surrender in the Spring of 1648. Charged with an arbitrary design "to overthrow the rights and liberties of the people," Charles I was tried and convicted of high treason and executed on January 30, 1649.[279]

An ardent enemy of individual liberty was gone, and many "looked across the ocean to new lands where the cause for which they were prepared to die . . . could breathe."[280] Those who suffered through those trying times knew the value of individual rights. They would never have surrendered their fundamental freedoms, *nor can we!*

---

[275]Churchill, *supra n.182*, Vol. 2, p. 185.
[276]See Halliday, *supra n.247*, p. 115.
[277]Churchill, *supra n.182*, Vol. 2, pp. 224-225.
[278]Churchill, *supra n.182*, Vol. 2, pp. 229-230.
[279]See Trial of Charles I, *supra n.199*, pp. 78, 129.
[280]Churchill, *supra n.182*, Vol. 2, p. 228.

**13. The English Commonwealth and Protectorate Under Oliver Cromwell (1649-1658).** Following the execution of Charles I, the office of king was formally abolished on February 7, 1649, and Oliver Cromwell became Chairman of the Council of State. Upon his dissolution of the "Rump Parliament" in April of 1653, he became "de facto king" with "a greater power and authority than had ever been exercised or claimed by any king" before him.[281] In his own mind, he was a modern-day Moses leading his faithful flock out of bondage into the Promised Land.[282]

In the annals of English history, no better illustration can be found for the futility of exchanging individual liberty for the prospect of economic prosperity than in Oliver Cromwell's reign. It was "a time of great peace and prosperity" in which the Commonwealth routed its enemies, both foreign and domestic, and became "the chief sea power in the world."[283] But power and prosperity were not without cost. In a constitutional sense, "these were hard times."[284] When "anarchy threatened," he "ruled by force."[285] "The one power left in England was the power of the sword."[286]

Oliver Cromwell was a man who "had a fatal disregard for civil and religious liberties"[287] and who "trampled underfoot the constitution."[288] In August of 1649, he led his "New Model Army" into Ireland where thousands were massacred at Drogheda and Wexford as part of a "deliberate policy of terror."[289] "Thousands perished by famine or the sword" and "shipload after shipload of those who surrendered were sent over seas to forced labor in Jamaica and the West Indies."[290]

---

[281] Cannon & Griffiths, *The Oxford Illustrated History of the British Monarchy*, pp. 391-396 (Oxford U. Press 1988).

[282] Morgan, ed., *The Oxford Illustrated History of Britain*, pp. 325-29 (Oxford University Press 1984).

[283] *See* Green, *History of the English People*, Vol. 3, pp. 267-325 (Hovendon Company 1874).

[284] Churchill, *A History of the English Speaking Peoples*, Vol. 2, p. 312 (Dorset Press 1956).

[285] Halliday, *A Concise History of England*, p. 3 of Table of Contents and p. 119 (Viking Press 1965).

[286] Green, *supra n.283*, p. 282.

[287] *Oxford Illustrated History, supra n.282*, p. 328.

[288] Green, *supra n.283*, p. 308.

[289] *The Cambridge Historical Encyclopedia of Great Britain and Ireland*, pp. 214-215 (Cambridge U. Press 1985).

[290] Green, *supra n.283*, pp. 293-294.

According to Green's *History of the English People*, under Oliver Cromwell, "no such doom has ever fallen on a nation in modern times as fell upon Ireland," and to this day, the worst curse an Irishman can cast upon an enemy is the "Curse of Cromwell."[291] Likewise, Winston Churchill wrote in 1956:

> ... *The consequences of Cromwell's rule in Ireland have distressed and at times distracted English politics even down to the present day. To heal them baffled the skill and loyalties of successive generations. They became for a time a potent obstacle to the harmony of the English speaking peoples throughout the world. Upon all of us there still lies "the Curse of Cromwell."*[292]

One positive aspect of the English Commonwealth under Oliver Cromwell was its attempt to establish a comprehensive written constitution[293] with some basic guarantees of individual liberty. In the *Agreement of the People* (1649), "having by our late labours and hazards, made it appear to the world at how high a rate we value our just freedom," the Commonwealth endorsed the principles of equal representation, equal protection and the constitutional supremacy of "the foundations of common right, liberty and safety."[294] In the *Instrument of Government* (1653), Cromwell's Council of Officers provided for a modified form of universal suffrage, freedom of religion, and the equal administration of law and justice.[295]

Although a guarantee of the right of trial by jury had been included in the Levellers' "Third Draft" of the *Agreement of the People*, attempts to obtain the approval of Cromwell and the army were unsuccessful.[296] "Too far advanced for its own day, it was to bear fruit in the American *Bill of Rights*."[297]

---

[291] Green, *supra n.283*, p. 294.

[292] Churchill, *supra n.284*, Vol. 2, p. 292.

[293] For a discussion of the basic differences in the British and American constitutions, *see* pp. 425-436 below.

[294] *See* Stephenson & Marcham, *Sources of English Constitutional History*, pp. 511-516 (Harper & Row 1937).

[295] *See* Adams & Stephens, *Select Documents of English Constitutional History*, pp. 407-416 (MacMillan 1908).

[296] Schwartz, *The Great Rights of Mankind: A History of the American Bill of Rights*, pp. 17-18 (Oxford Univ. Press 1977).

[297] Schwartz, *supra n.113*, Vol. 1, p. 23.

*Oliver Cromwell* installed as Lord Protector (1653)

**14.     The Jury Trials of John Lilburne (1649, 1653).** In December of 1637, at age 23, John Lilburne was arrested for allegedly importing "libellous and seditious books" from Holland into England. Standing on his privilege against self-incrimination, he was tried before the Court of the Star Chamber by affidavit and sentenced to a public whipping through the streets of London, a session in the pillory and a long term of solitary confinement.[298] In November of 1640, he was discharged by an order of Parliament and his sentence was later reversed by the House of Lords.

Lilburne later commanded a regiment of Dragoons in the Parliamentary Armory during the English Civil Wars (1642-1648), and became a leader in the Levellers Movement which advocated equality before the law and universal suffrage.[299] Having risen to the rank of Lieutenant Colonel, he refused to subscribe to the *Solemn League and Covenant* with Scotland, resigned from the army[300] and authored several books, including *The Fundamental Liberties of the People of England* (1649). For his criticism of Oliver Cromwell, he was imprisoned in the Tower of London, charged with high treason and brought to trial at the Guildhall of London on October 24, 1649.

Denied the right of counsel, the right of access to witnesses in his behalf, the right of effective cross-examination and hounded by a panel of unfriendly judges, John Lilburne demanded the right to trial by "a legal jury of my equals, constituted according to law," and conducted one of the most remarkable defenses in the history of Anglo-American law. Citing the *Magna Carta, The Petition of Right* and Sir Edward Coke's *Institutes on the Laws of England*, Lilburne insisted upon his right to an open, public trial and delivered a defense that brought forth a loud cry of "amen" from the assembled citizens of London.[301]

---

[298] *See* "The Trial of John Lilburne and John Wharton, For Printing and Publishing Seditious Books," 3 *How. St. Tr.* 1315-1368 (April 1638).

[299] *See The Cambridge Historical Encyclopedia of Great Britain and Ireland, supra* n.289, pp. 232, 359 and Davies, *The Early Stuarts* (1603-1660), pp. 75, 197 (Oxford University Press 2d ed. 1959). The Levellers, "a democratic faction in the government," was largely responsible for the recognition of the citizen's right against self-incrimination. *See* Perry & Cooper, *supra* n.98, pp. 134-136.

[300] *See Encyclopædia Britannica Micropædia*, Vol. VI, p. 221 (15 ed. 1979).

[301] *See* "Trial of Lieutenant Colonel John Lilburne," 4 *How. St. Tr.* 1269-1470 (1649).

In his closing speech to the jury, John Lilburne expressed his great faith in that institution that we so proudly call "the cornerstone of our judicial process."

> *I must speak in my own behalf unto the jury, my fellow countrymen, upon whose consciences, integrity and honesty, my life, and the lives and liberties of the holiest men of this nation, now lies. . . .*
>
> *. . . I leave it to your judgments and consciences to judge righteously between me and my adversaries. . . ; for I profess, I know of no wrong that I have done them. . . . My conscience is free and clear in the sight of God, and, I hope, of all unbiased men. . . .*
>
> *. . . With an upright heart and conscience, and with a cheerful countenance, I cast my life, and the lives of all the honest citizens of England . . . into the care and conscience of my honest jury and fellow citizens; whom I declare by the law of England, are the conservators and sole judges of my life, having inherent in them alone the judicial power of the law.*
>
> *. . . And therefore I desire you to know your powers, and consider your duty both to God, to me, to yourselves, and to your country. And may the gracious assisting Spirit and Presence of the Lord . . . go along with you, give counsel and direct you, to do that which is just. . . .* [302]

On Friday, October 26, 1649, at 5:00 p.m., the jury retired, and, one hour later they returned with a verdict of NOT GUILTY. When Lilburne was acquitted:

> *Extraordinary were the acclamations for the prisoner's deliverance, as the like hath not been seen in England; which acclamations and loud rejoicing expressions went quite through the streets with him . . . , and for joy the people caused that night an abundance of bonfires to be made all up and down the streets of London. . . .* [303]

---

[302] *Trial of John Lilburne*, supra n.301, pp. 1378-1395.
[303] *Trial of John Lilburne*, supra n.301, p. 1405.

But John Lilburne's troubles did not end there. Having incurred the ire of Oliver Cromwell, he was banished from the Commonwealth by the Rump Parliament in January of 1651 upon penalty of death should he return. But return he did and in July, 1653, he was arraigned and tried at the Old Bailey in London.

With a crowd of 6,000 in attendance, Lilburne again conducted a "notable defense." Calling the jury "the Keepers of the Liberties of England," he challenged the validity of the act of banishment as well as the validity of the Parliament that passed it. He argued that "all crimes whatever were to be heard, determined and judged at the common law" and that all acts of attainder were unlawful. On August 20, 1653, the jury returned a verdict of acquittal and "the joy and acclamation was so great after they had cleared him, that the shout was heard an English mile."[304]

For their verdicts, Lilburne's jury was summoned to account by Cromwell's Council of State. Unintimidated by this inquisition, the jury foreman, a candlestick maker named Thomas Greene, responded that he had "discharged his conscience" and that he would "give no other answer to any questions which shall be asked him upon that matter."

*The trial of John Lilburne was judged and conceived to be a matter of very great consequence; for on one side Cromwell being so highly set and incensed against him, and on the other side the people murmuring so much against such illegal and violent proceedings against the ordinary course and practice.*[305]

As a layman who successfully defended the constitutional liberties of England, John Lilburne believed that "the fundamental law is the perfection of reason."[306] His acquittal by two successive English juries was clear evidence of a national desire to uphold the supremacy of the law.[307] A commemorative medal was struck in honor of the event[308] as a milestone on the rocky road to the American Revolution.

---

[304] See 5 How. St. Tr. 407-444 (1653).

[305] 5 How. St. Tr. 445-450 (1653).

[306] Davies, supra n.299, p. 197.

[307] Holdsworth, supra n.14, p. 162.

[308] See M.D.A. Freeman, "The Jury of Trial," pp. 65, 66, 91, in Current Legal Problems 1981, Vol. 34 (Stevens & Sons 1981). The medal read: "John Lilburne saved the power of the Lord and the integrity of his jury who are judges of law as well as fact."

**Lt. Col. John Lilburne (1614-1657)**, *who believed that "the fundamental law is the perfection of reason." He called the jury "the Keepers of the Liberties of England."*

## 15. Restoration of the Monarchy Under Charles II

**(1660).** When Oliver Cromwell "quietly breathed his last" on September 3, 1658, he was succeeded by his son Richard, "a weak and worthless man." To a "nation sick of military rule," Cromwell's reign had been "the tyranny which England was resolute to throw off." Sir Ashley Cooper described him as "his highness of deplorable memory, who with fraud and force deprived us of our liberty."[309] It was no great surprise that Richard's rule lasted only eight months.

Upon threat of military intervention, Parliament was dissolved in April of 1659 and recalled in the following month. After a royalist insurrection in August, the army expelled Parliament again in October. Intensified opposition to military rule resulted in a restoration of the Long Parliament in December, 1659, where it sat continuously until its final dissolution in March of 1660, in the face of a widespread feeling that peace and prosperity "might be too dearly purchased if secured at the sacrifice of civil liberty."[310]

On April 4, 1660, Charles II agreed to the *Declaration of Breda* containing a general amnesty, a provision that "no man shall be disqualified or called into question for differences of opinion in matters of religion," and a promise to restore "the just, ancient and fundamental rights" of the citizens of England.[311]

On April 25, 1660, the Convention Parliament assembled at Westminster and on May 25, 1660, Charles II landed at Dover and ascended to the throne as "Puritanism laid down the sword" and "ceased from the long attempt to build up a kingdom of God by force and violence."[312] The restoration of Charles II "automatically restored the state of affairs as it existed on the eve of the civil war."[313]

> *His reign was declared to have begun at the moment of his father's death; those acts of Parliament to which his father had assented were enforced, all the rest were null and void.* [314]

---

[309] Green, *History of the English People, supra n.283*, pp. 320-322.

[310] Davies, *supra n.299*, pp. 189, 237-256.

[311] Stephenson & Marcham, *supra n.294*, pp. 532-533.

[312] Green, *History of the English People, supra n.283*, pp. 323-324.

[313] Plucknett, *supra n.217*, pp. 54-55.

[314] *Oxford Illustrated History of Britain, supra n.282*, p. 330. As to the lasting effects of the legislation of this period, *see* Holdsworth, *supra n.14*, Vol. 6, pp. 148-174.

**16. An Act of Rhode Island for Declaring the Rights and Privileges of His Majesty's Subjects Within this Colony (March 1, 1662).** Fifteen years after its original passage, the General Assembly of Rhode Island reenacted legislation containing provisions substantially identical to the provisions of the *Magna Carta*:

> *... That no free man shall be taken or imprisoned, or be deprived of his freehold, or liberty, or free customs, or outlawed, or exiled or otherwise destroyed, nor shall be passed upon, judged, or condemned, but by the lawful judgment of his peers....* [315]

**17. The Charter of Connecticut (May 3, 1662).** Two years after the *Restoration*, Charles II granted the *Charter of Connecticut* to John Winthrop and "all such others as now are or hereafter shall be admitted" to the company and society of that colony. In it, he guaranteed that "every subject who shall go and inhabit within said colony ... shall have and enjoy all Liberties and Immunities of free and natural subjects ... as if they and every one of them were born within the realm of England."[316]

**18. The Charter of Rhode Island and Providence Plantations (July 8, 1663).** As with the earlier charters, that of Rhode Island provided that citizens "shall have and enjoy all Liberties and Immunities of free and natural subjects ... as if they ... were born within the realm of England."

> *Like the Massachusetts Body of Liberties, the [Charter of Rhode Island] was prefixed with an affirmation of Chapter 39 of [the] Magna Carta....* [317]

Over a period of 57 years, commencing with the *First Charter of Virginia* in 1606, the Charters of five successive colonies had guaranteed the right of trial by jury in order to encourage English emigration to the vast American wilderness. It was a matter of great importance to the American colonists of the 17th century, just as it remains a matter of great importance to the American citizen of today. That it was regarded by them as an invaluable right is demonstrated by the events that followed.

---

[315] *The Earliest Laws of Rhode Island, supra* n.274, p. 139.

[316] Chafee, ed., *Documents on Fundamental Human Rights*, pp. 94-97 (Harvard University Press 1951).

[317] Perry & Cooper, *supra* n.98, pp. 177, 165.

**19. Resolutions of the House of Commons on the Punishment of Jurors (December 13, 1667).** The practice of juror intimidation was well known to early English common law. In 1554, when the court was dissatisfied with the verdict of the jury in Sir Nicholas Throckmorton's treason trial, it committed the jury to prison and imposed a heavy fine.[318] Ten years later in Sir Thomas Smith's famous book on *The Republic of England*,[319] the practice was condemned as "violent, tyrannical, and contrary to the liberty and custom of the realm of England."[320] But, as evidenced by the fate of John Lilburne's jury, it still persisted.[321] And on December 13, 1667, in a disciplinary proceeding against Chief Justice Keeling, the House of Commons declared that "the practice of fining or imprisoning juries is illegal."[322]

**20. John Locke's Fundamental Constitutions of Carolina (March 1, 1669).** John Locke (1632-1704), described as "The Theorist of the Glorious Revolution of 1688,"[323] wrote that the end of the law is to "preserve and enlarge freedom."[324]

His opinions on the dissolution of government significantly influenced Thomas Jefferson in his authorship of the *Declaration of Independence*[325] and his views on separation of powers had a material impact on the formulation of our *Constitution*. His first major contribution to the concept of constitutional law came in his *Fundamental Constitutions of Carolina* on March 1, 1669. In it, he provided that "no cause, whether civil or criminal, of any freeman, shall be tried in any court of judicature, *without a judgment of his peers.*"[326]

---

[318] 1 *How. St. Tr.* 900-902 (1554).

[319] Holdsworth, *supra n.14*, pp. 208-209.

[320] *Blackstone's Commentaries, supra n.123*, Vol. 4, p. 354.

[321] 5 *How. St. Tr.* 445-450 (1653).

[322] Browning, ed., *English Historical Documents,* Vol. VIII (1660-1714), pp. 85-86 (Oxford University Press 1953).

[323] William Seagle, *The History of Law,* p.204 (Tudor Publishing Co. 1946).

[324] Stedman, *Our Ageless Constitution,* p. 264 (The Stedman Liberty Library 1987).

[325] *See* A. J. Langguth, *Patriots: The Men Who Started the American Revolution,* pp. 354-355 (Simon & Schuster 1988).

[326] *See* Locke's *Constitution,* 111th paragraph, in Cooper, *The Statutes at Large of South Carolina,* Vol. 1, p. 55 (1836). John Locke's *Second Essay Concerning Civil Government* (1690) is included in Volume 35 of *The Great Books of the Western World* (Encyclopædia Britannica 1952).

***John Locke (1632-1704)***
*His Fundamental Constitutions of Carolina (March 1, 1669) provided that "no cause, whether civil or criminal, of any freeman, shall be tried in any court of judicature, without a judgment of his peers."*

**21.    The Trial of William Penn (August 31, 1670).** In the *Declaration of Breda* of August 4, 1660, as a condition to the *Restoration*, Charles II had committed to the proposition that "no man shall be disquieted or called into question for differences of opinion in matters of religion." To this commitment, however, the king had affixed the condition that such opinions "do not disturb the peace of the kingdom,"[327] a proviso which ultimately swallowed up the rule itself.

In return for the Anglican Church's adherence to the doctrines of the divine right of kings, passive obedience and non-resistance, the king agreed that if he could not compel his subjects to conform to the established Church of England, he would "at least make it unpleasant for those who refused to conform." Accordingly, Charles II "gave a free hand to the cavalier and Anglican majority in the Parliament of 1661."[328]

A steady stream of legislation which followed was aimed primarily at the nonconformist Society of Friends, commonly called "Quakers."[329] *The Corporation Act* of 1661 required all local office-holders to take the sacraments according to the rites of the Church of England. *The Act of Uniformity* of 1662 required all ministers to use the revised *Book of Common Prayer*. And the *Conventicle Act* of 1664 prohibited "any assembly for the exercise of religion" not held in accordance with the established liturgy of the Church of England. As a result, many Quakers were imprisoned, "and the state of the prisons was such that a sentence of imprisonment too often meant a sentence of death."[330]

> *From the Quaker Act of 1662 . . . , Friends were hounded by penal laws for not swearing oaths, for not going to the Church of England, for going to Quaker meetings, and for refusing tithes. Some 15,000 suffered under these laws, and almost 500 died in prison, but they continued to grow in numbers. . . .*[331]

---

[327] Stephenson & Marcham, *supra n.294*, p. 533.

[328] Holdsworth, *supra n.14*, Vol. VI, p. 197.

[329] *See* Norris, *Dictionary of Word & Phrase Origins*, p. 472 (Harper & Row 1971).

[330] Holdsworth, *supra n.14*, pp. 197-199.

[331] *Encyclopædia Britannica Macropædia* Vol. 7, p. 743 (15th ed. 1979). For the texts of these Acts, *see* Browning, ed., *English Historical Documents 1660-1714* (Oxford U Press 1953). *See also* Adams & Stephens, *Select Documents of English Constitutional History* (Macmillan 1908) and Stephenson & Marcham, ed., *Sources of English Constitutional History* (Harper & Row 1937).

One of the most influential converts to the Quaker cause was William Penn, son of a British admiral. His trial before "a formidable bench"[332] at the Old Bailey in September of 1670 has been described as "one of the landmarks of Anglo-American liberty."[333]

*Penn and a small group of Quakers held a meeting in Grace Church Street, London, in 1670, after being shut out of their meeting house by government soldiers. The meeting was thus held because the "Conventicle Act" declared unlawful any meetings for worship other than those of the Church of England. William Mead and Penn were indicted for illegally disturbing the king's peace "by preaching to an unlawful assembly and causing a great concourse and tumult."* . . .[334]

At age 26, Penn conducted his own defense. Three witnesses were called for the prosecution. They testified that they saw Penn speaking to the people, but none had heard what he said. The only evidence against Mead was that he was present when Penn spoke.

*The court ordered the jury to find them guilty, for, said the court, if the jury found the Quakers had met at all, then the very meeting by itself was unlawful and, therefore, it followed as a matter of course that the peace was disturbed.* . . .

But four members of the jury refused to vote for conviction and the presiding judge, London's Lord Mayor, Sir Samuel Starling, "used many unworthy threats to the four that dissented." Identifying Edward Bushel as the leader of the hold-outs, Judge Starling called him "an impudent fellow" and both he and the Recorder, Sir John Howell, threatened to have him branded.

---

[332]"The ten judges who heard the case were a formidable bench for they included the Lord Mayor, Starling, the Recorder, Sir John Howell, and other representatives of the government who were very partisanly concerned in enforcing the *Conventicle Act*. Hardly an impartial court!" Marke, *Vignettes of Legal History*, "Trial of William Penn: A Landmark in the Development of the Jury System," pp. 217, 220 (Fred B. Rothman & Co. 1965).

[333]Schwartz, *The Roots of the Bill of Rights*, Vol. 1, p. 131 (Chelsea House Publishers 1980).

[334]Marke, *supra n.332*, pp. 219-220.

The jury again retired and, after further deliberation, returned with a unanimous verdict:

> *We find William Penn guilty of speaking to an assembly in Grace-Church Street and that William Mead is not guilty of the said indictment.*

Dissatisfied that the jury failed to find Penn's conduct unlawful, the court had Bushel and his fellow jurors locked up in Newgate Prison without food or water.

> *The jury persisted in its course for two days and nights, refusing to bring in a different verdict, although kept without food, water and heat. Finally the court ended the trial abruptly, fining them each 40 marks and committing them to imprisonment until they paid their fines. Bushel and the other jurors obtained a writ of habeas corpus from the Court of Common Pleas.*

In response to Bushel's petition, the Court of Common Pleas ruled that the jurors were judges of the facts and could not be punished for their verdict, thus establishing "the right of trial juries to decide cases according to their convictions."

> *It may be said without exaggeration that the Penn trial and Bushel's case gave a new meaning to the institution we know as the jury system.* . . .[335]

The legacy of Bushel's case is marked for posterity by a plaque in the Old Bailey inscribed as follows:

> *Near this site William Penn and William Mead were tried in 1670 for preaching to an unlawful assembly in Grace-Church Street. This tablet commemorates the courage and endurance of the jury . . . who refused to give a verdict against them, although locked up without food for two nights and were fined for their final verdict of not guilty. The case of these jurymen was reviewed on a writ of habeas corpus and . . . the opinion of the court . . . established the right of juries to give their verdict according to their convictions.*[336]

---

[335]Marke, *supra* n.332, pp. 223, 224.
[336]Moore, *The Jury: Tool of Kings, Palladium of Liberty*, p. 89 (W. H. Anderson Co. 1973).

***Newgate Prison****, the residence of Edward Bushel and his fellow jurors following their acquittal of William Penn and William Mead in 1670.*

**22.    *The General Laws and Liberties of Connecticut* (October, 1672).** Ten years after the granting of the *Charter of Connecticut,* the General Court met at Hartford in October, 1672, and adopted *The General Laws and Liberties of Connecticut,* providing for the right of trial by jury in all civil actions where the amount in controversy exceeded 40 shillings.

> And all cases, where the debt or damage shall exceed 40 shillings, they shall be tried by a jury of twelve men, which men shall be empaneled and sworn to try betwixt party and party who shall find the matter of fact with the damages and costs according to law. . . .[337]

**23.    *The Charters of East and West New Jersey* 1677-1683.** In 1677, New Jersey became the seventh consecutive colony to guarantee the right of trial by jury. Chapter 17 of *The Charter of Fundamental Laws of West New Jersey* (March 13, 1677) provided:

> That no . . . inhabitants . . . of West New Jersey, shall be deprived or condemned of life, limb, liberty, estate, property, or any ways hurt in any of their privileges, freedoms or franchises, upon any account whatsoever, without a due trial, and judgment passed by twelve good and lawful men of his neighborhood first had.[338]

According to the American Bar Foundation's *Sources of Our Liberties,* the effect of the *Magna Carta* was nowhere more apparent than in New Jersey:

> The general influence of Magna Carta upon colonial lawmakers has been noted elsewhere. The effect of that document during the period following the Restoration in England was probably nowhere more apparent than in New Jersey. . . .The fundamental Constitutions of East Jersey, 1683, provided: "That no person or persons within the said province shall be taken or imprisoned, or be devised of his freehold, free custom or liberty, or outlawed or exiled, or any other way destroyed; nor shall they be condemned or judgment passed upon them, but by lawful judgment of their peers.". . .[339]

---

[337] *The Earliest Laws of the New Haven and Connecticut Colonies 1639-1673,* pp. 75, 111 (Michael Glazier 1977).
[338] *See* Perry & Cooper, *supra n.98,* p. 185.
[339] Perry & Cooper, *supra n.98,* p. 183.

**24. *The General Laws and Liberties of the Province of New Hampshire* (March 16, 1680).** The General Assembly of New Hampshire adopted *The General Laws and Liberties* of that province on March 16, 1680, providing for the right of trial by jury in all cases:

> *It is further enacted that all trials, whether capital, criminal, or between man and man, both respecting maritime affairs as well as others, be tried by a jury of twelve good and lawful men, according to the commendable custom of England. . . .*[340]

**25. *Certain Conditions or Concessions of the Province of Pennsylvania* (July 11, 1681).** As Proprietor and Governor of the Province of Pennsylvania, William Penn adopted *Certain Conditions or Concessions* on July 11, 1681, providing that "no man shall by any ways or means, in word or deed, affront or wrong any Indian" and:

> *That all differences between the planters and the natives shall be ended by twelve men, that is, six planters and six natives, that so we may live friendly together as much as in us lieth, preventing all occasions of heart burnings and mischief.*[341]

**26. *The Frame of Government of Pennsylvania* (April 25, 1682).** *The Frame of Government of Pennsylvania* guaranteed that its inhabitants would enjoy the protection of "Certain Laws Agreed Upon in England." Among them were the provision "*that all trials shall be by twelve men . . . of the neighborhood.*"[342]

Pennsylvania (1682) had followed Virginia (1606), Massachusetts (1629), Maryland (1632), Rhode Island (1647), Connecticut (1662), South Carolina (1669), New Jersey (1677-83), and New Hampshire (1680) to become the ninth consecutive colony to guarantee to its citizens the right of trial by jury. A pattern was thus established that would continue with New York (1683, 1691), Delaware (1727), Georgia (1732) and North Carolina (1746) as all 13 colonies adopted guarantees that the fundamental right of trial by jury would be preserved.

---

[340] *Acts and Laws of New Hampshire 1680-1726*, pp. 203, 216 (Michael Glazier, Inc. 1978).

[341] *The Earliest Printed Laws of Pennsylvania 1681-1713*, pp. 190, 192 (Michael Glazier, Inc. 1978).

[342] *See Frame of Government of Pennsylvania* (April 25, 1682) in Perry & Cooper, *supra n.98*, pp. 209, 217.

**27.** ***The Charter of Liberties and Privileges of New York* (1683).** Originally settled by the Dutch, New York was "clearly in the hands of the English by 1669" and was renamed for the Duke of York, who ascended to the British throne as James II in 1685.[343] As "the future James II was scarcely the ruler to look favorably upon a popular government," New York was not permitted to elect a General Assembly until 1683. "The very first law passed by the first General Assembly of New York" was the *Charter of Liberties and Privileges* of 1683, "a direct result of the successful struggle for self-government that had agitated the colony from the beginning of English rule."[344]

With respect to the right of trial by jury, the New York *Charter of Liberties and Privileges* provided:

> *All trials shall be by verdict of twelve men, and as near as may be peers and equals of the neighborhood and in the country, shire or division where the facts shall arise or grow, whether the same be by Indictment, Information, Declaration or otherwise against the Person, Offender or Defendant.*[345]

As James II was "not the man to acquiesce in a document like the *Charter of Liberties*, he vetoed that instrument in 1684."

> *... The New York colonists, however, continued undaunted in their devotion to the 1683 Charter. When, after the expulsion of James II they again received the right of self-government, one of the first things the General Assembly, meeting in April, 1691, did was to enact "An Act Declaring What are the Rights and Privileges of Their Majesties' Subjects Inhabiting Within the Province of New York."...*

This Act "repeated the rights guaranteed in the 1683 Charter," including the right to trial by jury.[346]

---

[343] *Encyclopædia Britannica Macropædia*, Vol. 13, p. 21 (15th ed.1979).

[344] Schwartz, *The Great Rights of Mankind: A History of the American Bill of Rights*, p. 43 (Oxford University Press 1977).

[345] "Jury Trial on Trial — A Symposium," 28 *N.Y.S.B. Bulletin* 322, 329 (1956).

[346] Schwartz, *supra n.333*, p. 44. *See also The Colonial Laws of New York*, Vol. 1, pp. 125-126, 226-227 (1896).

### James II, King of England (1685-1689)

*As James II was "not the man to acquiesce in a document like the Charter of Liberties, he vetoed that instrument in 1684." The New York colonists, however, continued undaunted in their devotion to the right of trial by jury, guaranteeing that fundamental right in the Declaration of Rights of 1691.*

## 28. The Trial of the Seven Bishops (June 29-30, 1688).

The Seven Bishops Trial has been called "one the best known incidents of English history," its importance enhanced by the fact that "a verdict was given against a whole system of government."[347] In *Gentlemen of the Jury* (1924), Francis Wellman called the trial "one of the most remarkable and renowned instances of the courage of a jury in resisting the arbitrary will of power and authority."[348]

The controversy from which the case arose sprang from the religious intolerance which had dominated English life since Henry VIII broke with Rome, confiscated the Catholic monasteries, and established the Church of England in 1534. Following these events, "the growing strife among religious factions"[349] and Mary I's desire to restore Roman Catholicism as the state religion, had led to a Protestant insurrection under the leadership of Thomas Wyatt and the trial of Sir Nicholas Throckmorton in 1554.[350] Thereafter, under Bloody Mary's iron rule:

> *For three years rebel bodies dangled from gibbets, and heretics were relentlessly executed, some 300 being burned at the stake.*[351]

Thirty-two years later, a "plot to assassinate Elizabeth I and bring about a Catholic uprising" led to the execution of Mary Queen of Scots, the mother of James VI of Scotland who later became James I of England (1603-1625). During the reign of his son, Charles I, this same religious strife contributed significantly to the English civil wars (1641-1649), persecution at first of, and then by, the Puritans, and emigration to America by the Pilgrims to Massachusetts Bay in 1620,[352] by British Catholics to Maryland in 1632 and by the Quakers to Pennsylvania in 1681.

---

[347] Ogg, *England in the Reign of James II and William III,* p. 198 (Clarendon Press 1955).

[348] Wellman, *Gentlemen of the Jury,* p. 51 (The Macmillan Company 2d ed. 1936).

[349] *Encyclopædia Britannica Macropædia,* Vol. 8, p. 772 (15th ed. 1979).

[350] *See* pp. 100-101 above.

[351] *Encyclopædia Britannica, supra,* Vol. 11, p. 565.

[352] Which, in turn, resulted in the founding of Rhode Island by Roger Williams in 1636 "under an edict of banishment from Massachusetts Bay Colony. . .for advocating freedom of conscience in religion." *Encyclopædia Britannica Macropædia, supra,* Vol. 15, p. 807.

Persecution by the party in power was the order of the day.

> *Indelible stains of innocent blood*
> *Inseminated English sod,*
> *As atrocities came like a furious flood*
> *In the Glorious name of Almighty God!*

It was against this background that James II issued a series of "Indulgences" in 1687 and 1688. The highest court in England had held that "it is an inseparable prerogative in the king of England" to dispense with laws enacted by Parliament. Relying on this authority, James II suspended certain acts of Parliament which had previously discriminated against Catholics and Protestant dissenters.[353]

On May 4, 1688, James II directed that his Indulgence be read in all churches throughout England on two successive Sundays. However, the Archbishop of Canterbury and six of his fellow Anglican bishops questioned the king's right to suspend existing acts of Parliament and petitioned the king, requesting that they be relieved from compliance.

> *Your Petitioners therefore most humbly and earnestly beseech Your Majesty that you will be graciously pleased not to insist upon their distribution and reading Your Majesty's said Declaration.*[354]

The king was enraged. He locked the Seven Bishops in the Tower of London and tried them for seditious libel at Westminster Hall on June 29, 1688. Tensions ran high.

> *Before the day of trial the agitation had spread to the farthest corners of the island. . . . The people of Cornwall, a fierce, bold, and athletic race . . . were moved by the danger to Bishop Trelawney, whom they revered. . . . All over the country the peasants chanted. . . . "And shall Trelawney die, and shall Trelawney die? Then 30,000 Cornish boys will know the reason why!"*[355]

---

[353] *Hale's Case* (1686), *see* Adams & Stephens, *Selected Documents of English Constitutional History*, pp. 450-454 (1908).

[354] Browning, ed., *English Historical Documents (1660-1714)*, p. 84 (Oxford University Press 1953).

[355] Presser & Zainalden, *Law and American History*, p. 19 (West Publishing Company 1980).

On the day of the trial, the courtroom was packed. The leaders of the British Bar appeared on both sides of the aisle. The Chief Justice summed up the evidence and instructed the jury that "anything that shall disturb the government, or make mischief and a stir among the people" was a seditious libel. However, one of his fellow justices was of the opinion that the Petition had been delivered "with all the humility and decency that could be" and that it was the right of every subject to petition the king.[356]

The jury not only exonerated the seven bishops, but toppled the government of the last of the Stuart kings.

> *When the verdict of "not guilty" was announced, the benches and galleries raised a shout and on the instant 10,000 persons who had crowded the court hall replied with a still louder shout. The boats which gathered on the Thames gave an answering cheer. As the news spread, streets, squares and marketplaces resounded with acclamations. The roar of the multitude was such that, during a half hour, scarcely a word could be heard in the court. The jury could hardly make their way out of the hall. They were forced to shake hands with hundreds. The streets were aglare with bonfires, surrounded by crowds singing good health to the bishops .... Windows were lighted with rows of candles, each row consisting of seven in honor of the seven bishops.*[357]

This event has been described as the crowning blow which led, not only to the abdication of one of the most unpopular sovereigns in the history of the English monarchy, but also to the enactment of the British *Bill of Rights*.

> *... On June 30, 1688, the defendants were acquitted, amid great public rejoicing and jubilation. On the same day Prince William of Orange was invited to come to England. The terms upon which William and Mary accepted the Throne included the enactment as law of the Bill of Rights.*[358]

---

[356] Stephenson & Marcham, *Sources of English Constitutional History*, p. 585 (1937) [Justice Holloway].

[357] Wellman, *supra* n.348, p. 51.

[358] Dumbauld, *The Constitution of the United States,* pp. 11-12 (University of Oklahoma Press 1964).

*The acquittal of the Seven Bishops is one of the most renowned instances of the courage of a jury in resisting the arbitrary will of power and authority.*
—**Francis L. Wellman (1924)**

## 29. The Abdication of James II (February 22, 1689).

James II had succeeded his brother as King of England on February 6, 1685. However, those who welcomed James II to the throne were in for a rude shock.

> *James was in fact a bigot. His government of Scotland in the early 1680's had been a most severe repression and extensive use of judicial torture against Protestant dissenters. . . .[359]*

He suppressed two popular rebellions with "great ferocity," packed the British bench with his political allies, and, when seven bishops petitioned him to withdraw his *Articles of Indulgence*, he prosecuted them for seditious libel.[360]

> *The struggle between Crown and Parliament which had dominated English life since the reign of James I had now come back to its starting point. Eighty years of fearful events . . . had brought the monarchy . . . to almost . . . absolutism. . . .[361]*

Weary of a long line of divine right kings, his subjects rebelled. Contending armies met again on English soil. Mass desertions from his mutinous ranks forced James II's flight to France. "On February 22, 1689, the Convention Parliament declared that James had abdicated, and the next day offered the Crown to William and Mary."

The end of an era had come. The British *Bill of Rights* followed shortly and the battlefield to save the jury system shifted from the streets of London to the virgin forests of America. In the 102 years that elapsed between the British *Bill of Rights* of 1689 and the American *Bill of Rights* of 1791, many American patriots risked their lives and fortunes to preserve that ancient right which the barons wrested from the tyrannical grip of King John on the great plain of Runnymede. They never wavered in their allegiance to the cause of freedom. To them, individual liberty came first, economic prosperity would inevitably follow. They never took the right of trial by jury for granted.

---

[359] *Oxford Illustrated History of Britain*, supra n.282, p. 337.

[360] *Encyclopædia Britannica Macropædia*, Vol. 10, pp. 23-24 (15th ed. 1979).

[361] Churchill, *A History of the English Speaking Peoples*, Vol. 2, p. 383 (Dorset Press 1956).

### 30. The British *Bill of Rights* (December 16, 1689).

Following the restoration of the monarchy in 1660, concerted attempts were made by the Stuart kings to undermine the effectiveness of the jury system in England, much in the same manner as the captains of American industry are seeking to undermine it here in America today. The primary difference was that the English kings used their power to control the juries through influence and intimidation while our modern-day aristocrats seek to circumvent the *Seventh Amendment* by penalizing the victim for exercising his constitutional right to a civil jury trial, or by establishing arbitrary limitations on recoverable damages.

> *Following the restoration of the monarchy in 1660, the Stuart kings were confronted with a difficult problem in their efforts to control the administration of justice by royal prerogative. Because the Court of Star Chamber had been abolished in 1641, neither Charles II nor James II had an administrative court capable of asserting wide powers. As a result, they were unable to draw cases from the protection of trial by jury... Abolition of the Star Chamber also meant a loss of the Crown's power to punish juries.... After the restoration the Crown could still control juries to some extent because the judges of the common law courts had authority to punish juries with whose verdict they disagreed. This power was abolished, however, in 1670 in Bushel's Case.... Thereafter the Stuart kings sought to control jury verdicts by influencing the manner in which they were selected.... The Corporation Act of 1661 gave the Crown wide authority over the appointment of the officials... who could be trusted to... empanel juries who could be trusted to give verdicts favorable to the Crown. It was this technique for the manipulation of juries which was condemned by the eleventh clause in the list of the Bill of Rights.*[362]

In the eleventh clause of the *Bill of Rights*, Parliament, acting as a "full and free representative of this nation" as our "ancestors in like case have usually done for the vindicating and asserting their ancient rights and liberties", declared that "jurors ought to be duly empaneled and returned." This action guaranteed in theory the impartiality which our American jury system enjoys in actuality today.

---

[362]Perry & Cooper, *supra n.98*, pp. 237-238.

> During the controversy with Great Britain, from 1763 to 1776, American editors frequently reprinted the English Bill of Rights, and American leaders hailed it as "the Second Magna Carta." After the Declaration of Independence, Americans framing their first state constitutions drew upon the Bill of Rights; certain clauses of the national Constitution and our own Bill of Rights . . . can also be traced to the English statute of 1689. . . .[363]

Upon the abdication of James II, the British throne was declared vacant on February 22, 1689, and a convention Parliament offered the throne to William III and Mary II as joint sovereigns subject to the provisions of the British *Bill of Rights*.[364] William and Mary accepted this condition and Parliament enacted the *Bill of Rights* on December 16, 1689.

> The Bill of Rights and other documents constituting the Revolution Settlement represented the triumph of the principles for which the recently formed Whig party had struggled against Charles II (1660-85) and James II (1685-89). These documents asserted the supremacy of Parliament over the claimed divine right of kings. The royal prerogative was sharply curtailed, and even the possession of the crown became a statutory right, not a hereditary right. Toleration for Protestant dissenters was assured, and a number of individual liberties, insisted upon as among the rights of the subject, were given formal recognition as part of the law of the land. The documentary counterparts of several of these rights appeared later in the Constitution of the United States and first ten amendments thereof. The Bill of Rights of 1689, therefore, may be regarded as one of the sources of some of the most important individual liberties enjoyed by American citizens.[365]

---

[363]Levy, ed., *Encyclopedia of the American Constitution*, p. 113 (Macmillan Publishing Co. 1986).

[364]*See* "The History of Britain and Ireland" in Vol. 3 of *Encyclopædia Britannica Macropædia*, pp. 198, 248 (15th ed. 1979).

[365]Perry & Cooper, *supra n.98*, p. 223. "The *Bill of Rights of 1689* may be considered, after *Magna Carta* and the *Petition of Right*, the third Great Charter of English Liberty." Schwartz, *supra n.333*, p. 40.

***William III (1689-1702) & Mary II (1689-1694)*** *shown consenting to the British Bill of Rights (December 16, 1689).*

**31.** ***An Act Setting Forth General Privileges in the Province of Massachusetts Bay*** **(October 13, 1692).** In a session of the General Court held at Boston on October 12, 1692, the Governor, Council and "Representatives of their Majesties' Province of Massachusetts Bay in New England" adopted *An Act Setting Forth General Privileges* providing that "the rights and liberties of the people" shall be "firmly and strictly holden and observed." Article I of this Act, in the language of the *Magna Carta*, provided as follows:

> That no free man shall be taken and imprisoned or be disseized of his freehold or libertys or his free customs, or be outlawed or exiled, or in any manner destroyed, nor shall be passed upon, adjudged or condemned, but by the lawful judgment of his peers or the law of this Province.[366]

Thirteen months later, on November 25, 1693, the General Assembly of Massachusetts Bay adopted "*An Act for the More Orderly Regulation and Establishment of Courts of Justice Throughout this Province.*" This Act provided that in all civil causes, "all matters and issues in fact arising or happening within the said Province, shall be tried by twelve good and lawful men of the neighborhood."[367] As evidence of Great Britain's deprivation of the colonists' right to trial by jury even at this early stage, both of these Acts were disallowed by the Privy Council on August 22, 1695.

In response, the General Assembly of Massachusetts Bay adopted *An Act for Establishing Courts* on June 19, 1697, containing provisions similar to the Act of August, 1695. It, likewise, provided that in all civil causes "all matters and issues in fact arising or happening in any county or place within this Province shall be tried by twelve good and lawful men of the neighborhood." This Act suffered a similar fate to the Act of August, 1695, and was disallowed by the Privy Council on November 24, 1698. A subsequent letter from the British Board of Trade to Governor Bellomont on February 3, 1689, stated:

---

[366] *The Acts and Resolves of the Province of Massachusetts Bay*, Vol. 1, p. 40 (Boston 1869). Article 6 of this Act further provided that "all trials shall be by the verdict of twelve men, peers or equals, and of the neighborhood and the county or shire where the facts shall arise and grow. . . ."

[367] *Acts of Massachusetts, supra* n.366, Vol. 1, p. 74, §§ 7-10.

*The Act entitled An Act for Establishing of Courts, providing, among other things, that all matters and issues of fact shall be tried by a jury of twelve men, has, in that particular, been looked upon to be directly contrary to the intention of the Act of Parliament . . . entitled An Act for Preventing Frauds and Regulating Abuses in the Plantation Trade, by which it is provided that all causes relating to the breach of the Acts of Trade may, at the pleasure of the officer or informer, be tried in the Court of Admiralty . . . ; Because the method of trial in such Courts of Admiralty is not by juries . . . it is necessary Your Lordship take special care that the intent of the . . . Act of Parliament relating to Courts of Admiralty in the Plantations, be duly complied with in that Province of the Massachusetts Bay.*[368]

**32. Denial of the Right of Trial by Jury Redressed by the Massachusetts General Assembly (September 29, 1696).** Pursuant to a complaint by Nathaniel Reynolds, a warrant was issued by a Justice of the Peace for Bristol County, Massachusetts, on October 2, 1694, under which 200 sheep belonging to John Wilkins were seized. Wilkins appeared at the Court of Quarter Sessions "and prayed that the matter of fact might be tried by a jury as the law directs." But his motion was denied and judgment entered against him on October 9, 1694. Wilkins then petitioned the Massachusetts General Assembly complaining that the Court of Quarter Sessions had deprived him of his right to trial by jury "contrary to the fundamental Rights and liberties of the Subject."

On June 9, 1696, the General Assembly ordered the Justices of the Peace to appear and answer for "the denial of a jury to one of His Majestie's Subjects" and on September 29, 1696, the House of Representatives declared that Wilkins' complaint against the Justices had been "well proved":

*That the said justices present at the denial of a Jury, be admonished by His Honour the Lieutenant Governor in the face of this whole Court; and shall repay the charge that . . . Wilkins sustained by their Judgment, and reimburse him his costs in prosecuting this Cause at this Court. . . .*[369]

---

[368] *Acts of Massachusetts, supra* n.366, Vol. 1, pp. 283-287.
[369] *Acts of Massachusetts, supra* n.366, Vol. 7, pp. 110-111, 491-493.

**33. An Act for Establishing of Courts of Massachusetts (June 19, 1697).** In 1696, Parliament adopted an *Act for Regulating the Plantation Trade* which provided "that all causes relating to the breach of the *Acts of Trade* may, at the pleasure of the officer or informer, be tried in the Court of Admiralty." When the General Assembly adopted *The Massachusetts Courts Act of 1697*, it guaranteed "that all matters and issues in fact arising or happening in any county or place within this Province shall be tried by twelve good and lawful men of the neighborhood." The British Board of Trade objected to this guarantee of the right of trial by jury and the Act was subsequently disallowed by the Privy Council on November 24, 1698.[370]

**34. An Act for Ascertaining the Qualifications of Jurors of New Jersey (November, 1703).** The General Assembly of New Jersey provided in 1703 for the summoning of jurors who "shall be of good fame, credit and reputation, and freeholders of the county in which they shall serve." The Act further provided that "in case any sheriff or coroner shall return any person or persons to serve on juries, not qualified, as directed by this Act, every plaintiff or defendant may have his challenge against such persons."[371]

**35. South Carolina's Adoption of the *Magna Carta* and *Petition of Right* (December 12, 1712).** On October 15, 1692, and again on January 14, 1694, the General Assembly of South Carolina adopted Acts providing for the selection of impartial jurymen "in all causes, civil and criminal." Later, in 1712, the General Assembly adopted certain English statutes in what *Wallace's History of South Carolina* called "the most notable legislation in our legal history."[372] This Act specifically adopted the *Magna Carta, The Petition of Right* and all English statutes declaring "the rights and liberties of the subjects and ... the better securing of the same." It specifically provided, however, that such Act should not be construed to alter the usual course of drawing or balloting of jurymen nor "alter the usual proceedings in our Courts in this Province, and the said Jury Acts."[373]

---

[370] *Acts of Massachusetts, supra* n.366, Vol. 1, pp. 283-287.

[371] *The Earliest Printed Laws of New Jersey 1703-1722*, pp. 27-28 (Michael Glazier, Inc. 1978).

[372] Wallace, *South Carolina: A Short History 1520-1948*, pp. 83-84 (University of South Carolina Press 1966).

[373] Cooper, *The Statutes at Large of South Carolina*, Vol. II, pp. 76, 96, 401-416 (1837) [South Carolina Bar Association 1970].

*Trial by jury is the most enduring of all institutions which have flourished among the English-speaking peoples. No other institution ever struck its roots so deep into their hearts. Its overthrow would be the end of popular government.*
—**Delphin M. Delmas,** *The Democracy of Justice* **(1918)**

36.     ***The Maryland Jury Act (1715).*** On June 3, 1715, the Council and Assembly of Maryland adopted an Act requiring that the sheriffs of each county "shall cause to come before the justices of the several and respective county courts, a competent and sufficient number of good and lawful men, of the best and most understanding freeholders of their several and respective counties, to serve as jurors of the several and respective county courts."[374]

37.     **Delaware's Adoption of the *Magna Carta* (1727).** In 1727, Delaware adopted *An Act of Privilege to a Free Man*, which provided:

> *That no free man within this government shall be taken or imprisoned, or disseized of his freehold or liberties, or be outlawed or exiled, or otherways hurt, damnified or destroyed, nor to be tried or condemned but by the lawful judgment of his twelve equals, or by the laws of England, and of this government.*[375]

38.     **The South Carolina *Jury Act of 1731*.** On August 20, 1731, the South Carolina General Assembly passed *An Act Confirming and Establishing the Ancient and Approved Method of Drawing Juries*, whose preamble read as follows:

> *Whereas by the ancient, known and fundamental laws and Constitution of the Kingdom of Great Britain, none of His Majesty's subjects shall be taken or imprisoned, or disseized of his free-hold, liberty or free customs, or shall be out-lawed, exiled or otherwise destroyed, or shall any judgment pass upon him without lawful trial of a jury by his peers: and whereas the equal, indifferent and impartial method of drawing juries by ballot, used and approved in this Province for many years past, hath greatly contributed to the due and upright administration of justice, and is the surest means to continue the same. . . .*[376]

By this date, "the ancient, known and fundamental laws and *Constitution* of the Kingdom of Great Britain" had guaranteed the right of trial by jury for 516 years. It was indeed "an ancient and approved" fundamental right whose roots had grown deep into the hearts of the American people.

---

[374] *The Laws of Maryland*, Vol. 1, Ch. 37 (April, 1715).
[375] *Laws of the State of Delaware*, Vol. 1, p. 119 (1797).
[376] Act 552 of 1731. See *The First Laws of the State of South Carolina*, Part 1, pp. 123-130 (Glazier 1981).

**39.  *The Charter of Georgia* (1732).**  The Charter of *Georgia* issued by George II in 1732 provided that all persons "which shall happen to be born within the said province, and every of their children and posterity, shall have and enjoy all liberties, franchises and immunities of free denizens and natural subjects . . . born within this our Kingdom of Great Britain. . . ."[377]

**40.  The Role of an American Jury in Establishing the Fundamental Right of Freedom of the Press: The Trial of John Peter Zenger (August, 1735).**  In the early 18th century, freedom of the press only meant freedom from prior restraint. Once an uncomplimentary article was published, its author was subject to prosecution for criminal libel.[378] Neither King nor Parliament could prevent publication, but once published, the author was subject to criminal prosecution. This was the status of the law in 1734 when John Peter Zenger lampooned the Royal Governor in the *New York Weekly Journal*. The Governor had Zenger indicted. "Unable to furnish the exorbitant bail, Zenger remained in jail for ten months until he came up for trial in August, 1735."[379] When the judge refused to allow Zenger's lawyer, Andrew Hamilton of Philadelphia,[380] to prove the truth of the articles as a defense, Hamilton closed his case without calling a witness and relied upon the innate sense of justice of an American jury.

> *. . . With rousing eloquence [Hamilton] maintained the jury's exclusive right to determine the truth as well as the source of an alleged libel and to exonerate the defendant if his comments were found valid. The jurors . . . jubilantly acquitted Zenger. That night Hamilton was honored at a civic banquet; vessels in the harbor boomed their cannon upon his departure for Philadelphia; and the Board of Aldermen sent after him the keys of the city in a gold box.*[381]

---

[377] Chafee, ed., *Documents on Fundamental Human Rights*, pp. 139, 141-142 (Harvard University Press 1951).

[378] *See* Blackstone's *Commentaries on the Laws of England*, Vol. 3, pp. 125-126 (1768) [Legal Classics Library 1983].

[379] Schlesinger, *The Birth of a Nation*, p. 163 (The American Heritage Library 1968).

[380] One of the leading lawyers in the American colonies, *see* Encyclopædia Britannica Macropædia Vol. 5, p. 661 (15th ed. 1991).

[381] Schlesinger, *supra* n.379, p. 163. For a full text of Andrew Hamilton's closing argument, *see* James Alexander, *The Trial of John Peter Zenger*, pp. 78-99 (Notable Trials Library 1989).

Thus, it happened that in 1735, an American jury had lit the lamps of freedom and fueled the fires of the American Revolution. Their verdict was widely acclaimed and did much to advance the cause of journalistic independence. The case of John Peter Zenger had "nerved" the early American press "to greater fearlessness thereafter and correspondingly deterred the authorities from seeking legal measures of restraint."

When the *Stamp Act of 1765* levied heavy duties on all newspapers, advertisements, and "virtually everything else printed in the colonies," angry articles "proliferated in the press flaying the act as unconstitutionally denying the principle of no taxation without representation." When the *Stamp Act* was repealed, other British abuses of the individual liberties of the American colonists followed:

> *At each successive stage, the [colonial] newspapers advanced almost as one; no more than a handful ever sided with Britain. For the war on words they drew heavily on leading patriots.... Vigorous controversialists leaped into the fray in every part of America....*[382]

Trial by jury had helped promote freedom of the press. Freedom of the press, in turn, helped to bring about the birth of a new nation based upon principles of representative government and a guarantee of fundamental freedom to every American citizen.

> *The Zenger trial turned out to be the cornerstone of the liberty of the press in this country. It provided a defense to arbitrary power and established the right of critical comment on the activities of public officials.*

> *Gouverneur Morris [a signer of the Constitution from Pennsylvania] ... recognizing how much his generation owed to the trial later said: "The trial of Zenger in 1735 was the germ of American Freedom, the morning star of that liberty which subsequently revolutionized America...."*[383]

---

[382]Schlesinger, *supra n.379*, pp. 163-164.

[383]Marke, *supra n.332*, "Peter Zenger's Trial: Cornerstone of the Liberty of the Press," p. 240. *See also* Geeting, "Trial by Jury Must be Preserved," 69 *Albany L.J.* 134-135 (1907) and Presser & Zainalden, *Law and Jurisprudence in American History*, pp. 34-54 (2d ed. 1989).

**Gouverneur Morris, a delegate to the Constitution Convention of 1787 from Pennsylvania**

The trial of John Peter Zenger in 1735 was widely acclaimed and contributed significantly to the cause of freedom of the press. Gouverneur Morris called it "the germ of American freedom, the morning star of liberty that revolutionized America."

**41.** ***An Act for Establishing the Courts of Justice of North Carolina* (1746).** The North Carolina *Act of 1746* guaranteed the right to trial by jury in all civil and criminal actions. It provided "that all issues in all actions and complaints, whether real, personal or mixt . . . shall be tried . . . by a jury of freeholders." It further provided that "all treasons, murders, burglaries, felonies, trespasses and crimes" shall be tried "by a jury of freeholders of the said respective county."[384] Thus North Carolina became the 13th American colony to guarantee to its citizens the right of trial by jury.

**42.** **The South Carolina General Assembly's *Resolution of 1751*.** The *South Carolina Jury Act of 1731* had restricted the jurisdiction of the nonjury Exchequer Courts because of "a set aversion of the colonists to the very nature of such a court, operating without a jury." When the Royal Governor criticized South Carolina's "time-honored jury law" in 1751, the General Assembly responded:

> . . . [W]e are firmly of the opinion that any person who shall endeavor to deprive us of so glorious a privilege as trials by jury . . . in this Province is an enemy to the same.[385]

**43.** **The Georgia *Jury Act of 1760*.** In 1760, the House of Assembly of Georgia adopted *An Act for Ascertaining the Qualifications of Jurors*. It provided:

> That from the jurors to be summoned and returned . . . for the trial of issues at the General Courts of Pleas, a jury shall be balloted and drawn for every cause in like manner as directed by an Act of Parliament of Great Britain, passed in the third year of the reign of His Present Majesty, entitled, An Act for the Better Regulation of Juries, and as has hitherto been used and accustomed in the said courts.[386]

---

[384] *The State Records of North Carolina,* Volume 23, pp. 252-254 (Nash Brothers 1904). For further evidence of North Carolina's reverence for trial by jury, *see* ¶ 53 on page 166 below (Resolution of August 25, 1774); The North Carolina *Declaration of Rights* of 1776 on page 178 below; and *Bayard v. Singleton* (1787) on page 430 below.

[385] Wallace, *A Short History of South Carolina,* pp. 115, 168 (University of S.C. Press 1966).

[386] *Georgia Colonial Laws 17 February 1755-10 May 1770,* pp. 71, 75-76 (Statute Law Book Company 1932).

**44. Resolution of the Town of Boston on Representation and Trial by Jury (1765).** Ten years before Paul Revere galloped off into the pages of American history, the town of Boston informed its representatives in the General Court that:

> *The most essential rights of British subjects are those of being represented in the same body which exercises the power of levying taxes upon them, and of having their property tried by juries: these are the very pillars of the British Constitution founded in the Common Rights of Mankind.*[387]

**45. John Adams on the *Stamp Act* (October 14, 1765).** John Adams characterized as "the most grievous innovation of all" of the obnoxious provisions of the *Stamp Act*, "the alarming extension of the Courts of Admiralty" into cases traditionally tried by civil juries. He viewed this as alarming because "in these courts one judge presides alone" and "no juries have any concern there." Referring to the *Magna Carta*, Adams and other American colonists believed that because "the law and fact are both to be decided by the same single judge ... this part of the act will make an essential change in the constitution of juries, and it is directly repugnant to the *Great Charter* itself."[388]

> *... So it is ... in the trial of causes between party and party. No man's property or liberty can be taken from him till 12 men in his neighborhood have said upon oath, that by the laws of his making it ought to be taken away.... [Representative government and trial by jury are] two popular powers, therefore, [that] are the heart and lungs, the mainspring and the center wheel, and without them the body [of liberty] must die, the watch must run down, the government must become arbitrary. ... In these powers consist wholly the liberty and security of the people. They have no other fortification against wanton, cruel power; no other indemnification against being ridden like horses, fleeced like sheep, worked like cattle, and fed and clothed like swine and hounds; no other defense against fines, imprisonments, whipping-posts, ... and racks.*[389]

---

[387]*See* Clinton Rossiter, *Seedtime of the Republic*, p. 388 (Harcourt, Brace & World, Inc. 1953).

[388]*Annals of America*, Vol. 2, pp. 154-155 (1976).

[389]Rossiter, *supra n.387*, pp. 388-389.

**46.    A *Declaration of Rights* by the Stamp Act Congress (October 19, 1765).** On October 19, 1765, delegates from nine colonies participating in the Stamp Act Congress, meeting in New York, petitioned the British Crown to repeal the Stamp Act, taking the same position John Adams had taken in Massachusetts. Their petition took the form of a *Declaration of Rights* setting forth "the most essential rights and liberties of the colonists." The seventh and eighth clauses of this *Declaration of Rights* read as follows:

> *That trial by jury is the inherent and invaluable right of every British subject in these colonies.*

> *That the [Stamp Act] . . . , by extending the jurisdiction of the Courts of Admiralty beyond its ancient limits, [has] a manifest tendency to subvert the rights and liberties of the colonists.*[390]

**47.    The "Regulators": Charles Woodmason, Lawlessness on the South Carolina Frontier (1767).** Opposition to Great Britain's denial of the colonist's right to trial by jury was not restricted to the colonial population centers along the Atlantic coast. Back-country settlers in North and South Carolina organized "Regulator" associations to enforce law and order on the frontier. They protested the fact that they had been denied the benefit of trial by jury in their own neighborhoods. In 1767, Charles Woodmason, an itinerant Anglican minister authored a pamphlet entitled, *Lawlessness on the South Carolina Frontier.* In it, he complained that access to trial by jury could not be obtained without traveling 200 miles to Charleston and petitioned that "juries be empaneled from . . . that country wherein crimes, trespasses, and damages have been committed or sustained — agreeable to *Magna Carta.*"

> *By our birthright as Britons we ought to be tried by a jury of our peers. This is the glorious liberty of freeborn subjects, the darling privilege that distinguishes Britain from all other nations. . . .*[391]

---

[390] Harvard Classics, *American Historical Documents, supra* n.207, pp. 147-148.

[391] Hooker, ed., *The Carolina Backcountry on the Eve of the Revolution: The Journal and Other Writings of Charles Woodmason, Anglican Itinerant,* p. 220 (UNC Press 1953).

*Jury Trial has been steadily regarded, from the earliest judicial history in England as the great safeguard of life, liberty and property. In our own country, almost from the earliest settlement, trial by jury was claimed by the people as the birthright of Englishmen, and as the most valuable of the rights of free men.*
     —**Chief Justice Charles Doe of New Hampshire (1882)**

**48.     Resolutions of the Virginia House of Burgesses (May 16, 1769).** In February, 1769, Parliament adopted an act directing the Governor of Massachusetts to arrest all persons responsible for disturbances in December, 1768, and send them to England for trial. "In protest, resolutions were adopted by the Virginia House of Burgesses and transmitted to the Assemblies of other colonies." These resolutions provided:

> .... [T]hat the seizing of any person or persons residing in this colony, suspected of any crime whatsoever committed therein, and sending such person or persons to places beyond the sea to be tried, is highly derogatory of the rights of British subjects, and thereby the inestimable privilege of being tried by a jury from the vicinage. . . .[392]

**49.     The Regulators of Anson County, North Carolina (October 9, 1769).** In the Regulators Movement in North Carolina, 260 residents of Anson County petitioned George III and "the several Boards in England" that Benjamin Franklin "or some other known patriot be appointed agent, to represent the unhappy state of this Province" in connection with a list of 17 grievances. The sixth grievance listed was:

> That all debts above 40 shillings and under 10 pounds be tried and determined . . . by a jury of six freeholders empaneled by a Justice and that their verdict be entered by the said Justice, and be a final Judgment.[393]

**50.     Proceedings of the Town of Boston (November 20, 1772).** A meeting of freeholders of the Town of Boston was held at Faneuil Hall beginning on October 28, 1772. A List of Infringements and Violations of Rights was adopted, including the following:

> Extending the power of the Courts of Admiralty to so enormous a degree deprives the people in the colonies in a great measure of their inestimable right of trials by juries: which has ever been justly considered as the grand bulwark and security of English property.[394]

---

[392]Chafee, ed., *Documents on Fundamental Human Rights*, pp. 150-151 (Harvard University Press 1951).

[393]Morrison, *Sources and Documents Illustrating the American Revolution*, pp. 83-87 (2d ed. 1929).

[394]Morrison, *supra n.393*, pp. 87, 94.

**51. Samuel Adams With Sword in Hand (November 20, 1772).** On November 20, 1772, Samuel Adams, a champion of the Revolution who "did more than any other American to arouse opposition against English rule in the colonies,"[395] authored a pamphlet entitled, *The Rights of the Colonists*. In it, he cited Justice William Blackstone, author of *Blackstone's Commentaries* (1765-1769), for the proposition that the *Magna Carta* had been "justly obtained" with "sword in hand" from King John:

> . . . [The] *Magna Carta* itself is in substance but a constrained declaration . . . of [our] original, inherent, indefeasible natural rights as . . . citizens. . . . That great author, . . . Mr. Justice Blackstone, holds that this recognition was justly obtained of King John, sword in hand. And . . . it must be one day, sword in hand, again rescued and preserved from total destruction. . . .[396]

**52. Thomas Jefferson, *A Summary View of the Rights of British America* (1774).** In 1774, the Virginia House of Burgesses protested the British blockade of the Port of Boston.[397] In retaliation, the Royal Governor of the Province promptly dissolved the House of Burgesses. Following the leadership of Patrick Henry, a special Virginia Revolutionary Convention gathered in August, 1774. This Convention commissioned Thomas Jefferson to draft a *Summary View of the Rights of British America*. In it, Jefferson wrote that many colonists had been "stripped of [their] privilege of trial by [a jury of their] peers" and transported to England where they were "tried by judges predetermined to condemn."[398]

---

[395] *Encyclopædia Britannica Macropædia*, Vol. 1, p. 80 (15th ed. 1979). As one of the planners of the Boston Tea Party, Samuel Adams was "one of the first American leaders to deny Parliament's authority over the colonies." He served as a member of the Provisional Congress of Massachusetts in 1774-1775, as Lieutenant Governor of Massachusetts from 1789-1793, and as Governor from 1794-1797. *Encyclopædia Britannica, supra.*

[396] Samuel Adams, *The Rights of Colonists* (November 20, 1772) [*Annals of America, supra* n.388, p. 219].

[397] *See* "Resolutions Against Trade with England," *Annals of America*, Vol. 2, pp. 256-257 (Encyclopædia Britannica 1976).

[398] *See* Thomas Jefferson, *A Summary View of the Rights of British America, Annals of America, supra* n.388, Vol. 2, p. 262.

**53.    The Provincial Congress of North Carolina (August 25, 1774).** On this date, the Provincial Congress of North Carolina resolved "that trial by juries of the vicinity, is the only lawful inquest that can pass upon the life of a British subject, and is a right handed down to us from the earliest ages, confirmed and sanctioned by the *Magna Carta* itself."[399]

**54.    The Continental Congress' *Declaration of Colonial Rights* (October 14, 1774).** The First Continental Congress convened on October 14, 1774, and adopted a *Declaration of Colonial Rights*. In it, the Continental Congress complained that the extension of jurisdiction of the Admiralty Courts and the transportation of colonists to trials in England had "deprive[d] the American subject of a constitutional trial by jury" in their own neighborhood.[400]

**55.    John Jay, An Address to the People of Great Britain (October, 1774).** John Jay, a member and later president of the Continental Congress, "was considered [by some] as second only to [George] Washington in service to his country."[401] In October, 1774, he was appointed by the First Continental Congress to draft an *Address to the People of Great Britain*. In it, he complained that through extension of the jurisdiction of the Admiralty Courts, the colonists had "lost the advantage of being tried by an honest, uninfluenced jury of the [neighborhood] and [were] subject to the sad necessity of being judged by a single man. . . ."[402]

> *Know then, that . . . we claim all the benefits secured to the subject by the English Constitution, and particularly that inestimable one of trial by jury. . . .*[403]

---

[399] Connor, "The Constitutional Right to a Trial by a Jury of the Vicinage," 48 *Univ. of Penn. L.R.* 197, 198 (1909).

[400] *Declarations and Resolves of the Continental Congress, Journals, I* (October 14, 1774) [*Annals of America, supra* n.397, Vol. 2, pp. 270-273]. The document refers to a "trial by jury of the *vicinage*." "Vicinage" is defined as "neighborhood; near dwelling; vicinity." *Black's Law Dictionary*, p. 1405 (5th ed. 1979).

[401] Biographical Note to *The Federalist, Great Books of the Western World*, Vol. 43, p. 24 (Encyclopædia Britannica 1952).

[402] John Jay, *Address to the People of Great Britain, Annals of America, supra* n.397, Vol. 2, p. 279.

[403] *Annals of America, supra* n.397, Vol. 2, p. 277.

*Know then, that we claim all the benefits secured to the subject by the English Constitution, and particularly the inestimable right of trial by jury.*

**—John Jay of New York (1774)**

# JOURNAL
## OF THE
## PROCEEDINGS
## OF THE
## CONGRESS,
### Held at PHILADELPHIA,
*September 5, 1774.*

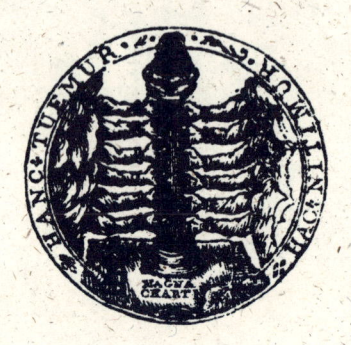

PHILADELPHIA:

Printed by WILLIAM and THOMAS BRADFORD,
at the *London Coffee-House.*

DCC,LXXIV.

**The Journal of the First Continental Congress**
*bearing the Seal of the Magna Carta.*

**56. The Continental Congress on Representative Government and Trial by Jury (October, 1774).** The First Continental Congress firmly believed that representative government and trial by jury were "the two most important principles on which to build a *Constitution* of free people." In October, 1774, Congress adopted a resolution which stated:

*The first grand right is that of the people having a share in their own government by representatives chosen by themselves....*

*The next great right is that of trial by jury. This provides that neither life, liberty nor property can be taken from the possessor, until twelve of his ... countrymen ... shall pass their sentence upon oath against him.*

John Adams called these two "popular powers" the heart and lungs of liberty, without which, "the body must die."[404]

**57. Patrick Henry Utters the Battle Cry of the American Revolution (March 23, 1775).** On March 23, 1775, Patrick Henry, that greatest of American patriots, the man who later "was largely responsible for the passage of the *Bill of Rights*,"[405] delivered the speech that became the battle cry of the American Revolution. An ardent proponent of the right of trial by jury in all civil actions at common law, Patrick Henry's ringing voice resounded through the pages of history:

*... If we wish to be free; if we mean to preserve inviolate those inestimable privileges for which we have been so long contending ..., we must fight! ... Is life so dear or peace so sweet as to be purchased at the price of chains and slavery?*

*Forbid it, Almighty God— I know not what course others may take; but as for me, give me liberty or give me death!*[406]

---

[404]Stedman, *Our Ageless Constitution*, supra n.324, p. 41.

[405]*Encyclopædia Britannica Macropædia*, Vol. 8, p. 775 (15th ed. 1979).

[406]William Wirt, *The Life and Character of Patrick Henry*, pp. 137-142 (DeSilver, Thomas & Co. 1836).

**58. The *Declaration of the Causes and Necessity of Taking Up Arms* (July 6, 1775).** Following the Battle of Lexington on April 19, 1775, the Continental Congress met on June 23 and appointed a committee consisting of John Rutledge of South Carolina, William Livingston of New Jersey, Benjamin Franklin of Pennsylvania, John Jay of New York, and Thomas Johnson of Maryland to draft a *Declaration of the Causes and Necessity of Taking Up Arms*. Later, John Dickinson of Pennsylvania and Thomas Jefferson of Virginia were added to the committee. The declaration was primarily prepared by John Dickinson with the concluding paragraphs written by Thomas Jefferson. Among the specific grievances listed against British colonial policy was that of "*depriving us of the accustomed and inestimable privilege of trial by jury, in cases affecting both life and property. . . .*"[407]

**59. The Continental Congress Rejects Lord North's Offer of Reconciliation (July 31, 1775).** Following Patrick Henry's stirring speech of March 23 and the Continental Congress' declaration of July 6, Lord North, the Prime Minister of Great Britain, presented an *Offer of Reconciliation* to the 13 Colonies in May of 1775. On July 31, Congress finally rejected Lord North's proposal upon the advice of a committee consisting of Benjamin Franklin, Thomas Jefferson, Richard Henry Lee and John Adams.[408] The *Message of Rejection*, adopted by the Second Continental Congress on July 31, 1775, stated in part as follows:

> We are of [the] opinion [that] the proposition is altogether unsatisfactory because . . . it does not propose to repeal the several acts of Parliament . . . taking from us the right of trial by jury . . . in cases affecting both life and property. . . .[409]

Beginning with the South Carolina General Assembly's Resolution of 1751, in a steady stream of complaints and protests extending over a quarter century, the American colonists had consistently demanded that the protection of the fundamental right to trial by jury be preserved inviolate. When Great Britain turned a deaf ear, they were ready to risk their freedom and fortunes to preserve one of the twin pillars of American liberty. Are we not willing to do the same today to preserve this legacy for countless generations of future Americans?

---

[407] *Annals of America, supra* n.397, Vol. 2, pp. 337, 338.

[408] "Reconciliation Rejected," *Annals of America, supra* n.397, Vol. 2, p. 353.

[409] "Reconciliation Rejected," *supra* n.408, p. 355.

**BENJAMIN FRANKLIN**

*On the recommendation of a committee headed by Benjamin Franklin, the Continental Congress rejected Lord North's Offer of Reconciliation because it did not "propose to repeal the several acts of Parliament taking from us the right of trial by jury in cases affecting both life and property."*

**60.    The *Constitution of South Carolina* (March 26, 1776).** A "congress" which convened in Charleston on November 1, 1775, was adjourned to March 1, 1776, when it adopted *A Constitution or Form of Government, Agreed to and Resolved Upon by the Representatives of South Carolina*. This document painted the following picture of colonial life on the eve of the American Revolution:

> Whereas, the British Parliament, claiming of late years a right to bind the North American Colonies by law, in all cases whatsoever, have enacted . . . unconstitutional and oppressive statutes . . . by which the powers of Admiralty Courts in the Colonies are extended beyond their ancient limits, and jurisdiction is given to such courts, in cases similar to those which in Great Britain are triable by jury — . . . the harbor of Boston was blocked up — . . . [and] the chartered Constitution of Government in that Colony [was] materially altered. . . . And whereas the delegates of all the Colonies on this Continent . . . assembled in a General Congress . . . [and] laid their complaints at the foot of the Throne, . . . these complaints being wholly disregarded. . . . And whereas large fleets and armies have been sent to America in order to enforce the execution of those laws, and to compel an absolute and implicit submission to the will of a corrupt and despotick administration, and in consequence thereof, hostilities having been commenced in the Massachusetts Bay . . . , and . . . there being just reason to apprehend that like hostilities would be committed in all other Colonies. The Colonists were therefore driven to the necessity of taking up arms, to repel force by force, and to defend themselves and their properties against lawless invasions and depredations.

Thus, this Congress created "the General Assembly of South Carolina", under a *Constitution* which provided:

> That all suits and processes pending in any court of law or equity : . . . [wherein] the judges of the courts of law shall cause jury lists to be made, and juries to be summoned, as near as may be, according to the directions of the acts of the General Assembly.[410]

---

[410]Cooper, *supra n.373*, pp. 128, 129, 133.

**61. The Virginia *Declaration of Rights* (June 12, 1776).** On June 12, 1776, three weeks before the *Declaration of Independence*, the Virginia Constitutional Convention adopted the *Virginia Declaration of Rights* authored by George Mason "as the theoretical foundation of all government." Section 11 of the *Virginia Declaration of Rights* provided:

> *That in controversies respecting property, and in suits between man and man, the ancient trial by jury is preferable to any other and ought to be held sacred.*[411]

**62. An Act to Abolish the Court of Appeals of New Hampshire (June 28, 1776).** On the eve of the American Revolution, the New Hampshire House of Representatives adopted an act "to prevent the absurd practice of granting appeals to the King of Great Britain in Council from the judgment of any Courts in this Colony." The preamble to this Act indicates that such practice had deprived the citizens of New Hampshire "of their great, inestimable and inherent right of trial by jury, and opening a door for arbitrary decisions of their property, even in causes of the greatest moment."[412]

**63. The *First Virginia Constitution* (June 29, 1776).** Following the *Virginia Declaration of Rights*, the *First Virginia Constitution* was adopted by a Provisional Convention on June 29, 1776, five days before the *Declaration of Independence*. In it, King George III was indicted "for depriving us of the benefits of trial by jury."[413] Article 3 of the *Draft Constitution for Virginia* (June, 1776) provided that:

> *All facts in causes whether of chancery, common, ecclesiastical, or marine law, shall be tried by a jury upon evidence given . . . in open court. . . .*[414]

Thus, on the eve of the American Revolution, colony after colony continued to claim the right of trial by jury as their inalienable birthright. The lessons of history should teach us all that this ancient fundamental right is no less important today than it was 200 years ago.

---

[411] *Annals of America, supra* n.397, Vol. 2, pp. 432-433.

[412] *The First Laws of the State of New Hampshire*, pp. 18-19 (Michael Glazier, Inc. 1981).

[413] *See* Jefferson, *Public and Private Papers*, p. 17 (Vintage Books/Library of America 1990).

[414] Jefferson, *supra* n.413, p. 17.

**64.     The *Declaration of Independence* (July 4, 1776).** Within a week of the adoption of the *First Virginia Constitution*, Thomas Jefferson authored and the Second Continental Congress adopted the *Declaration of Independence*, indicting the English Crown, "for depriving us, in many cases, of the benefits of trial by jury."[415]

The mood of the American people on the eve of the American Revolution was well expressed by Richard Bland of Virginia when he said that "trial by jury is hardly less important than representative government itself."[416] Our ancestors declared their independence and fought the Revolutionary War to protect this ancient right. They would not have sacrificed this fundamental freedom on the alter of economic necessity. *Nor should we!*

**65.     Arthur Schlesinger: "The Voice of the People".** In *The Birth of the Nation*, historian Arthur Schlesinger wrote that "along with liberal political institutions the colonists also inherited historic safeguards conferred by the English common law," foremost of which was trial by jury, "that firmest barrier of English liberty"-which serves as the "voice of the people."

> *. . . This body of unwritten legal principles [the English common law], evolved by judicial interpretation through the years, aimed to protect the individual against arbitrary acts, whether by government or by his fellows. It embraced such basic guarantees as the right of trial by jury chosen from the vicinity. . . . Trial by jury was in colonial minds "that firmest barrier of English liberty." Hence its denial helped light the fuse leading to independence when Parliament . . . gave power of enforcing the new trade and revenue legislation to the Crown-appointed juryless vice-admiralty courts. As John Adams put the matter, "Juries are taken . . . from the mass of the people, and no man can be condemned of life, limb, or property or reputation, without the concurrence of the voice of the people." . . .*[417]

Perhaps our legislators do not realize what a vital part the institution of trial by jury played in the creation of our country. Perhaps they never will. Time will tell.

---

[415] *Annals of America, supra* n.397, Vol. 2, p. 449.
[416] Rossiter, *Seedtime of the Republic: The Origin of the American Tradition of Political Liberty*, p. 276 (1953).
[417] Schlesinger, *supra* n.379, p. 15.

*Trial by jury and other rights and liberties of English subjects were claimed by the American colonies as their undoubted inheritance and birthright.*
—**Chancellor James Kent of New York (1827)**

### INDEPENDENCE BELL—JULY 4, 1776

As the bleak Atlantic currents
Lash the wild Newfoundland shore,
So they beat against the State House,
So they surged against the door. . . .

\* \* \*

So they surged against the State House,
While all solemnly inside,
Sat the Continental Congress,
Truth and reason for their guide,
O'er a simple scroll debating,
Which, though simple it might be,
Yet should shake the cliffs of England
With the thunders of the free.

That old State House bell is silent,
Hushed is now its clamorous tongue;
But the spirit it awakened
Still is living—ever young;
And when we greet the smiling sunlight
On the Fourth of each July,
We will ne'er forget the bellman
Who, betwixt the earth and sky,
Rung out, loudly, "Independence";
Which, please God, shall never die!

—*Anonymous*

# N. IMPACT OF THE CIVIL JURY ON RATIFICATION OF THE CONSTITUTION

**1. State Constitutions Adopted Between the *Declaration of Independence* and the Constitutional Convention of 1787.** Between July, 1776, and July, 1784, ten states adopted constitutional provisions guaranteeing the right of trial by jury in civil cases.

Section 22 of the *New Jersey Constitution* adopted July 2, 1776, provided:

> *That the inestimable right of trial by jury shall remain confirmed as a part of the law of this colony, without repeal, forever.*

In addition, §23 of the *New Jersey Constitution* provided that every person elected to the New Jersey legislature must take the following oath:

> *I will not assent to any law . . . which shall annul or repeal . . . that part of the twenty-second section in [the Charter of this colony] respecting the trial by jury.*[418]

Section 11 of the *Constitution of Pennsylvania* adopted August 16, 1776, provided:

> *That in controversies respecting property, and in suits between man and man, the parties have a right to trial by jury, which ought to be held sacred.*[419]

Section 13 of the Delaware *Declaration of Rights* adopted September 11, 1776, provided:

> *That trial by jury of facts where they arise is one of the greatest securities of the lives, liberties and estates of the people.*[420]

---

[418]Bernard Schwartz, *The Roots of the Bill of Rights: An Illustrated Source Book of American Freedom*, Vol. 2, pp. 260-261 (Chelsea House Publishers 1980).

[419]*See* Perry & Cooper, *Sources of Our Liberties*, p. 330 (American Bar Foundation, 1959).

[420]Perry & Cooper, *supra*, p. 339.

Section 3 of the *Constitution of Maryland* adopted November 3, 1776, provided:

> *That the inhabitants of Maryland are entitled to the common law of England, and the trial by jury, according to the course of that law, and to the benefit of such English statutes, as existed at the time of their first immigration. . . .*[421]

On December 14, 1776, North Carolina adopted a *Declaration of Rights* which provided in §14:

> *That in all controversies at law, respecting property, the ancient mode of trial, by jury, is one of the best securities of the rights of the people, and ought to remain sacred and inviolable.*[422]

Section 51 of the *Georgia Constitution*, adopted in early 1777, provided:

> *Freedom of the press and trial by jury [are] to remain inviolate forever.*[423]

Section 51 of the *New York Constitution*, adopted in April, 1777, provided:

> *And this convention doth further ordain, determine and declare, in the name and by the authority of the good people of this state, that trial by jury, in all cases in which it hath heretofore been used in the colony of New York, shall be established and remain inviolate forever.*[424]

The *Constitution of Vermont*, adopted on July 8, 1777, contained *A Declaration of the Rights* which provided in §13:

> *That, in controversies respecting property, and in suits between man and man, the parties have a right to a trial by jury; which ought to be held sacred.*[425]

---

[421]Perry & Cooper, *supra n.420*, p. 346.
[422]Perry & Cooper, *supra n.420*, p. 356.
[423]Schwartz, *supra n.419*, Vol. 2, p. 300.
[424]Schwartz, *supra n.419*, Vol. 2, p. 312.
[425]Perry & Cooper, *supra n.420*, p. 366.

*The state Constitutions demonstrated the great jealousy of the American people on the subject of jury trial. The judgment of a panel of twelve men has been an indispensable element in the judicial administration of the country.*
     —Justice Joseph N. Whitner, S.C. Court of Appeals (1856)

*The struggle for American independence was for chartered rights, for English liberties, for trial by jury, habeas corpus and Magna Carta.*

—John Quincy Adams (1839)

The *Constitution of Massachusetts* adopted October 25, 1780, provided for the right to trial by jury in civil cases in §15:

> *In all controversies concerning property, and in all suits between two or more persons, except in cases in which it has heretofore been otherways used and practiced, the parties have a right to a trial by jury; and this method of procedure shall be held sacred.*[426]

The *Bill of Rights* in the *Constitution of New Hampshire* dated June 2, 1784, contained identical language with respect to trial by jury in civil cases to that of the *Massachusetts Constitution* of October 25, 1780.

On Friday, July 13, 1787, the Continental Congress adopted *An Ordinance for the Government of the Territory of the United States Northwest of the River Ohio*. The second Article of that ordinance provided:

> *The inhabitants of the said territory shall always be entitled to the benefits of the writ of habeas corpus, and of trial by jury....*[427]

Can anyone who reads the history of the American Revolution ever doubt that the determination of our founding fathers to preserve the right of trial by jury both in civil and in criminal cases was one of the primary reasons that led to the founding of our country?

> *... Trial by jury was one of the "rights of Englishmen" brought to America by the earliest colonists, and the jury system became a fundamental feature of the administration of American justice. Infringements of that right by Great Britain furnished another motive for the American Revolution, and it was safeguarded by the Bill of Rights adopted by the states prior to the [federal] Constitution.*[428]

---

[426]Perry & Cooper, *supra n.420*, p. 376.

[427]Schwartz, *supra n.419*, Vol. 2, p. 400. Of the 18 votes recorded, 17 voted in favor of the adoption of this ordinance. One of them was William Few of Georgia, younger brother of the great-great-great-greatgrandfather of the author, and one of only ten members of Congress who served concurrently as a delegate the Constitutional Convention.

[428]Perry & Cooper, *supra n.420*, p. 406.

**2. Life Under the *Articles of Confederation* (1781-1787).** The *Articles of Confederation* were drafted by John Dickinson of Pennsylvania in July of 1776, revised and adopted by the Continental Congress in November of 1777, and eventually ratified by the states in 1781. They could well have been called the *Articles of Chaos*. There was no strong central government because the states were reluctant to surrender their sovereignty. "The states could ignore with impunity legislation passed by the Congress." In addition, "conflicts among the states made it difficult for Congress to shape a cohesive domestic policy." A huge war debt had piled up. Currency was scarce. "Farms were foreclosed and hundreds of men were thrown into debtors' prisons." In many states "bands of insurgent farmers gathered at courts and sheriff's auctions and closed them down."[429]

> *The trouble was that the Confederation which the Articles established was not a federation, though it was a good deal more, at least on paper, than a mere league between the states. It had no control over taxation and trade, it lacked both a federal executive and a federal judiciary, and it was entirely without sanctions by which Congress could enforce its will. The result was that relations within the Confederation were essentially international, while at the same time the states were without the resources to function as independent sovereignties. Such an arrangement could not last indefinitely; in fact, it was superseded within eight years by the government set up by the Constitution.*[430]

This situation came to a head in January, 1787, when a large band of poor farmers led by Revolutionary war hero Daniel Shays attacked an arsenal in Springfield, Massachusetts. The militia fired back, leaving three dead and one dying. Although this broke the back of the insurgency, "the impact of Shays' Rebellion on American public opinion was substantial." It "hung like a shadow" over Congress "and gave both impetus and urgency to the Constitutional Convention."[431]

---

[429] Collier, *Decision in Philadelphia: The Constitution Convention of 1787*, pp. 5-15 (Ballentine Books 1986).

[430] Poore, ed., *The Federal and State Constitutions, Colonial Charters and Other Organic Laws of the United States*, Vol. 1, pp. 7-12 (2d ed. 1877) [*Annals of America*, supra n.397, Vol. 2, p. 555].

[431] Collier, *supra* n.429, pp. 15-17.

### Shays' Rebellion
*In January, 1787, a large band of poor farmers led by Revolutionary War hero Daniel Shays attacked an arsenal in Springfield, Massachusetts.*

**INDEPENDENCE HALL**
*The delegates to the Convention believed that the right to trial by jury in civil cases was one of the most invaluable privileges a free country can boast.*
—American Biographer Andrew J. Bethea (1937)

**3.     The Constitutional Convention (May-September, 1787).** A corrupt colonial government had collapsed in Mexico, William Pitt became prime minister of Great Britain, and the last victims of the Spanish Inquisition were executed. The University of Georgia, Franklin and Marshall, Cokesbury College and the University of Pittsburgh had been founded. Noah Webster's *American Spelling Book* was published and the first American daily newspaper was distributed. Literature, music, medicine and science flourished. Emanuel Kant published the *Critique of Pure Reason*, James Boswell began *The Life of Samuel Johnson*, and Mozart composed the *Coronation Mass* and his *Symphony in C Major*. Astronomers discovered Uranus and observed the mists around Mars. Sophisticated slicing machines paved the way to microscopic study of human tissue, doctors clinically described the disease of alcoholism, uranium was discovered and Henry Cavendish told a waiting world that water was composed of hydrogen and oxygen.

With the winds of change came new inventions: the threshing machine, the cast iron plow, the fountain pen, false teeth, shrapnel, bifocals and hot air balloons. Rushing rivers powered modern cotton mills, steamships sailed up the Delaware River, New York installed the new nation's first town clock in the Old Dutch Church and the earliest American golf course opened to the public.[432]

In this enlightened age, 30 delegates from seven states met at Independence Hall in Philadelphia on May 25, 1787, at a time when appreciation of individual liberty had reached its zenith,[433] six years after 13 United States had, sword in hand, rescued the *Magna Carta* from the tyrannical grip of George III. When these delegates convened, however, their primary concern was the predicament that had evolved under the *Articles of Confederation*. They had preserved their historic right to trial by jury by invoking the aid of the God of Battles. The price they paid was dear. They had learned the hard way that fundamental freedoms don't come cheap.

---

[432] See generally The New York Public Library Book of Chronologies (Prentice Hall Press 1990).

[433] John Locke had published *An Essay Concerning the True Original Extent and End of Civil Government* in 1690 [see Great Books of the Western World, Vol. 35, pp. 25-84 (Encyclopædia Britannica 1952)]. Montesquieu had published *The Spirit of Laws* in 1748 and Rousseau had published a discourse on *The Origin of Inequality* in 1775 and *The Social Contract* in 1762 [see Great Books of the Western World, Vol. 38].

The *Articles of Confederation* had been a many-headed monster. Each state had its own agenda. Chaos reigned. The ox was in the ditch and it was their duty to get it out. It is not surprising, therefore, that their first order of business was to restructure the machinery of government. The *Bill of Rights* would wait.

The first two months of the Constitutional Convention were dedicated exclusively to the mechanics of government. Separation of powers, suffrage, apportionment and states rights were debated in detail. The first reference to trial by jury in James Madison's records of the Constitutional Convention came on Monday, August 6, 1787, when John Rutledge of South Carolina presented the report of the Committee of Detail.[434] Article XI, §4, provided for the right of trial by jury in criminal cases only.[435] One week later, John Dickinson of Delaware made his celebrated statement that "experience must be our only guide" because "reason may mislead us." He said that "it was not reason that discovered the singular and admirable mechanism of the English *Constitution*," nor could reason have discovered what was, "in the eye of those who are governed by reason, *the absurd mode of trial by jury.*"[436]

For by 1787, trial by jury was no recent scientific invention of an enlightened age of modern political philosophy, it was the full-grown child of ancient history sanctified by more than 500 years of human experience. It was, as Cicero has said, one of the "tidings of antiquity."

> *History is the witness that testifies to the passing of time; it illuminates reality, vitalizes memory, provides guidance in daily life, and brings us tidings of antiquity.*[437]

---

[434] Madison, *Records of the Debates of the Federal Convention of 1787*, p. 471 (Government Printing Office 1927) [Legal Classics Library 1989].

[435] "The trial of all criminal offenses (except in cases of impeachments) shall be in the state where they shall be committed; and shall be by jury." Madison, *supra* n.434, p. 479. The language of this proposal was modified slightly by unanimous consent on Tuesday, August 28, 1787, but the substance was the same. *See* Madison, *supra* n.434, pp. 626-627.

[436] Madison, *supra* n.434, p. 533. For more on John Dickinson's view of trial by jury, *see* pp. 201-203 below.

[437] Marcus Tullius Cicero (106-43 B.C.). *Bartlett's Familiar Quotations*, p. 110b (14th ed. 1968).

*Trial by jury is the foundation of our free Constitution: take that away and the whole fabric will soon moulder into dust.*
—**Charles Pratt, Lord Camden, Chancellor of England (1792)**

*The absence of any provision respecting the mode of trial in civil actions was so generally regarded as endangering the right of trial by jury, and evoked so much criticism on that ground, that the first Congress proposed the Seventh Amendment, which was promptly ratified.*

—**U.S. Supreme Court Justice Willis Van Devanter (1913)**

By the middle of August, the convention had been in continuous session for three long, hot months. There was a sense of "extreme anxiety" to bring the deliberations to an end.[438] No one had mentioned a *Bill of Rights* because bitter battles over apportionment, slavery and states rights had monopolized the time and sapped the strength of the entire convention. Clauses were discussed, debated, voted upon and brought back again for reconsideration. Presidential powers, impeachment, amendment, ratification, introduction of money bills, vetoes, terms of office, method of election and many other weighty matters were the subject of extended debate. Finally, through the unique American art of compromise, general agreement was reached. "They were tired and eager to go home."[439] No one got all they wanted, but the end result was sound, with one glaring exception, *there was no Bill of Rights.*

> *Guaranteed rights . . . were exceedingly important to Americans through the 1770's and 1780's. They were, in essence, what the country had fought the Revolution for. . . .*
>
> *As it turned out, what nearly sank the Constitution was the lack of a Bill of Rights. Those opposed to the Constitution . . . used it as a center point of their attacks.*[440]

---

[438]On August 18, 1787, John Rutledge of South Carolina "remarked on the length of the session, the probable impatience of the public and the *extreme anxiety of many members of the convention to bring the business to an end.*" Madison, *supra n.434*, p. 566.

[439]Collier, *Decision in Philadelphia: The Constitutional Convention of 1787*, p. 338 (Ballentine Books 1986). To the same effect, *see* Levy, *Encyclopedia of the American Constitution*, p. 113 (Macmillan Publishing Co. 1986), stating that "The weary delegates, after a hot summer's work in Philadelphia, were eager to return home."

[440]Collier, *supra n.439*, pp. 333-334, 342. To the same effect, *see* Morris, *The Forging of the Union: 1781-1789*, pp. 305-306 (Harper & Row 1987). *See also* Van Doren, *The Great Rehearsal: The Story of the Making and Ratifying of the Constitution of the United States*, p. 162 (Viking Penguin Inc. 1948, Penguin Books 1986).

**THE CONSTITUTIONAL CONVENTION OF 1787**

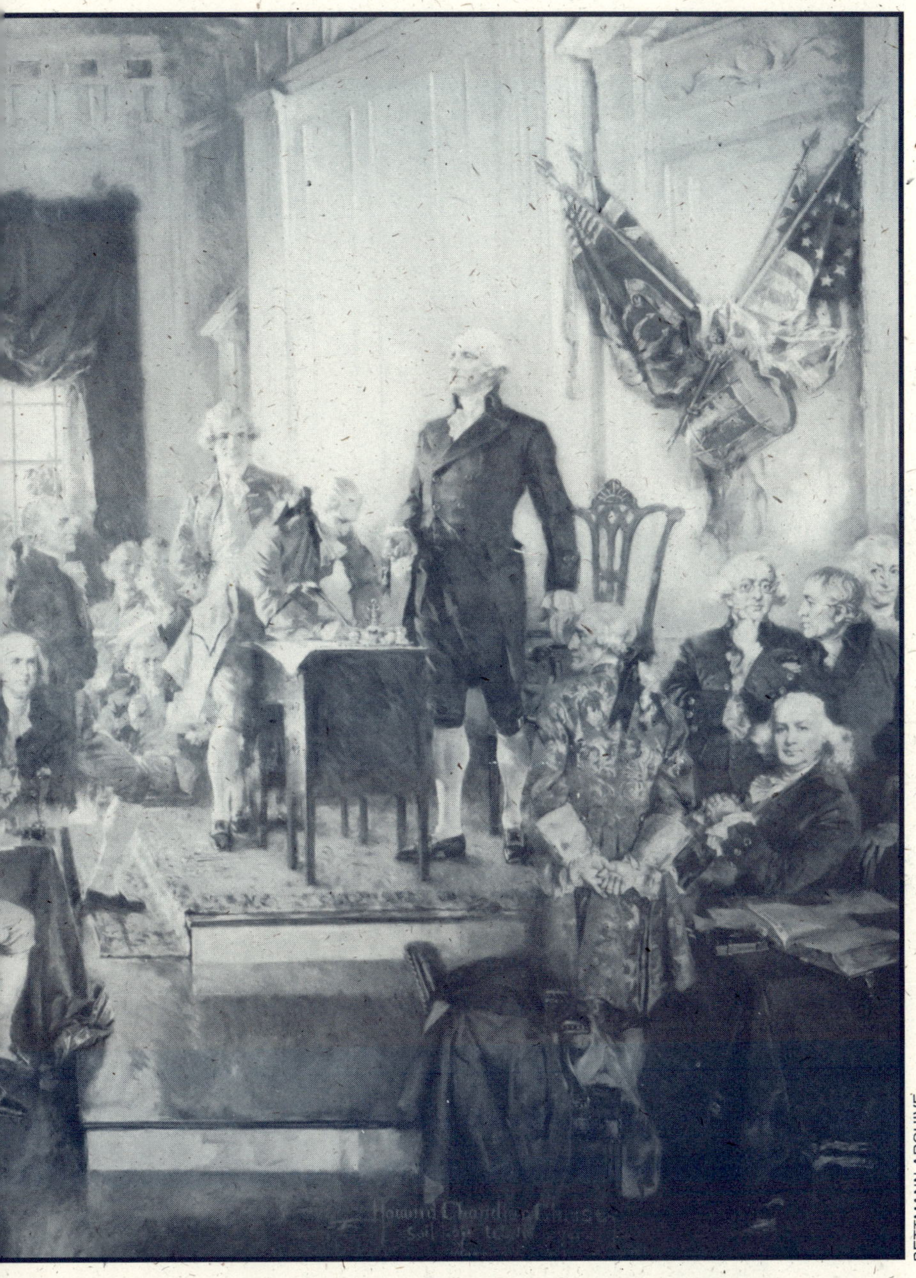

BETTMANN ARCHIVE

After almost four months, the Committee of Style presented the basic *Plan of the Convention* to the delegates on Wednesday, September 12, 1787.[441] The required vote to override a Presidential veto was reconsidered and revised.[442] Then Hugh Williamson of North Carolina "observed to the House that no provision was yet made for juries in civil cases and suggested the necessity of it."[443]

Two recognized champions of individual rights sprang forward to take up that great cause:

> Mr. [Elbridge] Gerry [of Massachusetts] urged the necessity of juries to guard against corrupt judges. He proposed that the Committee [of Style] should be directed to provide a clause for securing trial by juries.
>
> Colonel [George] Mason [of Virginia] perceived [that] . . . a general principle laid down on this and some other points would be sufficient. He wished the plan had been prefaced with a Bill of Rights, and would second a motion for that purpose. It would give great quiet to the people; and with the aid of the state declarations, a bill might be prepared in a few hours.
>
> Mr. Gerry concurred in the idea and moved for a committee to prepare a Bill of Rights. Colonel Mason seconded the motion.[444]

The mood of the convention was decidedly unreceptive. Roger Sherman of Connecticut "was for securing the rights of the people" where necessary. However, he said, "the state declarations of rights are not repealed by this *Constitution*; and being in force are sufficient." He felt that there were "many cases where juries are proper," but that "*the legislature may be safely trusted.*" George Mason responded that "the laws of the United States are to be paramount to state *Bills of Rights.*" This argument notwithstanding, Mason's motion went down to ignominious defeat.[445]

---

[441] *See* Madison, *supra n.434*, p. 702.

[442] Changed from three-quarters to two-thirds. *See* Madison, *supra n.434*, pp. 713-716.

[443] Madison, *supra n.434*, p. 716.

[444] Madison, *supra n.434*, p. 716.

[445] "On the question for a committee to prepare a *Bill of Rights,*" ten states voted "No" and Massachusetts abstained.

But the *Bill of Rights* did not die a quiet death. It was resurrected two days later, on Friday, September 14, 1787, when Elbridge Gerry of Massachusetts joined with Charles Pinckney of South Carolina in a motion to insert a declaration "that the liberty of the press should be inviolably observed."[446] Roger Sherman of Connecticut responded that this provision, which ultimately became the backbone of the *First Amendment*, was unnecessary because "the power of Congress does not extend to the press." Gerry and Pinckney's joint motion failed by a vote of seven to four.[447]

The following day, Saturday, September 15, Mr. Pinckney and Mr. Gerry moved to amend Article III, §2, §3, of the *Constitution* to add: "and a trial by jury shall be preserved as usual in civil cases." This motion also failed.[448]

Thus it was that the curtain came down on the Constitutional Convention. Edmund Randolph of Virginia spoke of "the indefinite and dangerous power given by the *Constitution* to Congress" and said that, without such amendments to the Plan as might be offered by the state conventions, he could not "put his name to the instrument." George Mason concurred, stating that "the dangerous power and structure of government" could lead to "a tyrannical aristocracy." He said that "as the *Constitution* now stands," he "could not give it his support or vote in Virginia." Elbridge Gerry listed eight specific objections to the structure of the proposed new government. These were not, however, the reason he withheld his support:

> *. . . He could, however, he said, get over all these, if the rights of the citizens were not rendered insecure, first, by the general power of the legislature to make what laws they may please to call necessary and proper; secondly, to raise armies and money without limit; [and] thirdly, [that] to establish a tribunal without juries, which will be a Star Chamber as to civil cases. . . .*[449]

---

[446]Madison, *supra n.434*, p. 726.

[447]Madison, *supra n.434*, p. 726. *See also* Chafee, *Freedom of Speech*, pp. 3-4 (Harcourt Brace 1920) [Legal Classics Library 1990].

[448]Madison, *supra n.434*, pp. 733-734.

[449]Madison, *supra n.434*, pp. 733-734, Mr. Gerry's remarks have been revised to reflect the changes to the transcript set forth in Madison, *supra n. 434*, nn.1-3 on p. 738.

The views of the remainder of the delegates were more closely those of Charles Pinckney who said:

> *These declarations from members so respectable at the close of this important scene, give a peculiar solemnity to the present moment. . . . He was not without objections as well as others to the plan. . . . But apprehending the danger of general confusion, . . . he should give the plan his support.*

The final day of the convention was Monday, September 17, 1787. Benjamin Franklin addressed the delegates:

> *I confess that there are several parts of this Constitution which I do not at present approve, . . . [but] the older I grow, the more apt I am to doubt my own judgment, and to pay more respect to the judgment of others. . . .*
>
> *. . . I agree to this Constitution with all its faults, if they are such; because I think a general government necessary for us, and there is no form of government but what may be a blessing to the people if well administered. . . .*

Having expressed these sentiments, Dr. Franklin "moved that the *Constitution* be signed by the members" and:

> *The Constitution being signed by all the members except Mr. Randolph, Mr. Mason, and Mr. Gerry who declined giving it the sanction of their names, the convention dissolved itself by an adjournment sine die —*[450]

Later events proved that the citizens of the several states were not satisfied with Roger Sherman's remark that "the Legislature may be safely trusted." As Chief Justice Rehnquist wrote in 1979:

> *. . . The founders of our nation considered the right of trial by jury in civil cases an important bulwark against tyranny and corruption, a safeguard too precious to be left to the whim of the sovereign.*[451]

---

[450] Madison, *supra n.434*, pp. 737-740, 745.
[451] Dissent of Justice Rehnquist in *Parklane Hosiery Co. v. Shore*, 439 U.S. 322, 337, 340, 343-344 (1979).

**Charles Pinckney**, *delegate from South Carolina to the Continental Congress of 1787, who joined with Elbridge Gerry of Massachusetts in an unsuccessful motion to guarantee the right of trial by jury in civil cases. This omission was later corrected by the Seventh Amendment ratified on December 15, 1791.*

**4.** **The Federalists (1782-1788).** The federalists were advocates of a strong central government and were the moving force behind the drafting, adoption and ratification of the *Constitution*. They were led by Alexander Hamilton and John Jay of New York and James Madison of Virginia. Together, they authored *The Federalist*: "a series of essays on the proposed new U.S. *Constitution* and the nature of representative government published in 1787-1788":

> *Taken together, they represented a masterly exposition of the new federal system and the major departments of the proposed central government....*
>
> *A general treatise on republican government, The Federalist is distinguished for its comprehensive analysis of the means by which the ideals of justice, the general welfare, and the rights of individuals could be realized. The possibility of good government lay in man's capacity to devise political institutions that would compensate for deficiencies in both reason and virtue in the conduct of government by ordinary men. This was the predominant theme in the late 18th century political thought in America and accounts in part for the elaborate system of checks and balances written into the Constitution.*[452]

As will be seen below, Hamilton, Madison and Jay were all strong supporters of the civil jury.

**(a)** **Alexander Hamilton (1757-1804).** Hamilton was a soldier, lawyer and statesman. In the Revolutionary War, he served as an artillery captain and as General George Washington's private secretary. He was a member of the Congress of Confederation from 1782-1783 and a delegate from New York to the Constitutional Convention in 1787.[453]

> *Hardly had the new government begun to function under the Articles of Confederation, when voices began calling for a stronger central authority. One such critic was Alexander Hamilton...*[454]

---

[452] *Encyclopædia Britannica Micropædia*, Vol. IV, p. 79.

[453] *See* Biographical Note to *The Federalist* in *Great Books of the Western World*, Vol. 43, p. 23 (Encyclopædia Britannica 1952).

[454] *Annals of America, supra* n.397, Vol. 2, p. 575.

Beginning in 1782, Hamilton authored a series of articles under the pseudonym, "The Continentalist", including "Arguments for Increasing the Power of the Federal Government" (July 4, 1782).[455] As a member of the Congress of the Confederation in 1783, Hamilton drafted a series of resolutions entitled, "Arguments For A Strong Federal Government."[456] Although his views commanded little popular support at the time, they formed the basis for his successful collaboration with James Madison and John Jay in the publication of *The Federalist*.

In *The Federalist* No. 83, Alexander Hamilton wrote:

> *The objection to the plan of the convention which has met with most success in this state, and perhaps in several of the other states, is that relative to the want of a constitutional provision for the trial by jury in civil cases. . . .*[457]

Although the federalists and the anti-federalists were bitterly divided on many issues, the one upon which they all could agree was the value that both sides placed upon the right of trial by jury. On this issue, Hamilton wrote:

> *The friends and adversaries of the plan of the Convention, if they agree in nothing else, concur at least in the value they set upon the trial by jury; or if there is any difference between them it consists in this; the former regard it as a valuable safeguard to liberty; the latter represent it is as the very palladium of free government. For my own part, the more the operation of the institution has fallen under my observation, the more reason I have discovered for holding it in high estimation. . . .*[458]

---

[455] John C. Hamilton, editor, *The Works of Alexander Hamilton*, Vol. 2, pp. 194-201 (1850-1851) *[see Annals of America, supra n.397, Vol. 2, pp. 575-579]*.

[456] *See* J. C. Hamilton, *supra* n.455, Vol. 2, pp. 269-275 and *Annals of America, supra* n.397, Vol. 2, pp. 612-616.

[457] *See Great Books of the Western World*, Vol. 43, p. 244 (Encyclopædia Britannica 1952).

[458] *Great Books of the Western World, supra* n.457, Vol. 43, pp. 245-246. According to Hamilton, "all are satisfied of the utility of the institution and of its friendly aspect to liberty."

Concerning "the excellence of the trial by jury in civil cases," Hamilton added:

> ... The strongest argument in its favor is that it is a security against corruption. As there is always more time and better opportunity to tamper with a standing body of magistrates than with a jury summoned for the occasion, there is room to suppose that a corrupt influence would more easily find its way to the former than to the latter. ...[459]

**(b)   James Madison (1751-1836).** James Madison was born in Port Conway, Virginia, on March 16, 1751. He attended the College of New Jersey, later Princeton University, and was elected to the Virginia Convention of 1776 where he drafted the state's guarantee of religious freedom. He served as private secretary to Governor Patrick Henry[460] and as a delegate to the Continental Congress where he soon rose to a position of leadership. He reentered the Virginia legislature in 1784 and was influential in bringing about the Constitutional Convention of 1787.[461]

> As a delegate to the Constitutional Convention of 1787, Madison earned the title Father of the Constitution for his role in drafting much of the document, arguing successfully for the creation of a strong central government, maintaining a comprehensive records of the proceedings, and marshalling public opinion in favor of its ratification. ...[462]

Following the ratification of the *Constitution*, on June 8, 1789, James Madison presented a proposed *Bill of Rights* to the House of Representatives. With respect to the guarantee of the right to a civil jury trial in the *Seventh Amendment*, Madison said:

> ... Trial by jury ... is as essential to secure the liberty of the people as any one of the pre-existent rights of nature.[463]

---

[459] *Great Books of the Western World*, supra n.457, p. 246.

[460] *See* Biographical Note on James Madison in *Great Books of the Western World*, supra n.457, Vol. 43, pp. 23-24.

[461] *Encyclopædia Britannica Macropædia*, Vol. 11, p. 281.

[462] de Gregorio, *The Complete Book of U.S. Presidents*, p. 60 (Dembner Books 2d ed. 1989).

[463] *Annals of America*, supra n.397, Vol. 3, pp. 358-359.

*In suits at common law, trial by jury is as essential to secure the liberty of the people as any one of the pre-existent rights of nature.*

—**James Madison (1789)**

**(c) John Jay (1745-1829).** John Jay was a delegate to the First Continental Congress in 1774 and was chosen President of the Continental Congress in 1778.[464] He later served as the first Chief Justice of the United States Supreme Court from 1789-1795.

> *John Jay, at the time The Federalist appeared, enjoyed the greatest prestige of any of the three men [Hamilton, Madison and Jay]. By some he was considered as second only to Washington in service to his country. . . . He served in the Continental Congress from its inception in 1774 and was later its president. In his own state he took a leading part in the revolutionary political developments. He was the author of the first New York Constitution and, after its establishment, its first Chief Justice. His greatest fame at the time, however, came to him as a result of his role as a diplomat. . . . He was sent to Paris to act with John Adams and Benjamin Franklin in negotiating the terms of peace with Great Britain. Described by Adams as "the Washington of the negotiations," [Jay] was instrumental in obtaining recognition of the independence of the United States which ended the Revolutionary War. . . .*[465]

John Jay composed *An Address to the People of Great Britain* in 1774 in which he wrote that the colonists rightfully claimed "all the benefits secured to the subject by the English *Constitution* and *particularly that inestimable one of trial by jury.*"[466] After becoming Chief Justice of the United States Supreme Court, speaking for a unanimous Court, three members of which had been delegates to the Constitutional Convention, Chief Justice Jay stated that "*juries are the best judges of the facts.*"[467]

---

[464] *Encyclopædia Britannica Micropædia,* Vol. V, p. 532 (15th ed. 1979). In 1776, John Jay was a member of the Provisional Congress of New York and was "instrumental in the formation of the *Constitution* of that state." In 1795, he was elected Governor of New York and served for two terms. *See Guide to American Law Encyclopedia,* Vol. 6, pp. 332-333 (West Publishing Company 1984).

[465] *See* Biographical Note to *The Federalist, Great Books of the Western World, supra* n.457, Vol. 43, p. 24.

[466] *Annals of America, supra* n.397, Vol. 2, p. 277. *See* pp. 194-195 above.

[467] *State of Georgia v. Brailsford,* 3 Dall. 1, 4, 1 L.Ed. 483, quoted in Justice Hugo Black's dissenting opinion in *Galloway v. United States,* 319 U.S. 372, 399 (1943).

**(d)  John Dickinson (1732-1808).** John Dickinson was born on November 8, 1932 in Talbot County, Maryland. He served in the colonial assemblies of Delaware and Pennsylvania and in the Stamp Act Congress where he drafted its *Declaration of Rights and Grievances.* He was a delegate from Pennsylvania to the First and Second Continental Congresses (1774-1776) and was the principal author of the *Declaration of the Causes and Necessities for Taking Up Arms.*[468] He was a brigadier general in the militia and a delegate to the Continental Congress (1779-1780) where he signed the *Articles of Confederation.* He was chief executive officer of both Delaware (1781-1782) and Pennsylvania (1782-1785) and served as a delegate to the Constitutional Convention of 1787.

> *Known as the "Penman of the Revolution," John Dickinson was a distinguished lawyer who wrote one historic document after another for more than 30 years during the Revolutionary period of American history. Because he maintained homes in both Delaware and Pennsylvania, he also had the unusual distinction of serving both these states alternatively as a legislator, as a congressional representative, and as chief executive officer.*[469]

As a Delaware delegate to the Constitutional Convention of 1787, Dickinson took an active part in its debates. He was the author of one of the best-remembered remarks from that historic assembly when he warned his fellow delegates that "experience must be our only guide" because "reason may mislead us."[470]

---

[468] *Encyclopædia Britannica Micropædia*, Vol. III, p. 531 (15th ed. 1979).

[469] Whitney, *Founders of Freedom in America: Lives of the Men Who Signed the Constitution of the United States*, p. 81 (J. G. Ferguson Publishing Co. 1965). Dickinson College at Carlisle, Pennsylvania, chartered in 1783, was named in his honor. On the occasion of his death on February 14, 1808, Thomas Jefferson wrote that "a truer patriot could not have left us. Among the first of the advocates of the rights of his country when assailed by Great Britain," Jefferson said, "he continued to the last the orthodox advocate of the true principles of our new government, and his name will be consecrated in history as one of the great worthies of the Revolution." Whitney, *supra,* p. 86.

[470] August 13, 1787. *See* Madison, *supra n.434,* p. 533.

John Dickinson was one of the leading federalists both at the Constitutional Convention and, later, as the author of the *Letters of Fabius* (1788). In *Letter IV*, he called trial by jury a "heaven-taught institution" which was one of the "cornerstones of liberty" and the birthright of every American citizen.

> *It would seem highly probable, that those who would reject this [Constitution], would also have rejected the heaven-taught institution of trial by jury, had they been consulted upon its establishment. . . .*
>
> *Happily for us our ancestors thought otherwise. . . .*
>
> *Perhaps they did not foresee, that from this acorn . . . , would be produced a perpetual vegetation of political energies, that would secure the just liberties of the nation for a long succession of ages, and elevate it to the distinguished rank it has for several centuries held. . . . This establishment originates from a knowledge of nature. With a superior force, wisdom and benevolence united, [trial by jury] rives the difficulties concerning administration of justice, that have distressed, or destroyed the rest of mankind. It reconciles contradictions — vastness of power, with safety of private station. It is ever new, and always the same.*
>
> *Trial by jury and the dependence of taxation upon representation, those cornerstones of liberty . . . must be preserved. . . .*
>
> *It is the duty which every man owes to his country, his friends, his posterity, and himself, to maintain to the utmost of his power this valuable palladium in all its rights; to restore it to its ancient dignity, . . . ; and [we must] above all . . . guard [it] with the most jealous circumspection against the new and arbitrary methods of trial, which, under a variety of plausible pretenses, may in time imperceptibly undermine this best preservative of liberty. Trial by jury is our birthright; . . . who in opposition to the genius of United America, shall dare to attempt its subversion.*[471]

---

[471] Schwartz, *supra* n. 419, Vol. 3, pp. 548-549.

*Trial by jury and the dependence of taxation upon representation, those cornerstones of liberty, must be preserved. Trial by jury is our birthright; who in opposition to the genius of United America, shall dare to attempt its subversion?*

**—John Dickinson (1788)**

**5.     The Anti-Federalists (1787-1788).** The anti-federalists were opposed to the ratification of the *Constitution* without a *Bill of Rights*. Their most effective and persistent argument against the Plan of the Convention was its failure to include a guarantee of the right of trial by jury in civil cases. Among the leading anti-federalists were Patrick Henry, George Mason and Richard Henry Lee of Virginia, Elbridge Gerry of Massachusetts, Melancton Smith of New York, Samuel Bryan of Pennsylvania, and Judge Alexander Hanson of Maryland.

**(a)     Patrick Henry (1736-1799).** By the Convention of 1787, the nation's most passionate patriot had served three terms as Governor of Virginia and commanded a loyal following. "Patrick Henry thought the *Constitution* might betray the democratic revolution, and Henry spoke for fully half the voters in the Union's largest state."[472] According to Justice Hugo Black, Henry "expressed the general conviction of the people of the 13 states" regarding the civil jury system when he said:

> *Trial by jury is the best appendage of freedom. We are told that we are to part with that trial by jury with which our ancestors secured their lives and property. . . . I hope we shall never be induced, by such arguments, to part with that excellent mode of trial.*[473]

**(b)     George Mason (1725-1792).** George Mason was born in Fairfax County, Virginia, in 1725. He was a leader of the Virginia patriots on the eve of the American Revolution and authored the *Virginia Declaration of Rights* (June 12, 1776), "the first authoritative formulation of the doctrine of inalienable rights."

> *. . . Mason's work was known to Thomas Jefferson and influenced his drafting of the Declaration of Independence. The model was soon followed by most of the other states. . . . He served as a member of the Virginia House of Delegates from 1776 to 1778.*[474]

---

[472] Banning, "1787 & 1776: Patrick Henry, James Madison, the *Constitution* and the Revolution," p. 59 in York, ed., *Toward a More Perfect Union* (Brigham Young Univ. 1988).

[473] *See* dissenting opinion of Justice Hugo Black in *Galloway v. United States*, 319 U.S. 372, 398 (1943).

[474] *Encyclopædia Britannica Micropædia*, Vol. VI, pp. 670-671 (15th ed. 1979).

At the Constitutional Convention, Mason warned his fellow delegates that the people of America were "jealous of their liberties" and he was the first to recommend that the *Constitution* be prefaced with a *Bill of Rights*.[475] When this proposal failed, he became one of only three delegates who refused to endorse the *Plan of the Convention*.[476] Mason objected to the *Constitution* because there was no declaration of rights and "no declaration of any kind, for preserving ... trial by jury in civil causes."[477]

> *... His criticism helped to bring about the adoption of the Bill of Rights. ...*[478]

**(c)  Richard Henry Lee (1732-1794).** Richard Henry Lee was born in Westmoreland County, Virginia, on January 20, 1732. He served in the Virginia House of Burgesses from 1758 through 1775, and was highly regarded as "Statesman of the Revolutionary War." He opposed the *Stamp Act* and, in March, 1773, together with colleagues Patrick Henry and Thomas Jefferson, he originated a plan for Inter-Colonial Committees of Correspondence.

> *Lee was an active member of the First Continental Congress, where admirers of his oratory compared him with Cicero. In the Second Continental Congress he introduced ... resolutions ... for declaring independence ("that these united colonies are, and of right ought to be, free and independent states. ...") His ... resolution was adopted on July 2 [1776] and the Declaration of Independence followed two days later. ...*
>
> *He opposed ratification of the federal constitution because it created a "consolidated" government and lacked a Bill of Rights. He served ... as senator from Virginia in the First Congress from 1789 to 1792.*[479]

---

[475] *See* Madison, *supra n.434*, p. 716.

[476] The others being Edmund Randolph of Virginia and Elbridge Gerry of Massachusetts.

[477] Ketcham, *The Anti-Federalist Papers and the Constitutional Convention Debates*, pp. 173-175 (1986).

[478] *Encyclopædia Britannica Macropædia*, Vol. 6, p. 670 (15th ed. 1979).

[479] *Encyclopædia Britannica Micropædia*, Vol. VI, p. 117 (15th ed. 1979).

A series of letters were published in the *Poughkeepsie Country Journal* over the pseudonym of "Letters from the Federal Farmer."[480] These letters "were long attributed to Richard Henry Lee."[481] One letter dated October 9, 1787, began as follows:

> *The essential parts of a free and good government are a full and equal representation of the people in the legislature, and the jury trial . . . in the administration of justice. . . .*
>
> *There are certain unalienable and fundamental rights . . . a free and enlightened people . . . will not resign . . . to those who govern. . . . These rights should be made the basis of every Constitution.*[482]

Enumerating these "unalienable and fundamental rights," Lee included the right of trial by jury.[483] In his *Letter IV* on October 12, 1787, he wrote:

> *. . . [T]rial by jury in civil causes, . . . trial by jury in criminal causes, [and] the benefits of the writ of habeas corpus . . . all stand on the same footing; they are the common rights of Americans. . . .*
>
> *Trial by jury is very important. . . . It is essential in every free country, that common people should have a part and share of influence, in the judicial as well as the legislative department. . . . [T]hey are not in a situation to . . . fill [the offices of senators, judges and offices to fill which an expensive education is required]; these, and most other offices of any considerable importance, will be occupied by the few. The few, the well-born, . . . in judicial decisions as well as in legislation are generally disposed, and very naturally too, to favor those of their own description.*[484]

---

[480] *See* Ketcham, *supra* n.477, pp. 256-257.
[481] *See* Pole, The American Constitution: For and Against, p. 27 (Hill & Wang 1987).
[482] Ketcham, *supra* n.477, pp. 264-265.
[483] Ketcham, *supra* n.477, pp. 264-266.
[484] Schwartz, *supra* n.419, Vol. 3, pp. 472-474.

ILLUSTRATION BY DANIEL MAFFIA

*Trial by jury in civil and criminal cases stand on the same footing. They are the common rights of Americans. It is essential in every free country, that common people should have a share of influence, in the judicial as well as the legislative department.*

—**Richard Henry Lee (1787)**

**(d)     Elbridge Gerry (1744-1814).** Born in Marblehead, Massachusetts, on July 17, 1744, Elbridge Gerry was a signer of the *Declaration of Independence*, a delegate to the Continental Congress (1776-1781), a member of Congress under the *Articles of Confederation* (1783-1785), a delegate to the Constitutional Convention of 1787, a member of Congress (1789-1793), governor of Massachusetts, and Vice President of the United States (1813-1814).

During the Constitutional Convention on September 12, 1787, Elbridge Gerry concurred in the need for a guarantee of civil juries and moved for a committee to prepare a *Bill of Rights*. When this motion failed, he moved jointly with Charles Pinckney of South Carolina, to amend Article III, §2, by adding a provision that "a trial by jury shall be preserved as usual in civil cases." When this motion failed, he declined to support or sign the *Constitution* insisting that "to establish a tribunal without juries . . . will be a Star Chamber as to civil cases."[485]

**(e)     Melancton Smith.** Melancton Smith was a prominent merchant from New York City. He had been a member of New York's First Provincial Congress, a delegate in the Continental Congress and sheriff of Dutchess County.[486] As a member of the Continental Congress, he joined Richard Henry Lee in opposing ratification of the *Constitution* because it did not "make the common law and trial by jury secure throughout the United States."[487]

Chancellor James Kent, author of *Kent's Commentaries on American Law* (1826-1830),[488] called Melancton Smith "the most prominent and responsible speaker on the part of the anti-federalist[s]."[489] In 1788, he authored "An Address to the People of New York on the Necessity of Amendments to the *Constitution*" in which he wrote that the advocates of the proposed new *Constitution* had admitted "that if alterations do not take place, a door will be left open for . . . encroachments on the liberties of the people."[490]

---

[485] Madison, *supra* n.434, pp. 716, 733, 738.

[486] Pole, *The American Constitution: For and Against*, p. 101 (Hill & Wang 1987).

[487] Van Doren, *The Great Rehearsal: The Story of the Making and Ratifying of the Constitution of the United States*, pp. 176-177 (Viking Penguin, Inc. 1948/Penguin Books 1986).

[488] For Chancellor Kent's views on trial by jury, *see* Vol. 2, p. 320, below.

[489] Van Doren, *supra*, p. 234.

[490] Schwartz, *supra* n.419, Vol. 3, p. 566.

> *It may be a strange thing to [the advocates of ratification without a Bill of Rights] to hear [that] the people of America are anxious for the preservation of their rights, but those who understand the true principles of liberty, are no strangers to their importance. The man who supposes the Constitution, in any part of it, is like a blank piece of paper, has very erroneous ideas of it. He may be assured every clause has a meaning, and many of them such extensive meaning, as would take a volume to unfold. . . .*[491]

He was concerned because "trial by jury, in all civil cases is left at the discretion of the general government," and said that if a *Bill of Rights* was "prefixed to our *Constitution*," then "every opposer of this system will be satisfied."

**(f) Samuel Bryan.** Samuel Bryan was a Pennsylvania anti-federalist who mounted "a fundamental attack on the whole idea that the intricate checks and balances of the new *Constitution* would protect liberty." Using the pseudonym "Centinel" he published a series of articles in the *Philadelphia Independent Gazetteer* which "set forth a basic anti-federalist argument about the nature of free government." On October 5, 1787, he wrote:

> *To the freemen of Pennsylvania:*
> *Your [state] Constitution further provides "that in controversies respecting property, and in suits between man and man, the parties have a right to a trial by jury, which ought to be held sacred." . . . Whether the trial by jury is to continue as your birthright, the freemen of Pennsylvania, nay, all of America, are now called upon to declare.*[492]

The words of Samuel Bryan, written 205 years ago, have a strange and ominous ring today. For the identical question has arisen again:

> *Whether trial by jury is to continue as our birthright, all Americans are now called upon to declare.*

---

[491] Schwartz, *supra* n.419, Vol. 3, p. 576. A more accurate prophecy is hardly to be found in the annals of American law.
[492] Ketcham, *The Anti-Federalist Papers and the Constitutional Convention Debates*, pp. 227-228 (1986).

**(g)	Judge Alexander Hanson (1749-1806).** Judge Alexander Hanson served in the Maryland state senate where he was an opponent of paper money and an advocate of separation of powers. He said that "the acts of almost every legislature have uniformly tended to disgust its citizens, and to annihilate its credit."[493] As an opponent of ratification of the *Constitution*, he authored an *Address on the Proposed Plan of a Federal Government, 1788*, under the pseudonym of Aristides. In it, he contended that although the delegates to the convention had been distinguished by their talents and services, that they had "combined for the destruction of [our] liberties." On the institution of trial by jury, he wrote:

> *The institution of the trial by jury has been sanctified by the experience of ages. It has been recognized by the constitution of every state in the Union. It is deemed the birthright of Americans; and it is deemed, that liberty cannot subsist without it . . . .*[494]

**(h)	John DeWitt.** On October 27, 1787, an unidentified Massachusetts anti-federalist using the pseudonym "John DeWitt" published an essay in the *Boston American Herald* warning the citizens of Massachusetts that under the proposed *Constitution*, "a trial of the cause by jury you shall not have a right to insist upon."[495]

**(i)	Impact of the Anti-Federalists.** Although they ultimately proved unsuccessful in their attempts to amend the *Constitution* prior to its ratification, the anti-federalists did succeed in bringing the debate over trial by jury and the *Bill of Rights* into the forefront of the controversy. As a result of their efforts, amendments were proposed by eight states and seven of those specifically called for a guarantee of the right of trial by jury in civil cases as currently set forth in the *Seventh Amendment*.[496] Those states recommending a guarantee of the right to a civil jury trial included Pennsylvania, Massachusetts, Maryland, New Hampshire, New York, Virginia and North Carolina.

---

[493] Wood, *The Creation of the American Republic, 1776-1787*, pp. 369-370, 406, 559 (University of North Carolina Press 1969).
[494] Schwartz, *The Roots of the Bill of Rights, supra n.419*, Vol. 3, pp. 540-542.
[495] Ketcham, *supra n.492*, pp. 189-198.
[496] *See* Schwartz, *supra n.419*, Vol. 5, p. 1167.

*The institution of the trial by jury has been sanctified by the experience of the ages. It has been recognized by the Constitution of every state in the Union. It is deemed the birthright of Americans; and it is deemed, that liberty cannot subsist without it.*

**—Judge Alexander Hanson (1788)**

## 6. The Views of Thomas Jefferson on Trial by Jury.

Born in Albemarle County, Virginia, on April 13, 1743, Thomas Jefferson studied law at William and Mary College under the direction of George Wythe, a signer of the *Declaration of Independence*. He was a member of the Virginia House of Burgesses (1769-1776) and of the Continental Congress (1775-1776), and the author of the *Declaration of Independence*. He was elected Governor of Virginia on June 1, 1779, and was appointed Minister to France in March of 1785. He served as Secretary of State under George Washington and as the third President of the United States (1801-1809).[497]

Unable to attend the Constitutional Convention due to his duties as Minister to France, on March 13, 1789, Jefferson explained why he was sometimes characterized as anti-federalist:

> You say that I have been dished up to you as an Anti-Federalist.... I am not a Federalist [either].... I approved, from the first moment, of the great mass of what is in the new Constitution.... What I disapproved from the first moment, also, was the want of a Bill of Rights ... to secure freedom in religion, freedom of press, freedom from monopolies, freedom from unlawful imprisonment, freedom from a permanent military, and a trial by jury, in all cases determinable by the laws of the land....[498]

In a letter from his diplomatic post in Paris on February 12, 1788, Jefferson wrote:

> ...With respect to the new government, nine or ten states will probably have accepted it by the end of this month. The others may oppose it. Virginia I think will be of this number. Besides other objections of less moment, she will insist on annexing a Bill of Rights to the new Constitution, i.e., a bill where the government shall declare that (1) religion shall be free. (2) printing presses free. (3) trial by jury preserved in all cases....[499]

---

[497] *See* Jefferson: Public and Private Papers, pp. 383-395 (Vintage Books/The Library of America 1990).

[498] Schwartz, *The Roots of the Bill of Rights*, supra n.419, Vol. 3, pp. 618-619.

[499] *See* Jefferson's Letter to C. W. F. Dumas dated February 12, 1788, in Schwartz, *supra* n.419, Vol. 3, p. 613.

In another letter from Paris dated February 7, 1788, Jefferson wrote to Alexander Donald:

> *I wish with all my soul that the nine first conventions may accept the new Constitution, because this will secure to us the good it contains, which I think great and important. But I equally wish that the four latest conventions, whichever they be, may refuse to accede to it till a declaration of rights be annexed. This would . . . give to the whole fabric, perhaps as much perfection as any one of that kind ever had. By a declaration of rights I mean one which shall stipulate freedom of religion, freedom of the press, trial by juries in all cases, . . . [and] habeas corpus. . . . These are fetters against doing evil which no honest government should decline. . . .*[500]

Anti-federalist or not, Thomas Jefferson was a dedicated champion of the right of trial by jury. In the *Declaration of Independence*, he indicted George III for depriving the colonists of the benefits of trial by jury. In his draft of the *Constitution of Virginia* in June of 1776, he proposed that "all facts and causes whether of Chancery, Common, Ecclesiastical, or Maritime law, shall be tried by a jury upon evidence given . . . in open court."[501] In his first inaugural address in March of 1801, he called trial by jury part of that "bright constellation which has gone before us and guided our steps through an age of revolution and reformation."[502] In his first annual message to Congress in December of 1801, he recommended that "the protection of the inestimable institution of juries" should be "extended to all the cases involving the security of persons or property"[503] and he also said:

> *I consider trial by jury as the only anchor ever yet imagined by man, by which a government can be held to the principles of its constitution.*[504]

---

[500]Schwartz, *supra n.419*, Vol. 3, pp. 611-612.

[501]*Public and Private Papers, supra n.497*, pp. 11,17.

[502]*Annals of America, supra n.397*, Vol. 4, p. 145.

[503]*Public and Private Papers, supra n. 497*, pp. 181-182.

[504]*The Writings of Thomas Jefferson*, p. 41. (Washington ed.), *see* dissenting opinion of Justice Hugo Black in *Galloway v. United States*, 319 U.S. 372, 396 n.1 (1943).

*I consider trial by jury as the only anchor ever yet imagined by man, by which a government can be held to the principles of its constitution.*

—**Thomas Jefferson (1788)**

*Trial by jury is part of that bright constellation which has gone before us and guided our steps through an age of revolution and reformation.*

—**Thomas Jefferson (1801)**

**7. Ratification of the *Constitution* (1787-1788).** Notwithstanding the objections of the anti-federalists, the *Constitution* was signed and submitted to the states by the Constitutional Convention on September 17, 1787. The ratification process was long and stormy, however, and the required number of 11 states did not ratify the *Constitution* until March 4, 1789. In the interim, the debate over the *Constitution's* failure to guarantee a civil jury trial continued. As will be seen below, that subject dominated the debates in several states.

**(a) The Pennsylvania Ratification Convention (*November 20 through December 13, 1787*).** Following Delaware's unanimous ratification of the *Constitution* on December 2, 1787, the second state to act was Pennsylvania, where the struggle between supporters and opponents was close. In Pennsylvania the lack of a *Bill of Rights* was one of the anti-federalists' main issues throughout the convention debate. The leading anti-federalists at the Pennsylvania ratifying convention included Robert Whitehill and John Smilie. John Smilie contended that the federal convention "ought to have declared that the legislature should establish the trial by jury by proper regulations." The principal anti-federalist speaker, however, was Robert Whitehill.

> ... On December 12, 1787, Whitehill introduced 15 proposed amendments for the convention to recommend as part of its ratification action. [The second of which guaranteed jury trials in civil cases] ...
>
> The amendments proposed by the Pennsylvania Convention minority are of great importance in the history of the federal Bill of Rights.... The example set by the Pennsylvania minority was soon followed by the Massachusetts ratifying convention itself, and then by the ratifying conventions of four other states (South Carolina, New Hampshire, Virginia and New York).
>
> The amendments proposed by the Pennsylvania minority bear a direct relation to those ultimately adopted as the federal Bill of Rights. Indeed, eight of the first ten amendments were first suggested as amendments in the proposals of the Pennsylvania minority....[505]

---

[505] Schwartz, *The Roots of the Bill of Rights*, supra n. 419, Vol. 3, pp. 627-628, 639.

Two of the leading federalists at the Pennsylvania ratifying convention were James Wilson and Thomas Hartley. Wilson was one of only six men who signed both the *Declaration of Independence* and the United States *Constitution*. He was a member of the Continental Congress and later served as an Associate Justice of the United States Supreme Court (1789-1798).[506] Thomas Hartley had practiced law in the Philadelphia area since 1769 where he was prominent in political and military affairs.[507] Both Wilson and Hartley were strong supporters of the institution of trial by jury.

At the Pennsylvania ratifying convention, James Wilson said:

*I think I am not now to learn the advantages of a trial by jury. It has excellencies that entitle it to a superiority over any other mode....*[508]

Likewise, Thomas Hartley told the convention that "trial by jury ... is the fundamental security for every enjoyment that is valuable in the contemplation of a free man."[509]

On December 12, 1787, after the Pennsylvania Convention had ratified the *Constitution* by a vote of 46 to 23, 21 members of the minority signed a dissenting address that appeared in the *Pennsylvania Packet and Daily Advertiser* stating in part as follows:

*... We entered on the examination of the proposed system of government, and found it to be such as we could not adopt, without ... surrendering up your dearest rights....*

The second objectionable omission from the *Constitution* of which the Pennsylvania Minority complained was:

*That in controversies respecting property, and in suits between man and man, trial by jury shall remain as heretofore, as well in the federal courts, as in those of the several states....*[510]

---

[506] Whitney, *supra* n.469, p. 231.

[507] Chroust, *The Rise of the Legal Professional in America*, Vol. 1, pp. 227-228 (University of Oklahoma Press 1965).

[508] Schwartz, *The Roots of the Bill of Rights*, *supra* n.419, Vol. 3, p. 638.

[509] Schwartz, *supra* n. 419, Vol. 3, p. 654.

[510] Ketcham, *supra* n. 492, pp. 237-239.

**(b) The Massachusetts Ratification Convention (January 31 through February 6, 1788).** The Massachusetts Ratification Convention met on January 31, 1788, to consider ratification of the *Constitution*. Proposed amendments were made by the convention president, who spoke for the membership as follows:

> ...[I]t is the opinion of this convention that certain amendments and alterations in the said Constitution would remove the fears and quiet the apprehensions of many good people in this commonwealth, and more effectively guard against an undue administration of the federal government....[511]

The *Eighth Amendment* proposed to the Massachusetts Ratification Convention read as follows:

> In civil actions between citizens of different states every issue of fact arising in actions at common law shall be tried by a jury if the parties or either of them request it.[512]

This proposal was accepted by the convention, which then ratified the *Constitution* on February 6, 1788, by a vote of 187 to 168.[513]

Two months later, George Washington wrote to the Marquis de Lafayette on April 28, 1788, as follows:

> You doubtless have seen ... that the convention of Massachusetts adopted the Constitution in toto, but recommended a number of specific alterations.... [T]here was not a member of the convention, I believe, who had the least objection to what is contended by the advocates for a Bill of Rights and trial by jury.... [I]t was only the difficulty of establishing a mode, which should not interfere with the fixed modes of any states, that induced the convention to leave it as a matter of future adjustment.[514]

---

[511] Schwartz, *The Roots of the Bill of Rights,* supra n.419, Vol. 3, pp.676-677.

[512] *See* Schwartz, *supra* n. 419, Vol. 3, pp. 677, 680. *See also* Ketcham, *supra* n.492, pp. 217, 219.

[513] Schwartz, *supra* n.419, Vol. 3, pp. 680-681.

[514] Schwartz, *supra* n.419, Vol. 4, pp. 987-988.

*There was not a member of the Constitutional Convention who had the least objection to what is contended for by the advocates for a Bill of Rights and trial by jury.*

—George Washington (1788)

**(c)** **The Maryland Ratification Convention (April 21-26, 1788).** The Maryland convention met on April 21, 1788, with a majority favoring ratification. A committee was appointed to draft "such amendments and alterations as may be thought necessary, in the proposed *Constitution*." This committee proposed 13 amendments. "Though not officially adopted by the Maryland convention, the proposed amendments of the Maryland committee were of great consequence." According to Bernard Schwartz, author of a five-volume treatise on *The Roots of the Bill of Rights*, these amendments "were another step in the direction of a federal *Bill of Rights*." The Maryland amendments were widely distributed and "apparently directly influenced the proposed amendments later recommended by Virginia, upon which [James] Madison drew in writing his draft of the *Bill of Rights*."[515] Trial by jury was the centerpiece of these proposals which read in part as follows:

> *That, in all actions on debts or contracts, and in all controversies respecting property, . . . the trial of facts shall be by jury, if required by either party. . . .*
>
> *That in all cases of trespasses . . . the party injured shall be entitled to trial by jury. . . .*

According to Bernard Schwartz, "the great objects of these amendments were, first, to secure the trial by jury in all cases, the boasted birthright of Englishmen and their descendants, and the palladium of civil liberty."[516]

As the ratification battle shifted to Virginia, trial by jury as "the boasted birthright of Englishman and their descendants," assumed an even greater role. As the first English colony on the North American continent to welcome the *Magna Carta* to its shores in 1606,[517] the Virginia Jury Act of 1642 [518] had guaranteed the right of trial by jury in the "Old Dominion" for 146 years by the time the Virginia Ratification Convention began in June of 1788.

---

[515]Schwartz, *The Roots of the Bill of Rights, supra* n.419, Vol. 4, p. 729.

[516]Schwartz, *supra* n.516, Vol. 4, pp. 732-733. Following a statement that "Congress shall exercise no power but what is expressly delegated by the *Constitution*," paragraphs 2, 3 and 5 of the Maryland committee report all related to the right of trial by jury.

[517]*See* p. 101 above.

[518]*See* p. 122 above.

**(d)** ***The Virginia Ratification Convention (June 2-27, 1788).*** The Virginia convention was closely divided. The federalist forces were led by James Madison, John Marshall, George Wythe, and Edmund Randolph. Its anti-federalist leaders were "among the best known men in the country": Patrick Henry, George Mason, and Richard Henry Lee.

> *For both supporters and opponents of the federal Constitution, Virginia was the crucial state in the ratification contest....*
>
> *All those who had been responsible for including the pioneer Declaration of Rights in the Virginia Constitution of 1776 were members of the 1788 convention.... They emphasized the lack of a similar Bill of Rights in the federal Constitution and argued against ratification until adequate protections for individual rights were included in it. As it turned out, this demand of the anti-federalists became the nub of the Bill of Rights debate in the Virginia convention....*[519]

The most moving, eloquent denunciation of the *Constitution* came from Patrick Henry, "one of the greatest orators in our history,"[520] who argued that under Plan of the Convention, trial by jury and other "great rights of free men" were endangered.

> *... [Y]ou ought to be extremely cautious, watchful, jealous of your liberty; for instead of securing our rights, you may lose them forever....*
>
> *... You are not to inquire how your trade may be increased, nor how you are to become a great and powerful people, but how your liberties can be secured; for liberty ought to be the direct end of your government. Is it necessary for your liberty, that you should abandon those great rights by the adoption of this system? Is the relinquishment of trial by jury and liberty of the press, necessary for your liberty; will the abandonment of your most sacred rights tend to the security of your liberty; liberty, the greatest of all earthly blessings — give us that precious jewel, and you may take everything else!...*

---

[519] Schwartz, *supra n.419*, Vol. 4, p. 762.
[520] Schwartz, *supra n.419*, Vol. 4, p. 763.

Patrick Henry's arguments were answered by John Marshall, who later served as Chief Justice of the United States (1801-1835).[521] Marshall countered:

> *... The exclusion of trial by jury, in this case, he urged to prostrate our rights ... [but] I hope that in this country, where impartiality is so much admired, the laws will direct facts to be ascertained by a jury. ...*[522]

Having heard the arguments of the anti-federalists, the Virginia Convention ratified the Plan of the Federal Convention on June 27, 1788, with the following recommendation:

> *... That there be a declaration or Bill of Rights asserting, and securing from encroachment, the essential and unalienable rights of the people, in such manner as the following:*

> *... That, in controversies respecting property, and in suits between man and man, the ancient trial by jury is one of the greatest securities to the rights of the people, and to remain sacred and inviolable.*[523]

Virginia produced as many genuine American patriots as any other state. Richard Bland, Patrick Henry, Thomas Jefferson, Richard Henry Lee, John Marshall, George Mason, James Madison and George Washington each made a significant contribution to the creation of that "patriot's dream that sees beyond the years."[524]

No state had a greater hand in crafting our *Declaration of Independence*, our *Constitution* and our *Bill of Rights*. These men believed that the preservation of trial by jury in civil as well as in criminal cases was absolutely essential to the preservation of that germ of American freedom which they had so carefully planted.

As will be seen below, the North Carolina Convention followed suit as the friends of individual liberty rallied to ensure that the ancient right of trial by jury, "one of the greatest securities to the rights of the people," remained sacred and inviolable.

---

[521] *See* "John Marshall and the Marshall Court," Ch. 3, p. 53 in Lieberman, *Milestones! 200 Years of American Law* (West Publishing Co. 1976).

[522] Schwartz, *supra n.419*, Vol. 4, p. 811.

[523] Ketcham, *supra n.492*, pp. 219-220.

[524] Katherine Lee Bates, *America the Beautiful* (1893).

*I hope that in this country where impartiality is so much to be admired, the laws will direct facts to be ascertained by a jury.*

—**John Marshall (1788)**

**(e) The North Carolina Ratification Convention (July 21 through August 2, 1788).** The North Carolina Ratification Convention was "dominated by a large anti-federalist majority."

> *Throughout the debate, the anti-federalists hammered at the Bill of Rights issue, saying that they would "never swallow the Constitution till it is amended."...*

> *...[Judge] Samuel Spencer expressed a widespread view when he declared, "I wish to have a Bill of Rights, to secure those inalienable rights, ... [to] satisfy the minds of the people."*[525]

James Bloodworth added that "the footing on which the trial by jury is, in the *Constitution*, does not satisfy me.... [If] our liberties cannot be secured, we can never hang long together. Interest is the bond of social union; and when this is taken away, the union itself must dissolve."[526]

Samuel Spencer followed up James Bloodworth's arguments by insisting:

> *Every person who is acquainted with the nature of liberty need not be informed of the importance of [trial by jury]. Juries are called the bulwarks of our rights and liberty; and no country can ever be enslaved as long as those cases which affect their lives and property are to be decided, in a great measure, by the consent of 12 honest, disinterested men.... It is highly improper that any clause which regards the security of trial by jury should be any way doubtful....*[527]

By an overwhelming majority, the North Carolina Ratification Convention approved a resolution that "a *Declaration of Rights*, asserting and securing from encroachment the great principles of civil and religious liberty, and the unalienable rights of the people ... ought to be laid before Congress." In its 11th and 12th clauses, the North Carolina *Declaration of Rights* stated:

---

[525] Schwartz, *supra* n.419, Vol. 4, p. 932. Samuel Spencer served on the Superior Court of North Carolina and joined Judge James Iredell in the Court's opinion in *Bayard v. Singleton* (1787). *See* Vol. 2, p. 430, below.

[526] Schwartz, *supra* n.419, Vol. 4, p. 944.

[527] Schwartz, *supra* n.419, Vol. 4, p. 946.

*That, in controversies respecting property, and in suits between man and man, the ancient trial by jury is one of the greatest securities to the rights of the people, and ought to remain sacred and inviolable.*

*That every free man ought to find a certain remedy, by recourse to the laws, for all injuries and wrongs he may receive in his person, property, or character; he ought to obtain right and justice freely, without sale, completely without denial, promptly without delay; and that all establishments or regulations contravening these rights are oppressive and unjust.*[528]

**(f)** ***The Margin of Victory.*** Primarily because of the omission of a *Bill of Rights*, the margin of victory in favor of ratification was close in many states.[529] In Virginia, the vote was 89 to 79.

*The [anti-federalists] . . . hope was a ratification of the Constitution conditional upon the adoption of amendments, and they proposed . . . a Bill of Rights of 20 Articles. . . . By a vote of 89 to 79, the convention ratified the Constitution unconditionally, with amendments recommended to the consideration of Congress.*[530]

The Pennsylvania Convention ratified the *Constitution* by a vote of 46 to 23, with 21 dissenting members publishing their opposition in the *Pennsylvania Packet*. The second "objectionable omission from the *Constitution*" which they mentioned was the failure to guarantee trial by jury in civil cases.[531] In Massachusetts, the vote was 187 to 168.

---

[528]Schwartz, *supra n.419,* Vol. 4, pp. 966-988. This last provision is taken substantially verbatim from *Blackstone's Commentaries on the Laws of England,* Vol. 1, p. 137 (1765) [Legal Classics Library 1983]. *See* p. 42 above.

[529]For a discussion of the ratification process, *see* Schwartz, *supra n.419,* Vol. 3, p. 627, through Vol. 4, p. 979. *See also* Rossiter, *1787 The Grand Convention,* pp. 274-298 (1966) and Bernstein, *The Making of the Constitution,* pp. 199-242 (1987).

[530]Morris, *The Forging of the Union 1781-1789,* pp. 311-312 (Harper & Row 1987).

[531]*See* p. 217 at n.510 above.

> *The most significant action of the Massachusetts convention and the step that . . . did most to win over enough dissenters, was the series of recommendatory amendments [containing the basic elements of the Bill of Rights] offered by John Hancock, amendments that "would remove the fears and quiet the apprehensions of many of the good people of the Commonwealth. . . ." These amendments removed the apprehensions of a sufficient number of anti-federalists to secure ratification . . . by the close vote of 187 to 168. As the first convention to propose recommendatory amendments, Massachusetts established a pattern. Of the seven states which had yet to ratify, only one . . . failed to take such action.[532]*

In New York, by the slim margin of 30 to 27, the convention ratified the *Constitution*. There, the anti-federalists focused on loading any adoption with conditional amendments in the form of a proposed *Bill of Rights*.[533]

> *The lack of a Bill of Rights proved to be the strongest argument of the opponents of ratification. . . .*
>
> *. . . Massachusetts led the way toward recommended amendments, and the last four states to ratify recommended comprehensive Bills of Rights. . . .*
>
> *In states where ratification was in doubt, especially New York, Virginia, and North Carolina, federalists pledged themselves to subsequent amendments to protect civil liberties, as soon as the new government went into operation.[534]*

As will be seen below, the federalists kept their promise, and a *Bill of Rights* was adopted and ratified shortly thereafter. It is this *Bill of Rights* which contains our guarantee of trial by jury in civil cases as one of those first ten amendments to our *Constitution* which are "every American's guarantee of freedom."[535]

---

[532]Morris, *The Forging of the Union 1781-1789*, pp.304-305 (Harper & Row 1987).

[533]Morris, *supra n.532*, p. 313.

[534]Levy, ed., *Encyclopedia of the American Constitution*, pp. 114-115 (Macmillan Publishing Co. 1986).

[535]*Memoirs of President Harry S. Truman*, Vol. 1., 19 (1955).

*At the time when the Constitution was submitted to the people for adoption, one of the most powerful objections urged against it was, that in civil causes it did not secure the trial of facts by a jury.*

—U.S. Supreme Court Justice Joseph Story (1833)

In "The Constitutional History of the Seventh Amendment," published in 1973, Professor Charles W. Wolfram wrote:

> *The institution of jury trial in civil cases was a familiar and well-ensconced feature of pre-1787 political life. . . . Legal writers and political theorists who were widely read by the colonists were firmly of the opinion that trial by jury in civil cases was an important right of free-men. . . . In fact, "[t]he right of trial by jury was probably the only one universally secured by the first American state constitutions. . . ."*
>
> *In short, the nascent American nation demonstrated at virtually every important step in its development that trial by jury was the form of trial in civil cases to which the people and their politicians were strongly attached. . . .*
>
> *Ratification was ultimately achieved probably only on the strength of assurances that the basic protections of a Bill of Rights would be incorporated as amendments. . . . [T]he entire issue of a Bill of Rights was precipitated at the Philadelphia Convention by an objection that the document under consideration lacked a specific guarantee of jury trial in civil cases.*[536]

The failure of the Constitutional Convention of 1787 to include a *Bill of Rights* guaranteeing the right to a civil jury trial dominated the ratification process. The right to a civil jury trial was important to our ancestors because its denial was fresh in their minds. To them, individual liberty was a sacred subject. Do we want less for ourselves today and our children tomorrow? Trial by jury is our birthright. It is the citadel of our freedom, our anchor against the storm of oppression, whether that oppression comes from our government, our industries, or the unpredictable whims of public opinion. The *Declaration of Independence* promises us life, liberty and the pursuit of happiness. Representative democracy and trial by jury place these essential rights within the reach of every American citizen.

---

[536] Wolfram, "The Constitutional History of the Seventh Amendment," 57 *Minn. L.R.* 639, 653-657 (1973).

## O. THE ADOPTION OF THE *SEVENTH AMENDMENT*

On July 26, 1788, after nine states had ratified the *Constitution*, Thomas Jefferson wrote to James Madison as follows:

> *I sincerely rejoice at the acceptance of our new Constitution by nine states. (It is a good canvas on which some strokes only want retouching). What these are, I think, are sufficiently manifested by the general voice from north to south which calls for a Bill of Rights. It seems pretty generally understood that this should go to juries, habeas corpus, standing armies, printing, religion, and monopolies....*[537]

The process of drafting a *Bill of Rights* was begun under the leadership of Alexander Hamilton: "200 proposals on basic rights were gathered from the states, narrowed to 12, and then to 10."[538] Then, on June 8, 1789, James Madison presented a proposed *Bill of Rights* to the House of Representatives. In his address to Congress, he characterized the right to a civil jury trial "as one of the best securities of the rights of the people":

> *... In suits at common law between man and man, the trial by jury, as one of the best securities to the rights of the people, ought to remain inviolate.*

* * *

> *... Trial by jury ... is as essential to secure the liberty of the people as any one of the pre-existent rights of nature....*[539]

---

[537] Ford, *The Writings of Thomas Jefferson,* Vol. 5, pp. 43-48 (In 10 volumes, New York and London, 1892-1899) [Republished in part in *Annals of America,* Vol. 3, pp. 304-305 (Encyclopædia Britannica 1976)].

[538] Stedman, *Our Ageless Constitution,* p. 45 (Stedman Liberty Library 1987). The two original recommendations not ratified by the states were a limitation on the number of members of the House of Representatives and a prohibition against raising the salaries of representatives without an election intervening. *See Annals of America, supra* n.537, Vol. 3, p. 364.

[539] *Annals of America, supra* n.537, Vol. 3, pp. 358-359.

Three-and-a-half months later, the *Bill of Rights* was adopted by Congress on September 25, 1789. On December 15, 1791, when Virginia became the 11th state to ratify them, the *Bill of Rights* became "the supreme law of the land."[540] As ratified, the *Seventh Amendment* provided:

> *In suits at common law, where the value in controversy shall exceed twenty dollars, the right of trial by jury shall be preserved, and no fact tried by a jury shall be otherwise examined in any court of the United States than according to the rules of the common law.*

The right to a civil jury trial as guaranteed by the *Seventh Amendment* is an inherent element of "the most comprehensive protection of individual freedom ever written."[541] As Thomas Jefferson has said, "a *Bill of Rights* is what the people are entitled to . . . and what no just government should refuse."[542]

> *Historically, the right to a civil jury has been one of the most prized and accepted of all those in the Bill of Rights. It was included in the original Jamestown Charter of 1607, and by 1776 all 13 colonies protected the right in some form. . . .*

> *[Since this] right was secured in 1791, the Supreme Court has repeatedly recognized that the right to a civil jury has "so firm a place in our history," and "is so fundamental and sacred to the citizen" that it must be "jealously guarded by the courts."*[543]

But the obligation to preserve, protect and defend the *Seventh Amendment* is not limited to the judiciary. It is the obligation of *every American citizen* to prevent *any infringement, however slight*, on this historic right, so fundamental and sacred to every American citizen, won for us on the great plain of Runnymede 777 years ago.

---

[540] *Annals of America, supra* n. 537, Vol. 3, p. 364.

[541] Alderman & Kennedy, *In Our Defense: The Bill of Rights in Action*, p. 15 (William Morrow & Co. 1991).

[542] *See* Stedman, *supra n.538*, p. 45.

[543] Alderman & Kennedy, *supra n.541*, p. 277. "Of course, the jury is thought to actually insure fairness as well. The *Seventh Amendment* places a high value on the collective 'wisdom of the community.'. . . ." Alderman & Kennedy, *supra* n. 541, p. 277.

## The Bill of Rights

Of these 12 proposed amendments, 10 were approved and ratified by the states on December 15, 1791. Since that date, the Seventh Amendment has guaranteed to every American citizen that "in suits at common law, where the value in controversy shall exceed twenty dollars, the right of trial by jury shall be preserved."

In *Decision in Philadelphia: The Constitutional Convention of 1787*, published in 1986, Clinton Collier wrote that, to the American citizen today, "the best known and most important part of the *Constitution* is the *Bill of Rights*":

> *Undoubtedly, to most Americans, the best-known and most important part of the Constitution is the Bill of Rights. Probably few of them could recite in detail what it actually contains, but almost all would know that it guarantees freedom of religion, freedom of speech, freedom of the press, the right to a fair trial, and some other freedoms about which they might be somewhat more vague. And from a certain point of view the Bill of Rights is the most important part of the Constitution. . . . Americans are justly proud of the Bill of Rights, for it is this section of the Constitution, more than any other, that has been a rallying cry for people all around the world.*[544]

Americans are also justly proud of our *Seventh Amendment* right to trial by jury. As Chief Justice Roger B. Taney wrote for a unanimous Supreme Court of the United States in 1851, trial by jury is one of "the most cherished and familiar principles of the common law" and our "best and only security for life, liberty and property."

> *The colonists who established the English colonies in this country . . . brought with them the common and statute laws of England, as they stood at the time of their emigration, so far as they were applicable to the situation and local circumstances of the colony. And among the most cherished and familiar principles of the common law was the trial by jury in civil, and . . . criminal cases. And, however the colonies may have varied in other respects . . . , trial by jury in all of them of English origin was regarded as a right of inestimable value, and the best and only security for life, liberty, and property."*[545]

---

[544] *See* "George Mason and the Rights of Man," Ch. 32, p. 332, in Collier, *Decision in Philadelphia: The Constitutional Convention of 1787* (1986).

[545] *United States v. Reid*, 13 L.Ed. 1023, 1024 (1851). As the fourth Chief Justice of the United States, Roger B. Taney of Maryland served on the Court from 1836 until his death in 1864.

Chief Justice Alexander W. Stowe of the Supreme Court of Wisconsin wrote in 1850:

> *... The trial by jury, as it existed of old, is **the** trial by jury secured by our national and state and constitutions. It is not **granted** by these instruments; it is more — it is **secured**. It is no American invention. Our forefathers brought it with them to this country more than two centuries ago, and, by making it a part of the Constitution, they intended to perpetuate it for their posterity, and neither legislatures nor courts have any power to infringe even the least of its principles. ...*[546]

And as Justice William Strong of the Supreme Court of Pennsylvania wrote in 1862, the right of trial by jury is one to which Americans have clung with an "unrelaxing grasp":

> *.... But if there is any right to which, more than all others, the people ... have clung with unrelaxing grasp, it is that of trial by jury. They brought it with them from the land of their fathers. In every constitution which has been adopted, they have taken care to secure it against infringement. ... What can this mean, but that the right of having controverted questions of fact in common law cases decided by a jury, should be beyond the reach of any department of the government ... ? This was the right which had always been enjoyed before, and if the constitutional provisions were not intended to protect that in all its length and breadth, they can mean nothing. ...*
>
> *Then, what has become of the constitutional right of the citizen? Such a doctrine would startle the people of this Commonwealth, and justly, for it would deprive them of one of their most valued privileges. No power in our government can take from the litigant the right to have his case tried by a jury, substantially [as it existed] when the Constitution ... was adopted.*[547]

---

[546] Dissenting Opinion of Chief Justice Stowe in *State v. Cameron*, 2 Pin. 490, 499 (Wis. 1850) [emphasis by Justice Stowe].

[547] *North Pennsylvania Coal Co. v. Snowden*, 6 Pa. 488, 492 (1862).

Mirroring these views, Justice Rufus P. Ranney of the Supreme Court of Ohio wrote in 1853:

> *The institution of the jury referred to in our constitution . . . is precisely the same in every substantial respect, as that recognized in the great charter and its benefits secured to the freemen of England, and again and again acknowledged in fundamental compacts as the great safeguard of life, liberty, and property. The same, brought to this continent by our forefathers, and perseveringly claimed as their birthright, in every contest with arbitrary power, and finally, an invasion of its privileges prominently assigned as one of the causes which was to justify them in the eyes of mankind, in waging the contest which resulted in independence. Nor did their affection for it then diminish or cool. They made it a cornerstone in erecting the State government; and after the adoption of the federal constitution, without a provision for security in it, they did not rest satisfied. . . .*
>
> *. . . An institution that has so long stood the trying tests of time and experience, that has so long been guarded with such scrupulous care, and commanded the admiration of so many of the wise and good, justly demands our jealous scrutiny when innovations are attempted to be made upon it.*[548]

Today, yesterday, tomorrow and forever, in the words of Thomas Jefferson, trial by jury is an essential star in "the bright constellation which has gone before us and guided our steps through an age of revolution and reformation":

> *The wisdom of our sages and the blood of our heroes have been devoted to [its] attainment. [It] should be the creed of our political faith, the text of civil instruction, the touchstone by which we try the services of those we trust; and should we wander from [it] in moments of error or alarm, let us hasten to retrace our steps and to regain the road which alone leads to peace, liberty, and safety.*[549]

---

[548]*Work v. Ohio*, 2 Ohio St. 296, 302-303 (1853).

[549]First Inaugural Address, March 4, 1801, in *The Annals of America, supra* n.537, Vol. 4, pp. 143-146.

*The wisdom of our sages and the blood of our heroes has been devoted to the attainment of trial by jury. It should be the creed of our political faith.*
        —**Thomas Jefferson, First Inaugural Address (1801)**

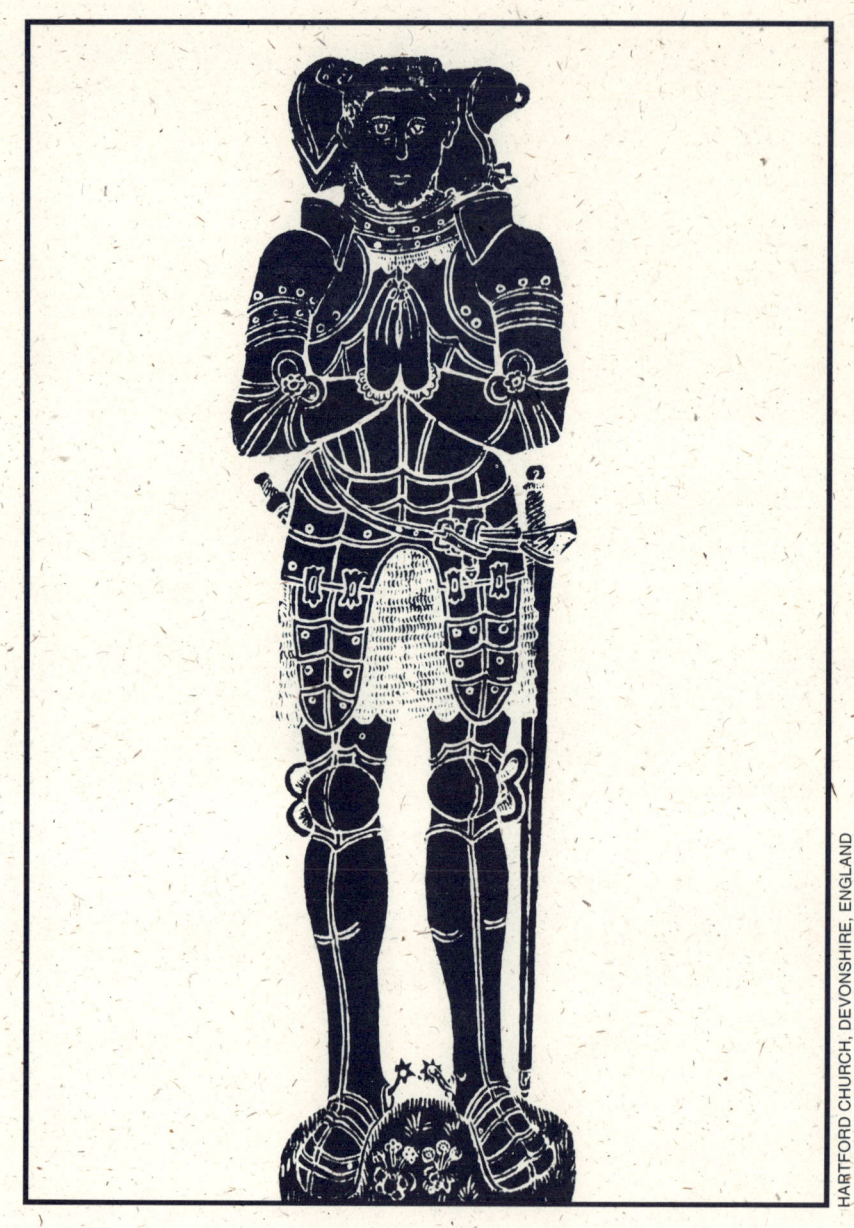

*Trial by jury is productive of far more justice than the trial of any other human law.*
—**Thomas Williams, Speaker of the House of Commons (1557)**

# P.  A CHRONOLOGY OF QUOTATIONS*

Set forth below are quotations on trial by jury from 182 sources. Additional quotations from appellate court opinions are set forth in Volume II, Appendix B and C, pp. 477-503 below.

*Trial by jury is the most rational and effective method for discovering the truth.*
    **—Sir John Fortescue, Chief Justice of the King's Bench (1468)**

*Trial by jury is a wise distribution of power which exceeds all other modes of trial.*
    **—Sir Edward Coke, Chief Justice of Common Pleas (1628)**

*Trial by jury is the most essential liberty of England. The lives and estates that it has preserved will never be forgotten.*
    **—William Walwin, *Juries Justified* (1651)**

*Jurors are the keepers of the liberties of England.*
    **—Lt.Col. John Lilburne (1653)**

*No cause, whether civil or criminal, of any freeman, shall be tried in any court of judicature, without a judgment of his peers.*
    **—John Locke's *Fundamental Constitutions of Carolina* (1669)**

*The excellent order of trial by jury carries a much greater preponderation to discover the truth than any other trial whatsoever.*
    **—Matthew Hale, Chief Justice of the King's Bench (1676)**

*Trial by jury is the impregnable fortress wherein the law preserves the just rights and liberties of this country.*
    **—Sir John Hawles, English Solicitor General (1680)**

*Trial by jury ranks among the choicest of our fundamental laws and whosoever shall openly suppress or craftily undermine it is an enemy and traitor to his king and country.*
    **—Henry Care, *English Liberties* (1680)**

*Trial by jury is our fence and protection against all frauds and surprises and against all storms of power.*
    **—Sir John Maynard, Serjeant at Law (1689)**

*Many of these quotations have been condensed due to space limitations.

*In the whole practice of law, there is nothing of greater excellency than trials by juries. Neither the wisdom of our ancestors could, nor could the present, nor after-ages invent a better.*
    —**Giles Duncombe, *The Law Concerning Juries* (1725)**

*The jury trial of Peter Zenger was the germ of American freedom, the morning star of liberty which revolutionized America.*
—**Gouverneur Morris, On the Trial of John Peter Zenger (1735)**

*The judiciary power ought to be exercised by persons taken from the body of the people.*
    —**Charles de Montesquieu, *The Spirit of Laws* (1748)**

*We are firmly of the opinion that any person who shall endeavor to deprive us of so glorious a privilege as trials by juries is an enemy to this province.*
    —**South Carolina General Assembly (1751)**

*Trial by jury is the best institution calculated for the preservation of liberty and the administration of justice that ever was devised by the wit of man.*
    —**David Hume, English Philosopher (1762)**

*The right of trial by jury cannot be guarded with too much vigilance, nor defended with too much ardor. If the people surrender it, their other rights will inevitably follow.*
    —**Joseph Towers, *The Rights and Duties of Juries* (1764)**

*Trial by jury is the inherent and invaluable right of every American.*
    —**The Stamp Act Congress (1765)**

*The most essential rights of the British subjects are representative government and trial by jury. These are the very pillars of the British Constitution founded in the common rights of mankind.*
    —**Resolution of the Town of Boston (1765)**

*Trial by jury is the glorious liberty of freeborn subjects, the darling privilege that distinguishes us from all other nations.*
    —**Charles Woodmason of South Carolina (1767)**

*Trial by jury is the principal bulwark of our liberties.*
    —**Justice William Blackstone (1768)**

*Representative government and trial by jury are the heart and lungs of liberty. Without them we have no other fortification against being ridden like horses, fleeced like sheep, worked like cattle and fed and clothed like swine and hounds.*

—**John Adams (1774)**

*The Magna Carta is a constrained declaration of our original, inherent, indefeasible natural rights as citizens.*
—**Samuel Adams of Massachusetts (1772)**

*The colonies are entitled to the great and inestimable privilege of being tried by their peers.*
—**Declaration of the First Continental Congress (1774)**

*We claim all benefits secured by the English constitution, particularly the inestimable right of trial by jury.*
—**John Jay of New York (1774)**

*The civil jury trial is preferable to any other and ought to be held sacred.*
—**Virginia Declaration of Rights (1776)**

*In civil suits the parties have a right to trial by jury, which ought to be held sacred.*
—**Pennsylvania Constitution (1776)**

*Trial by jury is one of the greatest securities of the lives, liberties and estates of the people.*
—**Delaware Declaration of Rights (1776)**

*The ancient mode of trial by jury in civil cases is one of the best securities of the rights of the people, and ought to remain sacred and inviolable.*
—**North Carolina Constitution (1776)**

*Trial by jury is hardly less important than representative government itself.*
—**Richard Bland of Virginia (1776)**

*The citizens of New Hampshire are entitled to their great, inestimable and inherent right of trial by jury.*
—**New Hampshire House of Representatives (1776)**

*Every free government should include a Bill of Rights containing the great principles of natural and civil liberty unalterable by human power. The right of redress by an appeal to public justice includes the right to trial by jury, a civil right common to both parties.*
—**Thomas Paine of Pennsylvania (1777)**

*In civil actions the parties have a right to trial by jury which ought to be held sacred.*
—**Vermont Constitution (1777)**

*In civil suits the parties have a right to trial by jury and this method of procedure shall be held sacred.*
—**Massachusetts Constitution (1780)**

*English liberty will subsist so long as trial by jury remains sacred and inviolate not only from all open attacks, but also from all secret machinations, which may sap and undermine it.*
—**Thomas Erskine, British Barrister (1784)**

*Trial by jury is a fundamental right guaranteed by our Constitution which the legislature cannot take away.*
—**James Mitchell Varnum,** *Trevett v. Weeden* **(1786)**

*The civil jury is a valuable safeguard to liberty.*
—**Alexander Hamilton of New York (1787)**

*In suits between man and man, the parties have a right to trial by jury which ought to be held sacred.*
—**Samuel Bryan of Pennsylvania (1787)**

*The right of trial by jury is a fundamental right of free and enlightened people and an essential part of a free government. Trial by jury in civil cases and trial by jury in criminal cases stand on the same footing: they are the common rights of Americans.*
—**Richard Henry Lee of Virginia (1787)**

*Trial by jury is the fundamental security for every enjoyment that is valuable in the contemplation of a free man.*
—**Thomas Hartley of Pennsylvania (1787)**

*Trial by jury has excellencies that entitle it to superiority over every other mode, in cases to which it is applicable.*
—**James Wilson of Pennsylvania (1787)**

*The jury is adapted to the investigation of truth beyond any other system the world can produce. A tribunal without juries would be a Star Chamber in civil cases.*
—**Elbridge Gerry of Massachusetts (1787-1788)**

*Trial by jury in all cases is the boasted birthright of Englishmen and their descendants, and the palladium of civil liberty.*
**—Maryland Ratification Convention Committee (1788)**

*In suits between man and man, the ancient trial by jury is one of the greatest securities to the rights of the people.*
**—Virginia Bill of Rights (1788)**

*I consider trial by jury as the only anchor ever yet imagined by man, by which a government can be held to the principles of its constitution.*
**—Thomas Jefferson (1788)**

*Trial by jury is the cornerstone of our liberty. We must guard it with jealous circumspection against those new and arbitrary methods of trial which may imperceptibly undermine it. Trial by jury is our birthright; who in opposition to the genius of United America, shall dare to attempt its subversion?*
**—John Dickinson of Delaware (1788)**

*It has been urged that the exclusion of trial by jury would prostrate our rights, but I hope that in this country, where impartiality is so admired, the laws will direct facts to be ascertained by a jury.*
**—John Marshall of Virginia (1788)**

*Juries are called the bulwarks of our rights and liberties; and no country can ever be enslaved as long as those cases which affect their lives and property are to be decided, in a great measure, by the consent of 12 honest, disinterested men.*
**—Samuel Spencer of North Carolina (1788)**

*There was not a member of the Constitutional Convention who had the least objection to what is contended for by the advocates for a Bill of Rights and trial by jury.*
**—George Washington (1788)**

*Trial by jury has been sanctified by the experience of the ages. It is deemed the birthright of Americans and liberty cannot subsist without it.*
**—Judge Alexander Hanson of Maryland (1788)**

*Trial by jury is the best appendage of freedom by which our ancestors have secured their lives and property. I hope we shall never be induced to part with that excellent mode of trial.*

—**Patrick Henry of Virginia (1788)**

*Trial by jury in civil cases is as essential to secure the liberty of the people as any one of the pre-existent rights of nature.*
—James Madison (1789)

*Trial by jury is the foundation of our free Constitution: take that away and the whole fabric will soon moulder into dust.*
—Charles Pratt, Lord Camden, Chancellor of England (1792)

*Trial by jury is part of the bright constellation which leads to peace, liberty and safety.*
—President Thomas Jefferson (1801)

*Trial by jury is the most cherished institution of free and intelligent government that the world has ever seen.*
—Justice Theodore Sedgwick of Massachusetts (1813)

*If the indifferent selection of impartial jurors can be achieved in France, we shall see the French regard trial by jury as one of their proudest privileges, and perform its duties with the same zeal, the same courage, and the same independence as their neighbors.*
—Monsieur M. Cottu, Counselor, Royal Court of Paris (1822)

*It is through trial by jury that the people share in government, a consideration which ought to make our legislators very cautious how they take away this mode of trial by new, trifling and vexatious enactments.*
—Lord John Russell, Prime Minister of England (1823)

*Trial by jury and other rights and liberties of English subjects were claimed by the American colonies as their undoubted inheritance and birthright.*
—Chancellor James Kent of New York (1827)

*The sacred privilege of trial by jury is the unadulterated voice of the people which should be heard in the sanctuaries of justice as fountains springing fresh from the lap of earth.*
—Henry Hallam, **The Constitutional History of England** (1827)

*What individual can so well assess the amount of damages which a plaintiff ought to recover for an injury he has received than an intelligent jury?*
—Henry Peter Brougham, Lord Chancellor of England (1828)

*As the great bulwark of English liberty, trial by jury is the best safeguard of a free Constitution. This mainspring in the machinery of remedial justice brings the law home to every man's door.*
— **Sir Francis Palgrave, On the English Commonwealth (1832)**

*The law of England has established trial by judge and jury in the conviction that it is the mode best calculated to ascertain the truth.*
— **Jeremy Bentham, English Philosopher (1832)**

*The inestimable privilege of trial by jury is conceded by all to be essential to political and civil liberty. It is justly dear to the American people, has always been an object of deep interest and solicitude and every encroachment upon it has been watched with great jealousy.*
— **U.S. Supreme Court Justice Joseph Story (1833)**

*Trial by jury is among the most inestimable privileges of an American citizen. It is a fundamental right which protects the lowest individual for which our union exists.*
— **U.S. Supreme Court Justice William Johnson (1833)**

*The right of trial by jury, being of the highest importance to the citizen, and essential to liberty, was not left to the uncertain fate of legislation, but was secured by the Constitution of this and all other states as sacred and inviolable.*
— **Chief Justice William L. Sharkey of Mississippi (1834)**

*The civil jury is the most effective form of sovereignty of the people. It defies the aggressions of time and man. During the reigns of Henry VIII (1509-1547) and Elizabeth I (1558-1603), the civil jury did in reality save the liberties of England.*
— **Alexis de Tocqueville, Democracy in America (1835)**

*No single institution that the wisdom of man has ever devised is so well calculated to preserve a people free, or make them so, as trial by jury.*
— **British Barrister J. Sydney Taylor (1838)**

*The struggle for American independence was for chartered rights, for English liberties, for trial by jury, habeas corpus and Magna Carta.*
— **Former President John Quincy Adams (1839)**

*Trial by jury is the glory of English law and the surest guardian of public justice. It is the most transcendent privilege which any subject can wish for and there can be no doubt that it has secured the just liberties of England for a long succession of ages.*
  **—Henry John Stephen, On the Laws of England (1844)**

*Our ancestors, both English and American, have resisted non-jury tribunals for reasons most vital to public liberty. They remonstrated on the abridgment of trial by jury even in the Declaration of Independence and it was a prominent cause of the Revolution.*
  **—U.S. Supreme Court Justice Levi Woodbury (1847)**

*Among the most cherished and familiar principles of the common law was trial by jury in civil and criminal cases. It was regarded as a right of inestimable value, and the best and only security for life, liberty, and property.*
  **—U. S. Supreme Court Chief Justice Roger B. Taney (1851)**

*A jury ensures to us that first and indispensable requisite of a judicial tribunal, integrity.*
  **—Massachusetts Lawyer Lysander Spooner (1852)**

*The right of being tried by his fellow citizens who simply decide according to what they believe to be the truth gives every man a conviction he will be dealt with impartially and inspires him to mete out to others the same measure of equity that is dealt to himself.*
  **—William Forsythe, History of Trial by Jury (1852)**

*The state Constitutions demonstrate the great jealousy of the American people on the subject of jury trial. The judgment of a panel of twelve men has been an indispensable element in the judicial administration of the country.*
  **—Justice Joseph N. Whitner, S.C. Court of Appeals (1856)**

*We are bound to the jury trial by all the holiest traditions of our past history; we esteem it as the very bulwark of our liberties.*
  **—American Author John Norton Pomeroy (1863)**

*The institution of trial by jury has been consecrated in the affections of the only nations of the earth truly free, and that security should forever be regarded as an inappreciable inheritance.*
  **—Eli K. Price, Discourse on Trial by Jury (1863)**

*The jury trial has borne the test of a longer existence better than any other legal institution that ever existed among men. England owes more of her freedom and prosperity to it than all other causes put together.*

**—Jeremiah S. Black, Chief Justice of Pennsylvania, U.S. Attorney General and Secretary of State (1866)**

*The right of trial by jury involves the very framework of the government and the fundamental principles of American liberty. The inestimable privilege of trial by jury is one of the most valuable in a free country.*
  —**U.S. Supreme Court Justice David Davis (1866)**

*We assent, fully, to all that is said of the inestimable value of trial by jury.*
  —**U.S. Supreme Court Chief Justice Salmon P. Chase (1866)**

*Jury trial, as an instrument of justice, as an educator of the people, and as a means of making them feel their responsibility in government, is by far the best system of trial yet devised.*
  —**Justice Thomas McIntyre Cooley of Michigan (1868)**

*To forego the good sense, practical experience and unbiased instincts of an impartial jury would do violence to history and injustice to the cause of personal liberty.*
  —**Emory Washburn, Study and Practice of Law (1871)**

*Twelve men in a jury box know more about the common affairs of life and can draw wiser and safer conclusions.*
  —**U.S. Supreme Court Justice Ward Hunt (1873)**

*The jury system is the handmaid of freedom. It takes on the spirit of liberty, and grows with the progress of constitutional government. Rome, Sparta and Carthage fell because they did not know it, let not England and America fall because they threw it away.*
  —**Charles S. May, Address to the Michigan Law School (1875)**

The English colonists settled here with a deep-rooted regard for trial by jury. They brought it with them and established it and cherished it as one of their dearest privileges. Ever since the Magna Carta, the right of trial by jury has been esteemed as a peculiarly dear and inestimable privilege by the English race.
  —**John Proffatt, A Treatise on Trial by Jury (1877)**

Typical of our democratic institutions, the jury is a fair sample of the community at large. For downright common sense and that sort of shrewdness which discerns the truth hidden in the bowels of a complicated dispute, we commend a jury of twelve plain men.
  —**Edward P. Wilder, New York Bar (1879)**

*The jury system involves a great number of persons in the discharge of justice. Much of the satisfaction with our system of justice may be traced to the large infusion of the popular element which the jury adds to the administration of justice.*
   —**John Duke, Lord Coleridge, Chief Justice of England (1879)**

*Trial by jury interests large numbers of people in the administration of justice and gives it a degree of power and popularity which could hardly be derived from any other source.*
   —**Sir James Fitzjames Stephen,**
   ***A History of the Common Law of England* (1883)**

*The right of trial by jury is expressly secured by the Seventh Amendment. The U.S. Supreme Court has always guarded this constitutional right with jealousy.*
   —**U.S. Supreme Court Justice Stanley Matthews (1885)**

*Trial by jury presents the foremost feature of the system of jurisprudence under which the English race has gained its liberties, and through which those liberties will in the future be preserved.*
   —**D. H. Chamberlain, *American System of Trial by Jury* (1887)**

*In the Declaration of Independence, the King of Great Britain was arraigned before the world for depriving us of trial by jury. This language evinces the purpose of our representatives to risk their lives and their fortunes to secure the ancient right of trial by jury.*
   —**Justice Alphonso C. Avery of North Carolina (1892)**

*Trial by Jury is one of the most important, most vital, most sacred of the institutions which maintain our free and popular government. It serves to bring the people into immediate participation in the administration of law and makes its administration tolerable.*
   —**Nobel Peace Prize Winner Elihu Root (1894)**

*Trial by jury has served as a potent promoter of the dispensation of justice for which no more perfect substitute has ever been devised.*
   —**American Author Maximus A. Lesser (1894)**

*The judgment by jurors is the true guarantee of individual liberty in England, and in every other country in the world where men aspire to freedom.*
   —**The French Author, Sikyes (1894)**

*The very essence of trial by jury is its principle of fairness. Twelve men of ordinary ability are just as capable of deciding today on the effect of evidence as they were in the infancy of the institution.*
   —**J.E.R. Stephens, *The Growth of Trial by Jury* (1896)**

*The judgment of twelve impartial men is more likely to be wise and safe than the conclusion of any single judge.*
   —**U.S. District Judge William Brawley (1897)**

*All attempts to tinker or tamper with trial by jury in civil causes should be discouraged as disastrous to the public welfare.*
   —**ABA President Joseph Choate (1898)**

*Nothing among the English was more ancient than the practice of popular justice. The jury system is characterized by its intrinsic fairness & is the most rational way of determining questions of fact.*
   —**James Bradley Thayer, Harvard Law Professor (1898)**

*The right of trial by jury is the palladium of our liberties.*
   —**Frederick Pollock, *The History of English Law* (1899)**

*Trial by judge and jury is immensely superior to any other mode of trial that the wit of man has ever devised; and evil will be the hour when the people of this country supinely acquiesce in its invasion.*
   —**Judge Henry Clay Caldwell, U.S. Court of Appeals (1899)**

*The jury are taken from the various walks of life, and their combined knowledge and experience afford the very best opportunity for safe and wise conclusions.*
   —**Chief Justice James H. Hazelrigg of Kentucky (1899)**

*Trial by jury is a fundamental guarantee of the rights and liberties of the people. English speaking people have for centuries regarded it as vital to personal security and the men of the Revolutionary period universally claimed it as the birthright of free men.*
   —**U.S. Supreme Court Justice John Marshall Harlan (1900)**

*Trial by jury is the best system yet devised. Its foundations are laid deep in the hearts of liberty loving Anglo-Saxons. Without it, the Republic would be deprived of one of its most effective weapons against absolutism, intolerance and greed.*
   —**Alfred C. Coxe, *The Trials of Jury Trials* (1901)**

*The preservation of the jury is a matter of great importance. It has been one of the most valuable institutions in our history.*
—U.S. Supreme Court Justice David J. Brewer (1902)

*We should at no time lose sight of the great safeguards of personal liberty. Like the right of suffrage, trial by jury is one of the instruments of the sovereignty of the people and is essential to both civil and political liberty.*
  —**William H. Holt, U.S. District Judge, Puerto Rico (1905)**

*Trial by jury has withstood the reign of tyrants, survived the overthrow of dynasties, and remains as one of the best expressions of free government. This heritage, coming from our liberty-loving ancestors, is one of the foundation stones of our commonwealth.*
  —**John F. Geeting,** *Trial by Jury Must be Preserved* **(1907)**

*The greatest and safest power of the English people was the right of trial by jury. Their heroism and sturdy spirit displayed as jurors formed themes for the strongest and most eloquent chapters in the history of this remarkable people.*
  —**Justice E. C. O'Rear, Kentucky Court of Appeals (1910)**

*Trial by jury is essentially a child of freedom. Where the scepter of the tyrant rules, it has no home. It is the greatest safeguard of liberty, and the greatest protector of its privileges.*
  —**Sam M. Wolfe,** *A Defense of the Jury* **(1911)**

*For a long time past Englishmen have been proud of their trial by jury, proud to see the nations of Europe imitating as best they might this "palladium of English liberties," this "bulwark of the British Constitution."*
  —**Frederic William Maitland,** *Collected Papers* **(1912)**

*The absence of any provision respecting the mode of trial in civil actions was so generally regarded as endangering the right of trial by jury, and evoked so much criticism on that ground, that the first Congress proposed the Seventh Amendment, which was promptly ratified.*
  —**U.S. Supreme Court Justice Willis Van Devanter (1913)**

*In the American colonies there was great popular enthusiasm for trial by jury as a bulwark of liberty. So highly prized by our ancestors, they put it beyond the power of the legislature to abolish.*
  —**Austin Wakeman Scott, President of Rutgers College (1918)**

*Trial by jury is the most enduring of all institutions which have flourished among the English-speaking peoples. No other institution ever struck its roots so deep into their hearts. Its decay would mark the decadence, and its overthrow be the end of popular government.*
    **—Delphin M. Delmas, *The Democracy of Justice* (1918)**

*The jury system appeals with peculiar force to the great masses of common people. Through their service on the jury, the shoulder of every citizen, whatever the accident of his birth or station, tingles with that matchless precept of the law that all men are born free, equal and independent.*
    **—Charles T. Coleman, *Origin of Trial by Jury* (1919)**

*The ancient and honorable institution of trial by jury has been universally considered the bulwark of our system of jurisprudence. It is a great popular university which has done a large part to perpetuate our American democracy.*
    **—Francis L. Wellman, *Gentlemen of the Jury* (1924)**

*Trial by jury plays a large part in the social and political life of a community. It also tends to foster respect for our courts, the last and final protecting tribunal of our liberties.*
    **—Marquette University Law Professor A. C. Umbreit (1924)**

*In most cases there is a better chance of justice from a jury of ordinary men than from any substitute.*
    **—Connor Hall, *The Present Day Jury* (1924)**

*The jury system is as fundamental as freedom of speech, habeas corpus, due process of law, or any of the other guarantees of the Bill of Rights.*
    **—Lester P. Edge, *Jury System? Yes.* (1925)**

*The jury system has for some hundreds of years been constantly bringing the rules of law to the touchstone of contemporary common sense.*
    **—W. S. Holdsworth, *A History of English Law* (1927)**

*The jury's homely experience, its touch with human affairs and its contact in everyday society endow it with a special ability to see and know what the real facts are.*
    **—Harold H. Corbin, *The Jury on Trial* (1928)**

*The jury must be preserved. It is the best system ever invented for a free people in the world's history. It supplies that flexibility of legal rules which is essential to justice and popular contentment.*
  **—Dean John Henry Wigmore, Northwestern Law School (1929)**

*There is no better or healthier system than to have disputed questions of fact, both in civil and criminal cases, passed upon by ordinary citizens of ordinary intelligence.*
  **—Judge Frederick E. Crane of New York (1929)**

*The traditions of English jurisprudence are the admiration of the world. The liberties of England are required to be construed not by technical persons, but by ordinary men who lead ordinary lives and think ordinary thoughts of ordinary people.*
  **—Lord Birkenhead, Chancellor of England (1929)**

*The right of trial by jury is as fundamental to democracy as the right of suffrage or the freedom of worship, press and speech. It cannot be surrendered without an equal loss of our faith in the fundamental principles upon which our government is founded.*
  **—John Shay, *A Defense of the Jury System* (1929)**

*Trial by jury is one of our cherished institutions. Often, in times of stress, it has stood as a bulwark against oppression. It is the layman's contribution to the administration of justice.*
  **—ABA President Clarence E. Martin (1934)**

*Jury trial offers the most satisfactory means of settlement of civil disputes and is looked upon today by American citizens as one of the most precious rights secured by our forefathers.*
  **—Stanley F. Brewster, *Twelve Men in a Box* (1934)**

*Maintenance of the jury is of such importance and occupies so firm a place in our history that any seeming curtailment of the right of trial by jury should be scrutinized with utmost care.*
  **—U.S. Supreme Court Justice George Sutherland (1935)**

*The delegates to the Constitutional Convention of 1787 believed that the right to trial by jury in civil cases was one of the most invaluable privileges a free country can boast.*
  **—American Biographer Andrew J. Bethea (1937)**

*The traditions of English jurisprudence are the admiration of the world. Our liberties should be construed by ordinary men who lead ordinary lives and think ordinary thoughts of ordinary people.*
—**Frederick William Smith, Lord Birkenhead, Chancellor of England (1929)**

*The founders of our government thought that trial by civil jury was an essential bulwark of civil liberty.*
— **U.S. Supreme Court Justice Hugo Black (1939)**

*The combined wisdom and experience through the centuries since Magna Carta have demonstrated that trial by judge and jury is the best that has ever been devised and the best machinery for bringing out a true result.*
— **Ashton File, President, West Virginia Bar Association (1940)**

*The jury has grown up as representative of the local community whose representative character appealed to democratic America. It seemed to Americans important to preserve the jury as a bulwark of political liberty.*
— **Roscoe Pound, Former Dean of Harvard Law School (1942)**

*The right of trial by jury in civil cases is so fundamental and sacred to the citizen that it should be jealously guarded by the courts.*
— **U.S. Supreme Court Justice Frank Murphy (1942)**

*The jury is a balance wheel in the administration of justice, it has been the protector of the people against tyranny, and it may be so against a militant bureaucracy.*
— **Resolution of the Boston Bar Association (1943)**

*Trial by jury has been the subject of countless eulogies as the very citadel of freedom.*
— **William Seagle, *The History of Law* (1946)**

*In the jury box, no less than in the polling booth, every day the American way of life is given its rebirth. American jurymen are the custodians and guarantors of the democratic ideal.*
— **Justice Bernard Botein of New York (1946)**

*The more I see of trial by judge, the more highly I think of trial by jury.*
— **Australian King's Counsel B. R. Wise (1948)**

*Trial by jury is one of our treasured legacies. To date, no finer or more just system of law has been devised anywhere.*
—**René A. Wormser, *The Law* (1949)**

*Trial by jury, where property, reputation and life are at stake, the jurors are chosen by lot, and democracy appears unalloyed.*
—**George Santayana, *Dominations and Powers* (1951)**

*It is difficult to exaggerate the esteem in which the American colonists held representative government and trial by jury. Few Americans believed that they could ever be improved upon as instruments of popular control of government. They are the means of defending all other fundamental rights.*
—**Clinton Rossiter, *Seedtime of the Republic* (1953)**

*Twelve heads are better than one, the joint effort of twelve people who are trying their best to do what is right is one product of our democracy for which we should be everlastingly grateful.*
—**Judge Harold R. Medina, U.S. Court of Appeals (1954)**

*Representative government and trial by jury are invaluable rights without which a people cannot be free and happy.*
—**U.S. Supreme Court Justice William O. Douglas (1954)**

*The jury system has come to stand for all we mean by English justice. The scrutiny of 12 honest jurors provides defendant and plaintiff alike a safeguard from arbitrary perversion of the law.*
—**Sir Winston Churchill (1956)**

*Since it was first recognized in the Magna Carta, trial by jury has been a prized shield against oppression. It is a right treasured by the American people.*
—**Albert Averbach, *Tampering With the Jury System* (1956)**

*The object of any tyrant would be to overthrow or diminish trial by jury, for it is the lamp that shows that freedom lives.*
—**Sir Patrick Devlin, British Lord of Appeal (1956)**

*To the American people the right to trial by jury is and has been a symbol of democracy. The jury box and the ballot box have frequently been called "the twin pillars of liberty."*
—**Clarence R. Runals, N.Y. State Bar Association (1956)**

*The right to trial by jury is one of the most valuable and most highly cherished rights guaranteed by the Constitution.*
—**Judge Elbert Parr Tuttle, U.S. Court of Appeals (1956)**

*The history of jury trial is a constant struggle to preserve the idea of laymen's justice. It offers an assurance of judgment by those who understand community values, a bulwark against the tyranny of headstrong judges & a means of softening the cold letter of the law.*
      —**University of Texas Law Professor Leon Green (1956)**

*Through 500 years of human history the jury trial has been regarded as an unalienable right cherished in the thinking of freedom-seeking peoples. It remains today a refuge against all those little tyrannies plotted behind hypocritical fronts in well-respected places theoretically dedicated to the preservation of basic civil liberties.*
      —**Judge William J. Palmer of California (1958)**

*As a tribunal for dispensing justice, the centuries have proved the civil jury to be without equal.*
      —**Canadian Queen's Counsel W. S. Martin (1959)**

*In the earliest colonies the jury system became a fundamental feature of the administration of American justice.*
      —**Perry & Cooper,** *Sources of our Liberties* **(1959)**

*Trial by jury is the most democratical of juridicial institutions and the cherished bulwark of constitutional liberty.*
      —**Theodore Plucknett, Literary Director, Selden Society (1960)**

*Trial by jury involves a carefully developed series of checks and balances equalled in no other method of trial.*
      —**Charles W. Joiner,** *Civil Justice and the Jury* **(1962)**

*Those who serve upon our juries have maintained a standard of fairness and excellence and demonstrated a vision toward the administration of justice that is a wellspring of inspiration.*
      —**U.S. Supreme Court Chief Justice Earl Warren (1962)**

*Jury trial represents courthouse democracy, the preservation of our funded experience in direct citizen participation in government.*
      —**Thomas F. Lambert, Jr., Suffolk Univ. Law Professor (1963)**

*In the course of many years of study I have become increasingly impressed with the humanity, strength, sanity, and responsibility of the civil jury.*
      —**Harry Kalven, Jr., Director, Chicago Jury Project (1964)**

*A jury provides a valuable array of experience in the problems of mankind and an acquaintance of the trials and obstacles that confront men in the pursuit of life, peace and security.*
—U.S. District Court Judge David Edelstein (1956)

*The collective judgment of twelve jurors is the nearest approach to perfect justice that can be achieved by man.*
—**Justice Howard T. Hogan, Supreme Court of New York (1964)**

*Created for the protection of individual rights and freedoms over the long pull of history, trial by jury has become one of the hallmarks of our civilization. To abolish trial by jury is to rupture a vital artery in the bloodstream of the democratic process.*
—**Jefferson F. Meagher,** ***A Fair Trial for Trial by Jury*** **(1964)**

*The right of trial by jury was gained through the blood of revolution and is part of the Constitution which has truly made this the land of the free.*
—**Donald K. Ross, Public Relations Director, Defense Research Institute (1965)**

*The stability of peoples of common law heritage may be attributed in a wholesome part to trial by jury, because it brought justice close to the people and put its dispensation largely in their keeping.*
—**H. H. Grooms, Alabama Federal District Judge (1965)**

*The civil jury is one of our best safeguards against tyranny and injustice, an ingenious and cherished element of Anglo-American jurisprudence, a bulwark of liberty and a cornerstone of democracy.*
—**Stanley E. Sacks,** ***Preservation of the Civil Jury System*** **(1965)**

*The collective conscience of the jury adds a humanistic touch to the strict demands of the law so as to allow a more equitable judgment.*
—**U.S. Supreme Court Justice Tom C. Clark (1966)**

*The right of trial by jury is a fundamental part of our state and federal systems of jurisprudence.*
—**Justice Alvin C. Strutz of North Dakota (1966)**

*Trial by a jury of one's peers is one of a democratic society's primary techniques for achieving truth. When we strengthen that institution we strengthen the framework of our democratic society.*
—**Judge Irving R. Kaufman, U.S. Court of Appeals (1967)**

*Those twelve citizens in the jury box are the cornerstone of our judicial process.*
—**Morris J. Bloomstein,** ***Verdict: The Jury System*** **(1968)**

*In the minds of the American colonists, trial by jury was the firmest barrier of English liberty; it survives today as the voice of the people.*
  —**Arthur Schlesinger, *The Birth of the Nation* (1968)**

*For almost eight centuries trial by jury remains the best, safest, surest and perhaps the only bulwark to protect the basic rights of the average citizen. It is still the "Lamp of Liberty" and it must be preserved.*
  —**Joseph T. Karcher, *The Case for the Jury System* (1969)**

*Justice can easily be banished from courts where juries are absent. But while the verdict of the court is in fact the verdict of a group of ordinary men, liberty can never be totally extinguished.*
  —**Henry Marsh, *British Documents of Liberty* (1971)**

*The cost of the jury system is insignificant. The delay caused by the jury system is minimal. The value of the jury system is immeasurable.*
  —**Rudolph Janata, President, Defense Research Institute (1974)**

*Trial by jury is the ultimate protector of individual liberties. It is the only real check against abuse of power. A jury ensures that our leaders are responsive and responsible. The power of wealth must be subject to the scrutiny of the average citizen in a democratic and just society.*
  —**Canadian Justice E. L. Haines (1979)**

*The right of trial by jury in civil cases is fundamental to our history and jurisprudence. The founders of our nation considered it an important bulwark against tyranny and corruption, a safeguard too precious to be left to the whim of the sovereign.*
  —**U.S. Supreme Court Chief Justice William H. Rehnquist (1979)**

*Trial by jury in all cases is the boasted birthright of Englishmen and their descendants, and the palladium of liberty.*
  —**Bernard Schwartz, *Roots of the Bill of Rights* (1980)**

*The competence of the common man and the validity of the jury trial are two basic, closely related notions upon which American democracy has always rested.*
  —**Richard H. Kuhlman, *Jury Trial, Progress & Democracy* (1981)**

*The jury represents democratic self government. Attacks on the jury system are attacks on the foundations of our political culture.*
—**M.D.A. Freeman,** *The Jury on Trial* **(1981)**

*The civil jury is firmly embedded in our system of justice. It is difficult to conceive of a better mechanism for establishing standards to which members of the community must conform.*
—**Peter W. Culley,** *In Defense of Civil Juries* **(1983)**

*The concept of the jury system is as close as any society has ever come to true democracy.*
—**Paula Di Perna,** *Faces of American Justice* **(1984)**

*Our constitutional right to trial by jury does not turn on the results of economic or fiscal calculations. There is no price tag on the continued existence of the civil jury system.*
—**Judge Stephen Reinhardt, 9th Circuit Court of Appeals (1986)**

*Juries are little democracies.*
—**Former Arkansas Governor Sidney S. McMath (1987)**

*The jury is the single most important institution in the history of Anglo-American law.*
—**U.S. District Judge Morris S. Arnold (1987)**

*Trial by jury is a cornerstone of our democracy.*
—**U.S. District Judge John V. Singleton (1987)**

*The civil jury performs a guardian role against oppression; it helps protect us against those who would threaten our health and safety and sets standards for responsibility and fair dealing.*
—**John Guinther,** *The Jury in America* **(1988)**

*Undermining and eroding Seventh Amendment guarantees is unacceptable, intolerable, and repugnant to the concept of Constitutional government.*
—**Paul B. Weiss,** *Reforming Tort Reform* **(1989)**

*Historically the right to a civil jury has been one of the most prized and accepted of all those in the Bill of Rights.*
—**Ellen Alderman & Caroline Kennedy**
*In Our Defense: The Bill of Rights in Action* **(1991)**

PHOTOGRAPH BY RON TUSO

*The civil jury was intended to serve as a means of political expression for average citizens. No other political institution can fulfill this role. Unless we find new respect for the Seventh Amendment, one of the basic elements of our democracy may be lost.*
—**Cynthia J. Cohen,**
**Whatever Happened to the Seventh Amendment? (1991)**

**STAND UP AND FIGHT FOR FREEDOM NOW**

It was a wild barbaric race
      Who settled on that ancient Isle,
Where once the God of Battles sat
      In solemn judgment at each trial.
Fierce native clans — by Saxons slain —
      In turn invaded by the Dane,
One thousand years of civil strife
      Had driven half of them insane.

But deep within each aching heart
      A small yet incandescent spark,
The pilot light of liberty
      Still faintly flickered through the dark.
It was this incandescent spark
      *That fateful day at Runnymede*
That sealed the *Magna Carta* with
      The sacred ink of freedom's creed.

For seven hundred years it's stood,
      Our faithful anchor through each storm,
Our basic and historic right
      Which needs no so-called *"tort reform."*
What enemy of liberty,
      What child of graft has got the greed
To undermine those ancient rights
      The people won at Runnymede?

What enemy of liberty,
      What freedom's foe would stoop so low
To undermine those rights we won
      Beside the Thames' triumphant flow?
*The citadel of freedom stands —*
      *Take heed, "the Hun is at the gate!"\**
*Stand up and fight for freedom now!*
      *Tomorrow may be far too late!*

                        —**J. Kendall Few (1992)**

\*"For all we have and are, for all our children's fate,
Stand up and take the war, *the Hun is at the gate!"*
                    —Rudyard Kipling (1914)